MW01504102

THE FOX MILLENNIUM

*1000 years of family survival
through wars and plagues*

(A documented historical narrative)

[Version: The Fox Millennium.387.wpd (August 17, 2020)]

ISBN: 9798674222927

Typesetting: WordPerfect (Times New Roman)
PDF, Adobe
Printer: kindle direct publishing/Amazon.com

My dad — besides having been a soldier of fortune, fighting for many armies in many wars — was a polygamist, con-artist, and habitual liar.

I didn't find out about his duplicity until I was about 50 years old, and he was long gone.

But his story is an integral although lesser part of this and some other books I've written.

THE FOX MILLENNIUM

PREFACE

A thousand years of my family origins and history (selective of course, but retaining basic context) is recalled and reported in this book. This is an epic autobiographical/biographical saga that a reader can vicariously appreciate and enjoy without actually coping with historical pitfalls and inadvertent misdirections.

The Author is a retired nuclear physicist and former U.S. Navy military officer who has extensively researched family origins. [His most extensive published autobiography appears online in association with SMA (Staunton Military Academy), and Linkedin has the author listed in connection with nuclear physics and engineering.]

While this **book is focused** on the author's origins and ventures, it's really about you or any other reader with wanderings through life. The book's been composed using WordPerfect word-processing software and its factual content validated when possible using the extensive online resource Wikipedia.

A particularly good and timely reason for reading this book now has to do with the current worldwide **Covid-19** corona-virus pandemic. Similar pandemics back in the middle ages strongly affected our ancestors (of the author and readers), which is one reason that much attention is paid in this book to the impact of pandemics.

WordPerfect (WP) is a computerized word-processing application, with a long functional history on multiple personal-computer platforms, and now owned by Corel (headquartered in Canada). At the height of WordPerfect's popularity in the 1980s and early 1990s, it was dominant in the word-processor market.

WP was originally developed for use on a minicomputer in the late 1970s. While not able to recall precisely, I must have adopted one of its earliest versions. The WP feature list was then considerably more advanced than its main competition.
It gained praise and rapidly displaced other systems, especially after its 1986 release, and it became the standard in the DOS market by 1989. WP's early popularity was partly because of extensive, no-cost support. It also has had available an extensive list of word-processing tools and options.

Microsoft Word later took over much of the word-processing market, helped by aggressive bundling deals that ultimately produced Microsoft Office; so by the mid-1990s WordPerfect was no longer the standard word processor. Nevertheless, it has essentially all the features needed for document creation. Since 1996 Corel has made regular releases to the product, often in the form of office suites under the WordPerfect name that include Quattro Pro spread-sheet, Presentations slides-formatter, and other applications. The common filename extension of WordPerfect document files is .wpd.

Wikipedia is a multilingual online encyclopedia. Its website was created and is maintained as an open-source collaboration project by a community of volunteer editors. It is the largest and most popular general reference work on the World Wide Web and is also one of the 20 most popular websites. It features free content exclusively, no commercial ads, and is owned and supported by the Wikimedia Foundation, a non-profit organization funded primarily through donations.

Wikipedia was launched in 2001. Now with 6.1 million articles, the English version is the largest of the more than 300 Wikipedia encyclopedias. Overall, Wikipedia articles attract 1.5 billion unique visitors per month.

Figure 1. Logo for Wikipedia, the free encyclopedia, available on-line in world-wide use.

In 2005, *Nature* published a review comparing 42 science articles from Encyclopædia *Britannica* and Wikipedia, finding that Wikipedia's level of accuracy approached that of *Britannica*. The following year, *Time* magazine stated that the open-door policy of allowing anyone to edit had made Wikipedia the biggest and possibly the best encyclopedia in the world. Its ingrained process of editing and updating material is undoubtedly a major factor in Wikipedia's sustained relevance and utility.

At this time of publication the author is probably the eldest descendent in the Volpi family line — in my case the De Volpi (or DeVolpi) lineage, which traces back a thousand years.

For this books's authorship and composition, I accept sole responsibility, having adopted my own preferred style. Some of the choices are for convenience such as indexing, while others are guided by presentation clarity.

There are many qualified kinfolk who can continue this family legacy.

CHAPTER I: A MILLENNIUM OF FOXES

This verifiable and venturesome family <u>saga</u> extends back in history at least 1000 years (a millennium) — as far in the past that is demonstrably provable from Western human records (according to information reliably reported in Wikipedia).

At the current time of publication (2020), coping with the corona virus (Covid-19) and its stay-at-home predilection, this book connects past to present with many relevant and historically similar situations, not the least appropriate being some episodes of pestilence spreading throughout Italy hundreds of years ago.

In terms of verified family history, our present story focuses on one specific human clan (anthropoid, hominid), the *Volpi* (Fox) kinship, documented to have originated near Como in the northen Italian lake region sometime during the first historical millennium. According to records discovered, Volpi-family members gradually migrated to regions further north, east and south on the boot-shaped peninsula protruding into the Mediterranean Sea.

That's a thousand years of post-Roman history in ancient Italy. In primordial times, aboriginal human species would have been able to have inhabited, in particular, the relatively isolated land mass known as the Italic Peninsula jutting into the Mediterranean Sea. Much much later, humans emigrated to or from the mid-East, Asia and central Europe to the peninsula that eventually became known as Italy. A bit of that migration ultimately evolved into the present-day Volpi and DeVolpi family descendants, and that is what this is about.

Throughout the book, you will find separated into double-lined "boxes" (as the one below) many informative details (and some curiosities) that I've unearthed in the course of researching background information for this book. After all, a lot happened to humans and to civilization in the past millennium. In those boxes, particularly, specific effort is made to provide historical, environmental and situational context. In this book I've also inserted as many copyright-permissible illustrations as possible.

Foxes (*vulpes or volpe* in Latin) are small four-footed mammals that have survived with omnivorous diets everywhere in nature. They are a relatively unusual animal species perhaps 2 million years old; it would simply guesswork to figure out why a particular human family in northern Italy would be named after them. However, it is not unusual for human families to have inherited animal-category names in various cultures and languages. Some native-American Indians are said to have chosen a baby's name from the first thing seen looking out of the teepee.

Being omnivorous, foxes are a *genus* of animals prone to scavenging. The foods of choice for *Vulpes* consist of invertebrates, a variety of small vertebrates, grasses and some flowering plants. The typical intake per day is a couple of pounds — about 1 kg. True foxes exhibit hoarding behavior or caching, storing food for another day out of sight from other animals. A fox could lose its kill to a bear, wolf, or even an eagle.

Foxes can dwell in a number of habitats, including alpine, forest, desert, coastal, farm and urban areas, but thrive in environments rich in food and shelter. They can now be found in great numbers in suburban/residential regions in some countries, such as Italy, Britain and the United States. For the most part, this coexistence is compatible for both fox and humans, but can sometimes result in house pet (cat) disappearances. On the other hand, wolves (*cannis lupe*) are more dog-like and mainly carnivores.

According to Wikipedia, **wild foxes** are small to medium-sized, omnivorous (animal- or plant-eating) mammals belonging to several *genera* of the family *Canidae*. They have flattened skulls, upright triangular ears, a pointed, slightly upturned snout, and a long bushy tail. Twelve species belong to the monophyletic "true foxes" group of genus *Vulpes*. (See Figure 2).

Figure 2. A fox with prey. (Note similarity of image to heraldic coat of arms for Volpi family, as shown in Figures 13 and 14.)

ABOUT FOXES AS MAMMALS

Not only does the saga in this book geographically traverse what is now ancient northern Italy, the ancestors (father and mother) of the present-day De Volpi family in the United States crossed the Atlantic in modern times, settling mostly in the United States, where specifically this book has been authored by a descendent now living in southern California.

In terms of time in history that it covers, this saga reaches from ancient to modern times — a thousand years overall. Moreover, it will sometimes drift into some fascinating details, slipping back and forth between history and memoir.

Fact Checking. My initial professional undergraduate college education (to be a journalist) and eventual professional career (as a nuclear physicist) trained me to routinely check and recheck facts and to review composed documents before sending them out and whenever available for reexamination. Such a process reduces but doesn't necessarily eliminate errors.

This book has been contemporized in terms of relevant information and history, as well as family relationships and relevant anecdotes.

Wikipedia Attribution. In this book, informative messages such as this one illustrated in such bounded clusters are often based on information from online Wikipedia without making specific attribution or copyright violation. Wikipedia is an open free-of-cost public source for information and images. Nowadays it is a rather dependable, reliable, convenient and verified source of contemporary worldwide information and pictorial representations and maps.

I justify my frequent use of Wikipedia not only on the grounds that it is free and convenient for public use, without running afoul of publication or plagiarism practices and laws, but also because I once contributed (in a very minor way) as one of its information sources, which made me familiar with its information-vetting processes. You can't imagine how much research time Wikipedia has saved me now compared to the time I used to spend in libraries and book stores for my earlier research and publications.

Having evolved professionally as a journalist and a nuclear scientist, it has been difficult for me to cite useful information or images without providing at least some deserved attribution. I'm not saying Wikipedia is error-free, but it is now a big improvement over older methods of cross-checking data and supplying supportive information.

ANCIENT HUMAN HISTORY, PRE-ROMAN TO ROMAN ERA

Absent trustworthy and specifically relevant records, it would be largely speculation or guesswork about the Volpi family lineage going back further to Roman times or earlier, although some generalized inferences are made in this book in order to establish a plausible historical framework.

Figure 3. Map of ancient Europe hundreds of years BC, dominated by the Celts (from the middle of the continent, gradually conquering outward the central region of Europe). Notice that northern Italy came under early Celtic domination 370 BC or so (England much later).

Logically one should start with the Celts, a collection of Indo-European peoples, although their exact geographic origin (Figure 3) is still disputed. According to one theory, the common root of the Celtic tribes and language arose in the Late Bronze Age culture of Central Europe, which flourished from around 1200 BC.

Christianity

Following the 5th-century Fall of Rome, Europe entered its Middle Ages, during which period the Catholic Church filled the power vacuum left in the West by the collapsed Roman Empire, while the Eastern Roman Empire (Byzantine Empire) endured for centuries.

The Italic Tribes

The Italics were an ancient Indo-European ethnolinguistic group identified by their use of what are called eponymously the "Italic" languages. The tribes that spoke these languages descended from Indo-Europeans who migrated into Italy in the second millennium BC.

In the course of time, another millennium or so later, Latins achieved a dominant position among these Italic tribes, gradually establishing the ancient Roman civilization.

Indo-European. Present-day Indo-European languages are a large human-communication category that originated in western Eurasia. The category now comprises most of the languages of Europe, together with those of the northern Indian Subcontinent and the Iranian Plateau.

The Indo-European category consists of several language or dialect branches, the largest now being Indo-Iranian, Germanic, Romance, and Balto-Slavic. The most populous within them are Spanish, English, Hindustani, Portuguese, Bengali, Punjabi, and Russian, each with over 100 million speakers, while German, French, Marathi, Italian, and Persian languages each have more than 50 million. In total, nearly half of the world's (3.2 billion) population speaks an Indo-European language as a first tongue, by far the highest of any language family. There are nearly 150 Indo-European language variations, over 100 of them belonging to the Indo-Iranian branch.

All Indo-European languages are descendants of a single prehistoric language, spoken sometime in the Neolithic era. Its precise geographical location and the Indo-European origin are unknown and has been the object of many competing hypotheses. By the time the first written records appeared, Indo-European had already evolved into numerous languages spoken across much of Europe and south-west Asia. Written evidence appeared during the Bronze Age in the form of Mycenaean Greek and the Anatolian languages. The oldest records are isolated Hittite words and names — interspersed otherwise in the unrelated Old Assyrian, a Semitic language — found in the texts of an Assyrian colony in eastern Anatolia in the 20th-century BC.

Although no older written records of the original Proto-Indo-Europeans remain, some aspects of their culture and religion can be reconstructed from later evidence in their cultures. The Indo-European language family possesses the second-longest recorded history, after the Egyptian language and the Semitic languages.

Documented historic representations exist of Western civilizations before and after the BC/AC juncture marked by the birth of Jesus Christ. In Europe, the expansive Roman Empire evolved starting about the 8ᵗʰ century BC until its collapse in the 5ᵗʰ century AC.

Historic Western civilization traces its roots back to Europe and the Mediterranean. It is linked to ancient Greece, the Roman Empire and with Medieval Western Christendom which emerged from the Middle Ages to experience such transformative episodes as the Renaissance, the Reformation, the Enlightenment, the Industrial Revolution, scientific revolution, and the development of liberal democracy. The civilizations of Classical Greece and Ancient Rome are considered seminal periods in Western history; a few cultural contributions also emerged from the pagan peoples of pre-Christian Europe, such as the Celts and Germans....

Origins of the Romans

The Roman civilization itself had begun as an Italic settlement within the Italian Peninsula, traditionally dated to 753 BC, which became the start of the Roman calendar. Two years later the Greeks established colonies in Italy and Sicily.

Although earlier events within the Grecian empire had a significant effect, that specific Italic settlement along a river estuary in Italy grew into the city of Rome which subsequently gave its name to the empire over which it ruled and to the widespread civilization which the empire developed.

When ruled by its first king Romulus, Rome adopted the Etruscan alphabet, which had been had adopted from the Greeks. However, Roman numerals are a system that originated in ancient Rome and remained the usual way of writing numbers throughout Europe well into the Late Middle Ages. Numbers in that system are represented by combinations of letters from the Latin alphabet.

Most ancient Umbrian cities were settled in the 9ᵗʰ century BC to the 4ᵗʰ century BC on easily defensible hilltops. Umbria was bordered by the Tiber and Nar rivers and included the Apennine slopes on the Adriatic.

The Greeks in Ancient Italy

Greek people in Southern Italy initially arrived in numerous waves of migrations, the ancient Greek colonization of Southern Italy and Sicily as mentioned in the 8ᵗʰ century BC up to the Byzantine Greek migrations of the 15ᵗʰ century driven by the Ottoman conquest.

Causes of the 8ᵗʰ- and 7ᵗʰ-century-BC migrations included demographic crises (famine, overcrowding, climate change, etc.); the search for new commercial outlets and ports; and forced expulsion from homeland. For some of those reasons about that time, Greeks began a large colonization drive into surrounding lands along the Adriatic and Mediterranean, particularly including southern Italy.

ANCIENT HISTORY, ROMAN TO CHRISTIAN ERA

The Roman Empire

From about to 400 BC, for nearly a millennium to about 600 AD, having conquered the Greeks, the Roman Empire dominated Europe, mostly around the periphery of the Mediterranean. (Figure 4 represents the ancient Roman empire in the middle of that 1000-year period.). Later, there was transition to a Republic, and even later the Ottomans gained ascendency. Geographically in the middle, originally Rome was the center of power, ruling mostly by military force.

Humans, Domains, and Empires. This is not a book about the history of humans, their domains, and their empires. Nevertheless it is important to note for context the role of empires: that the Persian empire reigned from 6th century BC, until the Greek empire dominated from the 12th to 9th centuries BC, the Roman empire (Figure 4) before and afer the birth of Christ, and the Ottoman empire from the 14th and early 20th centuries AD. This book focuses primarily on my documented or inferred family history, stretching from 1000 AD into the present second millennium.

Figure 4. Map of ancient Roman empire, 40 BC, with the Roman Empire at its widest extent (credit for this map due to Pinterest on the Internet).

Christianity

Following the 5th-century Fall of Rome, Europe entered its Middle Ages, during which period the Catholic Church filled the power vacuum left in the West by the collapsed Roman Empire, while the Eastern Roman Empire (Byzantine Empire) endured for centuries.

15

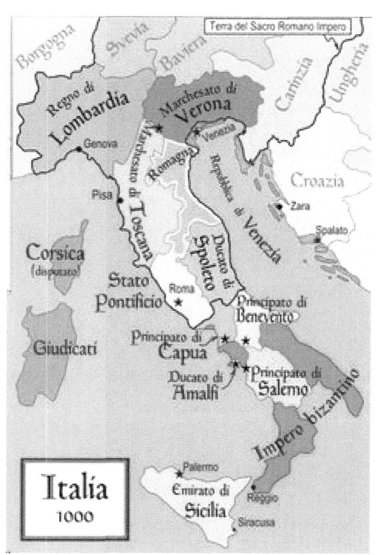

Figure 5. Provincial map of Italy, circa 1000 AD, when the Romans dominated.

CHAPTER II: THE ITALIAN ERA
(FROM 1861)

Modern Italy became a single independent nation-state during the *Risorgimento* (uprising) in 1861, when most of the states of the Italian Peninsula and the Kingdom of the Two Sicilies were united under king Victor Emmanuel II of the House of Savoy, hitherto king of Sardinia, a realm that had included Piedmont.

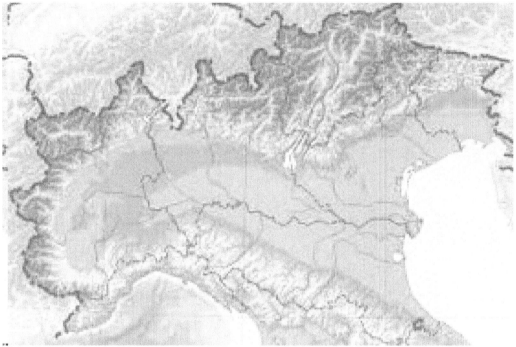

Figure 6. Geographical map of northern Italy. Note verdant plains (in green) receiving fresh water from mountain streams (darker lines) to the north. To the right of center is the fresh-water Como lake region full of fish and wildlife.

Italian unification, also known as the *Risorgimento*, was the 19th century political and social movement that consolidated different states of the Italian peninsula into the single Kingdom of Italy in 1861.

Volpi Family Connection in Distant Italian History

As explained with more detail in *Lover, Soldier, Reprobate* — Amazon.com, 2011), the present Volpi family came to be of some prominence during the earliest stages (*risorgimento*) in formation of the independent nation of Italy:

> *In those days horses were absolutely essential in armies. Bonaventura's grandfather Alessandro Volpi (after whom I was apparently named) was a famous veterinarian in Italy. He served as such in the regular army, but when Garibaldi began his insurrection against the government, Dr. Volpi became Garibaldi's surgeon-general. Veterinary service was a Volpi family tradition.*

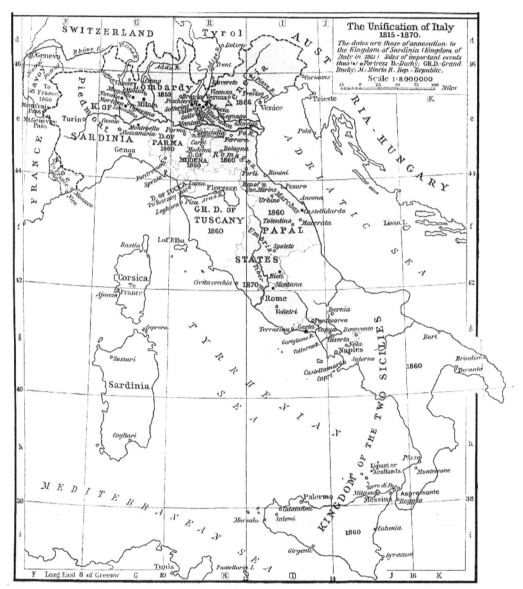

Figure 7. Map for Kingdom of Italy, 1861, at the height of the *risorgimento*.

Giuseppe Maria Garibaldi (1807 – 1882) was an Italian general and patriot. He fought for Italian unification and the creation of the Kingdom of Italy. Considered to be one of Italy's "fathers of the fatherland," Garibaldi is also known because of his military enterprises in South America and Europe.

Garibaldi was a follower of the Italian nationalist Mazzini, and embraced the republican nationalism of the Young Italy movement. He became a supporter of unification under a democratic Republican government. After participating in an uprising in Piedmont, he was sentenced to death, but escaped to South America; he spent 14 years in exile, taking part in several wars and learning the art of guerrilla warfare. In 1835, in Brazil, he took up the cause of the *Riograndense* in its attempt to proclaim another republic. Garibaldi also became involved in the Uruguayan Civil War, raising an Italian force known as Redshirts, and is still celebrated as an important contributor to Uruguayan independence.

In 1848, Garibaldi returned to Italy and commanded and fought in military campaigns that eventually led to Italian unification. The provisional government of Milan made him a general. When the war of independence broke out in April 1859, he led his Hunters of the Alps in the capture of Varese and Como. The war ended with Italy's acquisition of Lombardy.

In 1860, with the consent of Victor Emmanuel II, Garibaldi led an expedition that concluded with the annexation of Sicily, Southern Italy, Marche and Umbria to the Kingdom of Sardinia, before the creation of a unified Kingdom of Italy in 1861. His last military campaign took place during the Franco-Prussian War.

Garibaldi became an international figurehead for national independence and republican ideals. He was showered with admiration and praise by many intellectuals and political figures. In the popular telling of his story, he is associated with the red shirts that his volunteers, the *Garibaldini*, wore in lieu of a uniform.

Heraldry: Coats of Arms.
Heraldic eagles (as depicted in Figure 8) have been featured throughout world history, as in the ancient Achaemenid Empire (first Persian domain around 300 to 700BC), or nowadays flags of contemporary countries in the Baltic region.

The European post-classical symbolism of the heraldic eagle is connected on the one hand with the nonsectarian Roman Empire (especially in the case of the double-headed eagle), and on the other hand with the sectarian religious Saint John the Evangelist.

Figure 8. A bald eagle. The term "eagle" was used for a United States $10 gold coin issued by the United States Mint from 1792 to 1933.

The Golden Eagle in Italy

In present-day Italy, the Golden Eagle occupies alpine and subalpine habitats, as well as hills and sometimes lowland areas in the Alps, Apennines and major islands.

The golden eagle has always fascinated humans. It is a central character in most ancient mythologies, and a symbol of strength, intelligence and courage, especially in northern Italy.

Both the Golden Eagle and he Bald Eagle are large birds with dark brown bodies. The adult bald eagle has a noticeable white head and tail while the golden eagle has a brown head with "golden" feathers on the back of their necks. The adult bald eagle has a large, yellow beak, while the golden has a slightly smaller black beak

With its imposing wingspan of up to 2.3m (about 7 feet) and its weight that can reach 6kg (about 13 lbs), the golden eagle is the biggest day-time bird of prey in Europe. It is a fully protected species in the state of California where I now live. Although the bald eagle is honored as the U.S. national symbol, the golden eagle is also the national symbol of Mexico, Albania, Germany, Austria, and Kazakhstan — making it the most common "national" animal in the world. The golden eagle is national animal of Kazakhstan.

There is no visible difference between the sexes for eagles, except the size: the female is definitely larger. Eagle wings are rather narrow; they have a regular silhouette and become noticeably smaller where they are attached to the body. The dominant color of the golden eagle's plumage is dark brown; it's the nape that is golden yellow. The beak is strong and curved, and the feet are covered with feathers and equipped with very strong talons. Young birds have white spots on their feathers. The golden eagle's flight is characterized by very little wing movement, and when it glides along, the wing-quills are particularly extended and turned upwards. This monogamous species can reach over thirty-five years of age, and in captivity the record is fifty years. Towards the end of March, the female will lay one or two eggs. From the first egg, a chick will hatch after forty-five days. In most cases, only one of the young will survive.

Eagle Watching on the Mississippi River. Every year tens of thousands of people flock to the Mississippi River to take part in Bald Eagle Watches. They have come to catch a glimpse, perhaps for the first time, of our national symbol.

Up to 2500 bald eagles winter along the Mississippi near the lock and dams. Turbulence created below the dams provide open water and a smorgasbord of stunned fish for eagles to feast upon. In addition, wooded bluffs that overlook the Mississippi are excellent habitat for roosting and an increasing number of nesting. Bald Eagle Watches occur throughout January and February, but eagles can be seen from mid December through early March. It all depends on the weather. As warm weather arrives, most eagles will begin their journey back north to northern Minnesota, Wisconsin, and Canada to prepare for the nesting season.

Eagles are large, powerfully built birds of prey, with heavy heads and beaks. Even the smallest eagles have relatively long and broad wings, and more direct, faster flight. Most are larger than any other raptors apart from some vultures. Like all birds of prey, eagles have very large, hooked beaks, strong legs and powerful talons. Eagles' eyes are extremely powerful, leading to the definition of "eagle eye": the ability to see or observe keenly.

Adult golden and bald eagles have distinguishing characteristics in their coloring making it easy to identify the species. Both are large birds with dark brown bodies. The adult bald eagle has a noticeable white head and tail while the golden eagle has a brown head with "golden" feathers on the back of their necks. The adult bald eagle has a large, yellow beak, while the golden has a slightly smaller black beak.

Eagles normally build their nests, called eyries, in tall trees or on high cliffs. Due to their size and power eagles are ranked at the top of the food chain in the avian world. The type of prey varies. Some eagles prefer to capture fish and water birds. Most grab quarry without landing and take flight with it, so the prey can be carried to a perch and torn apart.

The bald eagle is noted for having flown with the heaviest load verified to be carried by any flying bird. Moreover, eagles may target prey considerably heavier than themselves.

Gulls are seabirds, most closely related to terns and only distantly related to auks, skimmers, and more distantly to wading birds. An older name for gulls is *mews*, connected with German *Möwe*, Danish *måge*, Dutch *meeuw*, and French *mouette*.

Gulls are typically range in size medium to large, usually grey or white, often with black markings on the head or wings. They have harsh wailing or squawking calls; stout, longish bills; and webbed feet. Most gulls are ground-nesting carnivores which take live food or scavenge opportunistically. Live food often includes crabs and small fish. Gulls have unhinging jaws which allow them to consume large prey and they are typically coastal or inland species, rarely venturing far out to sea. The larger gulls in the species take up to four years to attain full adult plumage, but two years is typical for small gulls. Large white-headed gulls are typically long-lived birds, with a maximum age of 49 years recorded for the herring gull.

Gulls nest in large, densely packed, noisy landward colonies. They lay two or three speckled eggs in nests composed of vegetation. Gulls are resourceful, inquisitive, and intelligent, the larger species in particular, demonstrating complex methods of communication and a highly developed social structure. Many gull colonies display mobbing behavior, attacking and harassing predators and other intruders. Certain species have exhibited tool-use behavior, such as the herring gull, using pieces of bread as bait with which to catch goldfish, for example. Many species of gulls have learned to coexist successfully with humans and have thrived in human habitats. Others rely on feeding from prey or other food that was caught, collected, or prepared by another animal, including stored food. Gulls have been observed preying on live whales as they surface, landing on them to peck out pieces of flesh.

Something that caught my attention recently was a newspaper "Earthwatch" item about seagulls starving in Italy, hunting rats, pigeons, and other small birds ever since the Corona virus took began depriving them of their usual scraps from tourists.

Figure 9. An "eagle" was the name used for a U.S. $10 gold coin issued by the United States Mint from 1792 to 1933.

Italian Heraldry

There's no particular reason to believe that heraldry in ancient Italy was basically much different in purpose than anywhere else. Of course various heraldic motifs with recurring shapes, creatures, and colors would reoccur as dominions and rulers changed.

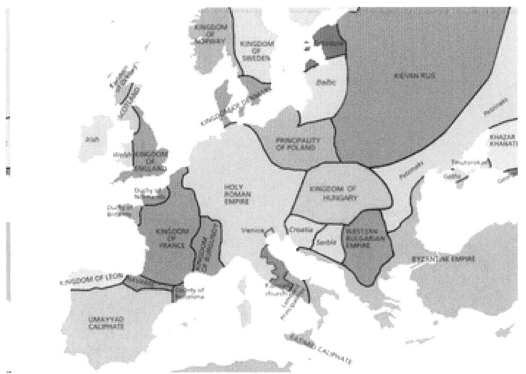

Figure 10. Map of ancient Europe around 1000 AD dominated the Celts (in the middle of the continent, gradually conquering outward the central region of Europe). Notice that northern Italy came under early Celtic domination 370 BC or so (England much later).

Italian Titles and Ranks (source: Louis Mendola)
Principe, Principessa (Prince, Princess). This is the highest Italian title of nobility, and also the title accorded members of the royal families. Many of Italy's noble princes, particularly in northern regions, are princes of the Holy Roman Empire, and lack feudal territorial designations attached to their titles. Some southern princes descend from the most ancient medieval feudatories. In most cases, the holder of a princely title in Italy is the descendant of forebears who in antiquity were barons or counts, the family having been elevated through the nobiliary ranks over the centuries.

Duca, Duchessa (Duke, Duchess). This title originally was reserved to the sovereign rulers of important territories. Dukedoms were sometimes borne by nobles whose early medieval forebears were barons, knights or other feudatories.

Marchese, Marchesa (Marquess, Marchioness). The term derives from the Old Italian marchio, referring to the man charged with guarding a march, or border territory.

Conte, Contessa (Count, Countess). The word traces its origin from the Latin for a military companion. It is noteworthy that conte is one of the few Italian titles sometimes – though rarely – inherited by all heirs male, depending on the terms set forth in the patent of creation.

Visconte, Viscontessa (Viscount, Viscontess). Originally vice comes, for the attendant of a count, this is the rarest of the modern Italian nobiliary titles, almost unknown in some regions.

Barone, Baronessa (Baron, Baroness). The title is probably of Germanic origin; the Latin root baro referred to a simpleton, but by the Middle Ages baronis was a title of nobility or, more often, a nobiliary rank employed in reference to holders of feudal property or any wealthy landholder. Heraldic regulation in the Kingdom of Italy further established that the sons of barons could no longer appropriate cavaliere as a courtesy title. Barone is the most frequent of the modern Italian noble titles.

Signore (seigneur). Originally a feudal lord, the title was introduced into Italy by the Franks and Normans. Formerly a minor rank, the title is rarely used today because most signori bear greater titles by which they are commonly known, and because, in common parlance, *signore* has come to mean "Mister."

Patrizio (Patrician). Rare in Sicily, the term obviously derives from that used to describe the aristocratic class of ancient Rome, and identifies the urban patriciate of certain northern Italian cities. A *patrizio* is said to be "of" a certain place, such as Venice or Florence, without it being his "feudal" seat (patricians were an urban aristocracy).

Nobile (untitled Nobleman). In the Dark Ages, local leaders known to their people were *nobiliti*, from the Latin *nobilitas*, meaning, appropriately, "known." The rank denotes some — though not all — aristocratic Italian families which bear historic coats of arms but lack titles of nobility.

Cavaliere Ereditario (Hereditary Knight Bachelor). This rank, usually transmitted by male primogeniture but sometimes to ordinary male heirs male, is quite similar to a British baronetcy but older. Most *cavalieri ereditari* descend from the younger sons of nobles or from historically untitled families ennobled with this form of knighthood in the fifteenth or sixteenth centuries in Sicily, Sardinia and some parts of mainland Italy.

The Ancient Volpi Clan in Italy (Beginning ~700 AD?)

Roughly the year 700 AD would be the earliest we should speculate that a particular family named Volpi (among possibly many others thus or similarly named in various regions of Italy) might have begun the heritage of my specific Volpi clan.

While 700 AD is indeed very, very long ago, it is not so much earlier than the date 1000 AD to which the Volpi family clan was genealogically traced rather objectively in the 1700s (as substantiated with details in my book *Lover, Soldier, Reprobate*).

Family heritage and the inheritance of heirs had long been important, particularly when land ownership and other manifestations of wealth and social station were involved. In fact, the lamentable saga about necessarily searching for male Volpi heirs was long ago included in a documented search hundreds of years ago by the last surviving female in the Volpi family of the Como region. (She had no idea that related Volpi family members had crossed the mountains over to Trento or had dodged the plague and survived far away in the Bari region of southern Italy.)

We now know about that because a member of the Volpi branch in Bari (a thousand miles away in southern Italy) traced his ancestral roots in the mid-1700s. He wrote it up in a book of which two copies — one in a library in Bari and the other in a library in Naples — have survived to this day. There will be more about that book later on.

Como is a city at the southern tip of **Lake Como** in northern Italy (see Figure 11). The city is known in tourism for its Gothic *Como Cathedral*, a popular scenic funicular railway, and a beautiful waterfront promenade. The *Museo Didattico della Seta* traces the history of Como's silk industry, while the *Tempio Voltiano* museum is dedicated to Italian physicist Alessandro Volta. Just north are the lakeside gardens of the palatial Villa Olmo, as well as other stately and ancient villas that surround the lake. Not so long ago Lake Como had fishing as an important means of commerce.

Figure 11. Map of the Lake Como region in northern Italy with Switzerland cutting through to the west (left on the map) and the city of Como to the far south of the Lago di Como (towards bottom of the map).

Alessandro Volta was an Italian physicist, chemist, and pioneer of electricity and power credited as the inventor of the electric battery and the discoverer of methane. He invented the Voltaic pile in 1799. With this invention Volta proved that electricity could be generated chemically and debunked the prevalent theory that electricity was generated solely by living beings. Volta's invention sparked a great amount of scientific excitement and led others to conduct similar experiments which eventually led to the development of the field of electrochemistry.

The 40 BC Roman Empire map earlier (shown in Figure 4) implies that the region in which my specific Volpi clan arose was then dominated by the ancient Celts. Of course, that map provides no guidance whether our particular Volpi family might have actually existed there during that early Celtic period of domination. To the contrary, judging from other indications, our family debut is likely to have been much later. That particular period in Roman history is somewhat after the course of ancient migration from the Grecian peninsula peaked.

Reiterating the line of reasoning: While historically well-established after 1000 AD, it's not unreasonable speculation to extrapolate Volpi family origination further back in time; to roughly 700 AD in northern Italy, more likely than not in the lake region not too far from Lake Como. That would be fully a thousand years after the Celts trudged through central Europe, gradually taking over that warmer region south across the Alps into Italy.

While there's no particular reason to reflect on it now, birds no-doubt flew around and alighted on trees and landed on the ground then, just as they do nowadays — good prey for foxes and other hunting animals — even becoming sport quarry for humans. Eagles have appeared in family crests as in Figure 6 (and in the following figures for the Volpi clan registered at various recorded stages). The eagle, in particular, has been used in heraldry variously as a consigned symbol, a military supporter and in family crests.

Here on following pages are examples of ancient Volpi family crests, as uncovered from various records and books. Even though the Como, Bari, and Trento families were separated by long distances and mountains, there are consistent features that unite these family crests, such as inclusion of the fox and the chevrons. The fox would usually have chicken in his mouth. Even in those days, these coats of arms were in color, and the chevrons (for example) were in blue on a white background.

Volpi Coat of Arms in Como

In the ancient Volpi (*De Vulpis*) family coat of arms as utilized in Como around the first millennium, we see the fox having caught a chicken. The banner above the fox says *Sta Fort* (Be Brave or Be Strong) which is thus the family motto.

On the bottom half of Figure 12, the chevrons (that would be in blue) would normally be painted or stained on representations of family coats of arms. This particular example was retrieved from my computer files.

In order to convey the basic family recognition information, the ancient recorded renderings of coats of arms would be described in words, for example "blue and white chevrons," that could be written and transmitted to others.

Figure 12. Coat of Arms for Volpi family in Como, circa 1000 AD, with the family motto *sta fort* (be brave, or strong) inscribed on the upper right.

Incidentally, not all that many historic families have found themselves both a coat of arms, but also a family motto that has been passed down for generations.

The inscription *sta fort* (be brave) on Figure 13 was added on my copy of the document by me (in blue ink). That is the actual Volpi family motto, carried over 1000 years from ancient times. Not many families can claim to have an ancient family slogan.

Volpi Coat of Arms in Modern Trento

One of the reasons that I was able to piece together the ancient Volpi family kinship in locations of very-distant cities and regions of Italy is the commonality of the respective family crests. Trento is in a valley north and east of Como. It is at a distance and mountain-surrounded location too far for ordinary people to have crossed from Como so long ago over the cragged terrain into the Trentino valley. (Nowadays, to go from Como to Trento you could span the mountains by driving on routes to the north, but better

Figure 13. Coat of Arms for Trento Branch of Volpi family in northern Italy

to swing around on *autostrada* to the south and head up north — a road distance of about 260 miles.)

Back then it would have been a big deal, but somehow it appears that a someone in the military made the difficult trek across or around from Como and settled down in Trento, establishing the Volpi family in the region, where family members still live and work.

Having driven from Trento to Como over the modern mountain-road route, I can only imagine the difficult trek it would have been in those days, maybe a thousand years ago — at least a few hundred years ago.

I once drove the mountain roads in a rental car across from Trento to Como. It's quite a haul for bicyclists, and you could tell that with no established trail it would have been a long and arduous journey on foot, mule, or horseback in the 1700s.

More likely, the Trento Volpi family originated from a calvary contingent that entered the valley from the South, having followed the river northward.

I have visited Trento many times, and sometimes met enduring family members in the city and its suburbs. On one occasion I gave a formal presentation (on the status of E-W negotiations regarding nuclear arms control) that was translated to a large high-school audience. One resident (Mirco Elena) who became a long-term friend had arranged for me to carry out the visit, translated conversations, and otherwise helped in my family searches in the Trento region.

In fact, Figure 13 is a copy of a resplendent coat of arms that I photographed in the apartment of one of the eldest Volpi family members I found in Trento decades ago. Note, in particular within the figure, ancestral commonality of the fox with a chicken clutched in its mouth.

To my knowledge, copies of this coat of arms have proliferated among present-day members of the De Volpi family in the United States. Just before my first visit to Trento (accompanied by professional family researcher and translator Trafford Cole), one of the last surviving male members of the current-generation Volpi family was killed in an automobile accident. Subsequently, I met some female members in the Volpi legacy of Trento.

Figure 14 exhibits the Volpi ancestral family tree, going back to the 1300s.

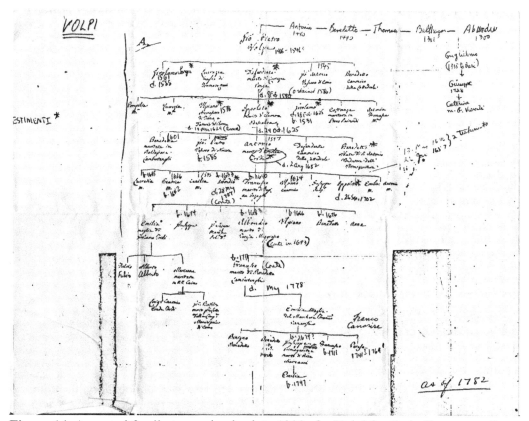

Figure 14. Ancestral family tree going back to 1300s for Volpi family in Trento, as of 1782.

Members of various Volpi family branches now live on and thrive in the Trentino region. Decades later I uncovered the family links between me, my father, his father, and the rest of the family. A treasured friend, Mirco Elena, was often able to provide guidance for me in Trento. I also visited or detoured there when the two-week "course" of the Italian peace movement held its biennial meetings, sometimes every other summer, sometimes every other winter, in and around Trento or in Venice.

Venice (Italian: *Venezia*) is a unique city of canals in northern Italy known both for tourism and industry, and is capital of the *Veneto* region. The city historically was an independent city-state known as the "*La Serenissima* (the most serene)." It is one of Europe's most romantic destinations.

Venice stretches across 117 small islands in the marshy Venetian Lagoon along the northeast Adriatic Sea. The Republic of Venice was a major maritime power during the Middle Ages and Renaissance, and a staging area for the Crusades. It was very important as a center of art and commerce (especially silk, grain and spice trade) in the 13th century up to the end of the 17th century. This made Venice wealthy throughout most of its history. Contemporary Venice has managed to preserved much of its age-old appearance with canals, bridges, and narrow walkways and no cars.

There is a long and controversial political and military history of the disputed Trentino valley, sometimes having been under control of Austria and the Austrian-Hungarian Empire and eventually conceded back to Italy (after World War I). The coat of arms for the Volpi family of Trento previously shown in Figure 14 emphasizes the earlier Austrian-Hungarian governing status, partly by the symbolic and elegant armoury in that figure surrounding the central coat of arms.

Heraldic designs came into general use among European nobility in the 12th century. The basic designs of heraldry are illustrated in Figure 15. Today, in the United States, copyright protections exist for the commercial equivalent.

Systematic, heritable heraldry had developed by the beginning of the 13th century. Exactly who had a right to use arms, by law or social convention, varied to some degree between countries. Early heraldic designs were personal, used by individual noble families. Arms become hereditary by the end of the 12th century, in England by King Richard I during the Third Crusade (1189–1192).

Figure 15. The basics of heraldry illustrated in this generic sketch: at the top would be a slogan or battle cry above a crown and battle cry, with supporters to the side, and a motto or family name at the bottom

Burgher arms are used in Northern Italy in the second half of the 13th century, and in the Holy Roman Empire by the mid 14th century. In the late medieval period, use of heraldic arms spread to the clergy, to towns as civic identifiers, and to royally chartered organizations such as universities and trading companies.

The term "coat of arms" itself in origin refers to the surcoat with heraldic designs worn by combatants, especially in the knightly tournament, and in Old French *cote a armer*. The sense is transferred to the heraldic design itself in Middle English, in the mid-14th century.

Genealogical Research in Italy for Ancient Volpi Family

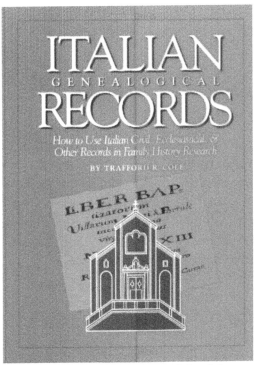

In order to discover Volpi family origins in Italy and determine which Volpi's now living might be related, I hired a genealogical researcher, Trafford Cole. He had been trained as an LDS family-history researcher in Utah and was living with his family in Italy. I could communicate with him readily because his native language was English, but he was well versed in Italian (and Latin). Trafford not only included searches for my Volpi family origins along with his other commissioned searches, but he also accompanied me on some of my visits to various cities in Italy in searching for relatives and records.

Figure 16. Cover of large, thick book by professional genealogist Trafford Cole who helped track my ancient Volpi family roots in Italy.

Trafford R Cole, is author of the impressive book, *Italian Genealogical Records*: *How to Use Italian Civil, Ecclesiastical & Other Records in Family History*, (651pp, hardcover – 16 September 1995) — cover displayed in Figure 16.

Trafford was the commissioned genealogist living in Italy who on my behalf uncovered and translated many of the Volpi family records. In fact, you will find many pages of his book filled with some of these Volpi records.

In his professional role he has performed genealogical research in state archives, diocesan archives, parishes, and townships in all of Italy and some nearby countries. His expertise in reading Medieval texts and in researching records in Italian, Latin and local dialects is important in family-history research.

Heraldry tradition has governed its design and use. Some nations, like England and Scotland, still maintain the same heraldic authorities that traditionally granted and regulated coats of arms for centuries and still continue to do so. In England, for example, the granting of heraldry is and has been controlled by the College of Arms. Unlike seals and other general emblems, heraldic "achievements" have a formal description called a blazon, which allows for consistency in heraldic depictions. Heraldic coats of arms are still in use by a variety of institutions and individuals: for example, many European cities and universities have guidelines on how their coats of arms may be used, and protect their use as trademarks. Many common-interest groups exist that aid in design and registration of personal coats of arms.

Historical References to Volpi in Bari

On at least one trip to Italy I searched for any surviving members or vestiges of the Volpi family in Bari. There was no sign that family members were still extant in the Bari or the surrounding region region. No Volpi was listed in contemporary directories (or cemeteries).

Even though I had a rental car that allowed me to drive around the city and the suburbs, I could find no indications of the ancient Volpi family.

However, the local central library had plenty of reminders of the family's role in regional history. There was ample enduring evidence of the historical Volpi family once present. For example, as shown in Figure 17, the arch above the entrance to the Bari historical library (*Arcivo di Stato di Bari*) bore a nameplate which honored three families that presumably contributed to either the history of Bari or the foundation of the library.

Figure 17. Nameplate above door to Bari National Library honoring Sagarriga, Visconti, and Volpi families prominent in the history of Bari.

(The Visconti's were a prominent family in northern Italy back in the middle ages and, presumably the Sagarriga's as well).

Moreover, formal paintings on the ceiling and walls of the Bari National Library were replete with images of community leaders from the Volpi family, such as Giuseppe Volpi in Figure 19. He was prominent in Bari during in the mid-1700s.
Trafford Cole, who discovered in the Library holdings one of the two copies known to exist of the ancient Volpi book, was allowed to photocopy the entire edition, some pages of which are rendered in figures that follow.

Here, for example, are some reproductions in the several following pages in the ancient Volpi family book at the Bari library that Trafford was allowed to photocopy carefully and gingerly:

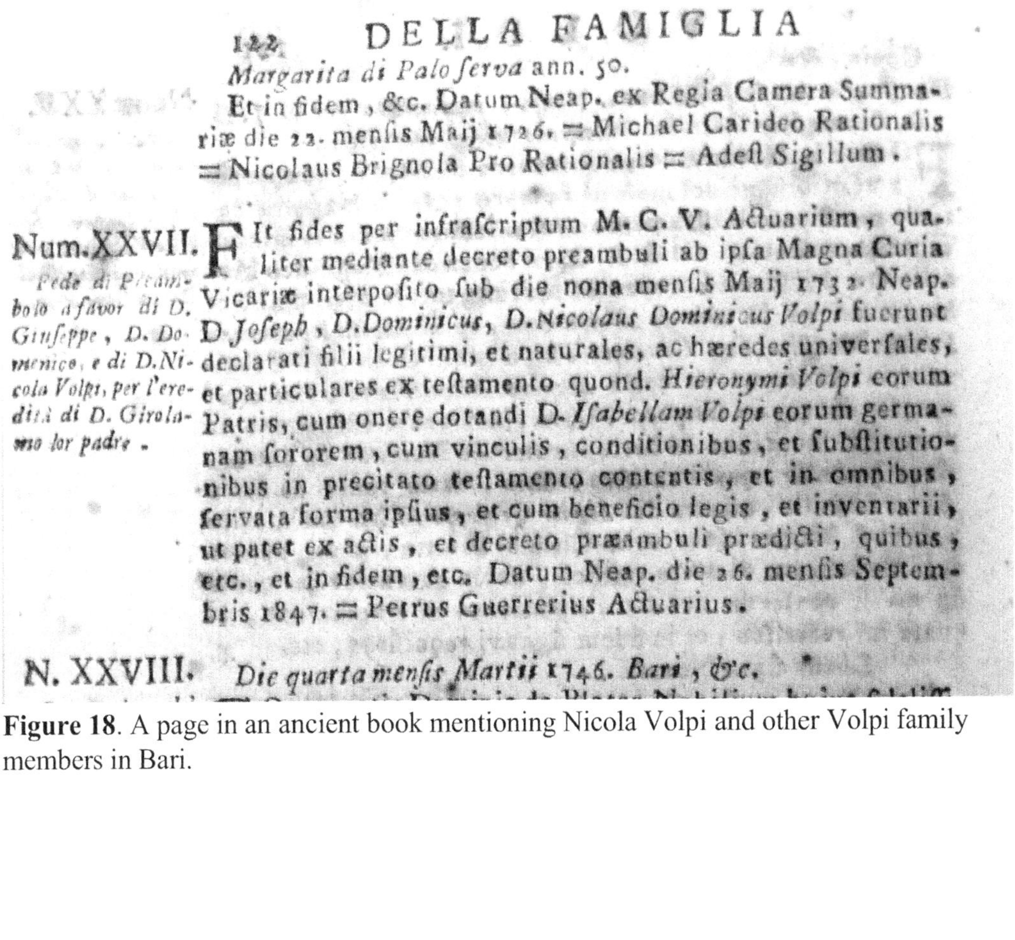
122 DELLA FAMIGLIA

Margarita di Palo ſerva ann. 50.

Et in fidem, &c. Datum Neap. ex Regia Camera Summariæ die 22. menſis Maij 1726. = Michael Carideo Rationalis = Nicolaus Brignola Pro Rationalis = Adeſt Sigillum.

Num. XXVII. *Fede di Preambolo a favor di D. Giuſeppe, D. Domenico, e di D. Nicola Volpi, per l'eredità di D. Girolamo lor padre.*

Fit fides per infraſcriptum M. C. V. Actuarium, qualiter mediante decreto preambuli ab ipſa Magna Curia Vicariæ interpoſito ſub die nona menſis Maij 1732. Neap. D. *Joſeph*, D. *Dominicus*, D. *Nicolaus Dominicus Volpi* fuerunt declarati filii legitimi, et naturales, ac hæredes univerſales, et particulares ex teſtamento quond. *Hieronymi Volpi* eorum Patris, cum onere dotandi D. *Iſabellam Volpi* eorum germanam ſororem, cum vinculis, conditionibus, et ſubſtitutionibus in precitato teſtamento contentis, et in omnibus, ſervata forma ipſius, et cum beneficio legis, et inventarii, ut patet ex actis, et decreto præambuli prædicti, quibus, etc., et in fidem, etc. Datum Neap. die 26. menſis Septembris 1847. = Petrus Guerrerius Actuarius.

N. XXVIII. *Die quarta menſis Martii 1746. Bari, &c.*

Figure 18. A page in an ancient book mentioning Nicola Volpi and other Volpi family members in Bari.

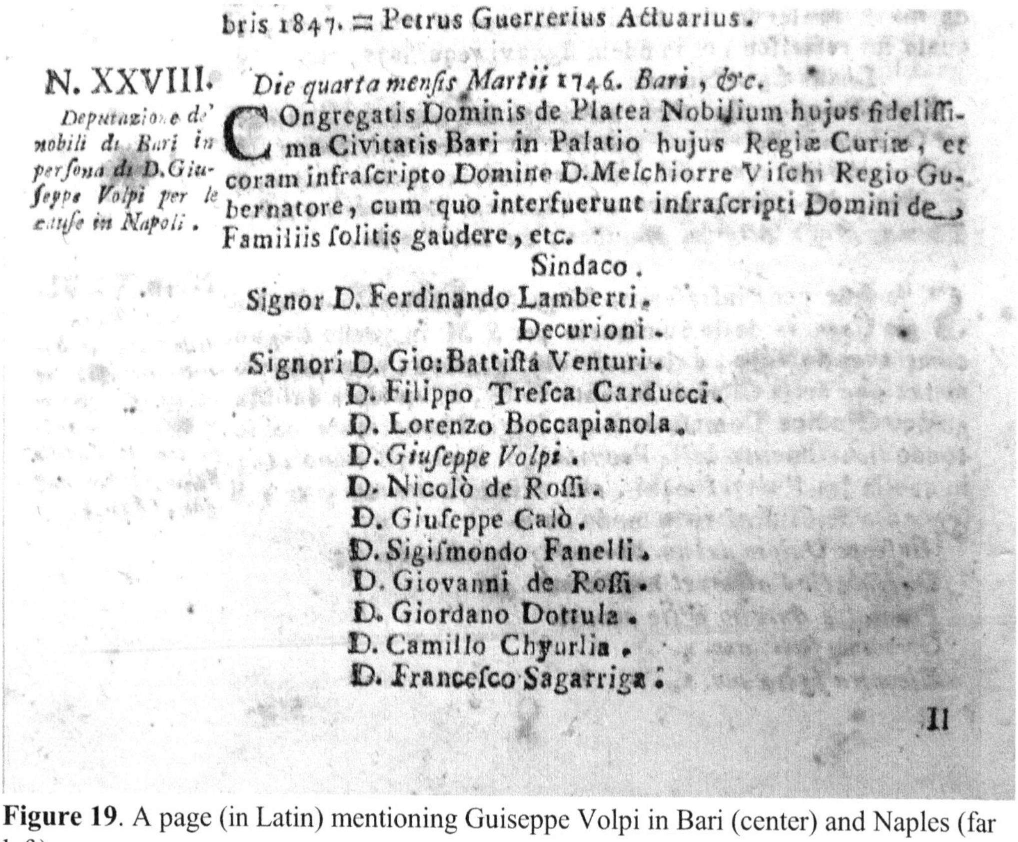

bris 1847. = Petrus Guerrerius Actuarius.

N. XXVIII.
Deputazio.e de' nobili di Bari in persona di D. Giuseppe Volpi per le cause in Napoli.

Die quarta mensis Martii 1746. *Bari , &c.*

Congregatis Dominis de Platea Nobilium hujus fideliſſima Civitatis Bari in Palatio hujus Regiæ Curiæ , et coram infraſcripto Domine D. Melchiorre Viſchi Regio Gubernatore, cum quo interfuerunt infraſcripti Domini de Familiis ſolitis gaudere , etc.

Sindaco.
Signor D. Ferdinando Lamberti.

Decurioni.
Signori D. Gio: Battiſtà Venturi.
D. Filippo Treſca Carducci.
D. Lorenzo Boccapianola.
D. Giuſeppe Volpi.
D. Nicolò de Roſſi.
D. Giuſeppe Calò.
D. Sigiſmondo Fanelli.
D. Giovanni de Roſſi.
D. Giordano Dottula.
D. Camillo Chyurlia.
D. Franceſco Sagarriga.

II

Figure 19. A page (in Latin) mentioning Guiseppe Volpi in Bari (center) and Naples (far left).

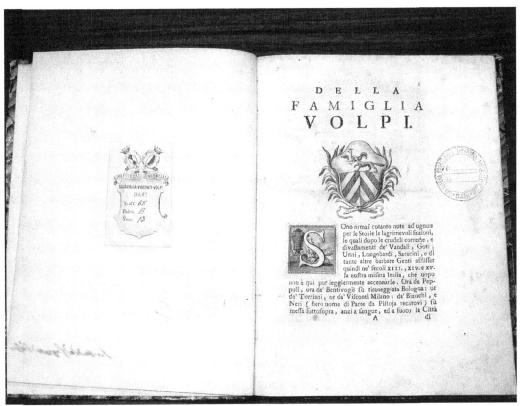

Figure 20. Title page of the Volpi family history book in the *Biblioteca Nationale* of Bari. The family coat of arms starts off ahead of the explanation for the contents of the book.

Figure 21. Volpi Family Crest in Bari National Library (note fox with prey)

Figures 22 and 23 below provide a comparison of family crests discovered for ancient Volpi families who lived 600 miles apart (and maybe 300 years in time), one family having thrived in Como at or about 1000 AD, the other becoming prominent in Bari, far south in the Italic peninsula hundreds of years later. (The Bari branch likely had become separated from the northern Como branch in the middle ages due to outbreaks of deadly pestilence, causing them to migrate south to Bari. Most likely, in those three or so centuries, the two families that coexisted so far apart lost track of each other's presence and survival, but still retained some vestiges of their relationship.)

Figure 22. Coat of Arms for Volpi Family in Como.

Figure 23. Coat of Arms for Volpi
family in Bari.

The proof in the pudding, as the expression implies, is in the similarity (and dissimilarity) of central (and repeated) features in these coats of arms: the fox, the prey, and the chevrons. The similarities and dissimilarities are consistent with what was likely, as commonly practiced in those days: that is, renderings of slightly different word-described, rather than ink-copied representations of their respective coats of arms.

Eventually, according to the research, writing and publication of the book *Della Famiglia Volpi* of Bari by Signor Don Guiseppe Volpi, the lineage had been (semi-officially) recognized, but not until the mid-1700s.

Keep in mind, of course, that in the 1300s there was no *autostrada*, no high-speed rail, nor air transport in those days. Being 600 miles apart then was essentially being disconnected for an eternity in time and distance.

I vaguely recall — through persevering research in American libraries such as at Dumbarton Oaks, Harvard, and Chicago — discovering the existence of the book in the libraries of Naples and Bari which had the only two surviving copies. That became a target of my genealogical research, partly commissioned through the professional services of Trafford Cole.

Figure 24 is one page from the ancient document (mentioning Guglielmo Volpi of Bari in 1735:

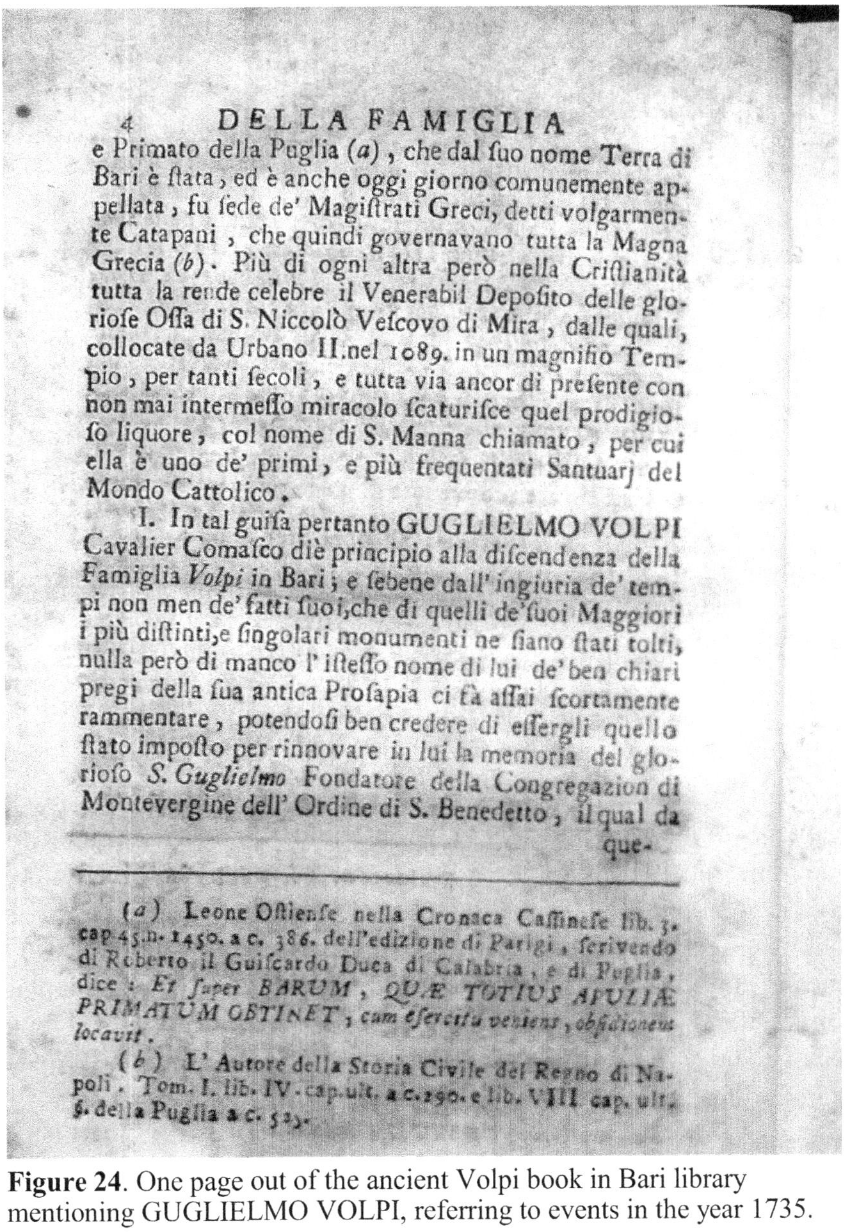

4 DELLA FAMIGLIA

e Primato della Puglia (*a*), che dal ſuo nome Terra di Bari è ſtata, ed è anche oggi giorno comunemente appellata, fu ſede de' Magiſtrati Greci, detti volgarmente Catapani, che quindi governavano tutta la Magna Grecia (*b*). Più di ogni altra però nella Criſtianità tutta la rende celebre il Venerabil Depoſito delle glorioſe Oſſa di S. Niccolò Veſcovo di Mira, dalle quali, collocate da Urbano II. nel 1089. in un magnifio Tempio, per tanti ſecoli, e tutta via ancor di preſente con non mai intermeſſo miracolo ſcaturiſce quel prodigioſo liquore, col nome di S. Manna chiamato, per cui ella è uno de' primi, e più frequentati Santuarj del Mondo Cattolico.

I. In tal guiſa pertanto GUGLIELMO VOLPI Cavalier Comaſco diè principio alla diſcendenza della Famiglia *Volpi* in Bari; e ſebene dall' ingiuria de' tempi non men de' fatti ſuoi, che di quelli de' ſuoi Maggiori i più diſtinti, e ſingolari monumenti ne ſiano ſtati tolti, nulla però di manco l' iſteſſo nome di lui de' ben chiari pregi della ſua antica Proſapia ci fà aſſai ſcortamente rammentare, potendoſi ben credere di eſſergli quello ſtato impoſto per rinnovare in lui la memoria del glorioſo *S. Guglielmo* Fondatore della Congregazion di Montevergine dell' Ordine di S. Benedetto, il qual da que-

(*a*) Leone Oſtienſe nella Cronaca Caſſineſe lib. 3. cap. 45. n. 1450. a c. 386. dell'edizione di Parigi, ſcrivendo di Roberto il Guiſcardo Duca di Calabria, e di Puglia, dice: *Et ſuper BARUM, QUÆ TOTIUS APULIÆ PRIMATUM OBTINET, cum exercitu veniens, obſidionem locavit.*

(*b*) L' Autore della Storia Civile del Regno di Napoli. Tom. I. lib. IV. cap. ult. a c. 290. e lib. VIII cap. ult. §. della Puglia a c. 523.

Figure 24. One page out of the ancient Volpi book in Bari library mentioning GUGLIELMO VOLPI, referring to events in the year 1735.

Figure 25. Leading page of ancient book found in Bari Library, with another (and only other) copy of the book ascribed to the Naples library as well).

One thing particularly satisfying was that close examination and translation (by Cole) of the contents of the book in Bari made it possible to trace Volpi family origins to a time and place in Italy 1000 years ago. That's quite an achievement in ancestral research. Of great importance and key to the tracing is that the coat of arms in the Bari book is essentially the same as that heralded by the Volpi family in Como, as mentioned in connection with Figures 26 and 27. But possibly even more significant is that back in the 1700s the author of the book (Gugliemo Volpi) had found enough information to track the family roots back to a specific individual and city in northern Italy at around the year 1000 AD.

CHAPTER III: WHAT'S IN A NAME?
(FROM 1861)

The Family Name "Volpi" in Contemporary Italy

Of course there were many individuals and families named Volpi, Volpe, and some variations like De Volpi and Di Volpi to be found in Italy (elsewhere too in the present-day world). Only a few of the same-spelling families have some logical claim to the earlier Volpi heritages back to the middle ages, or earlier.

On some of my trips to Europe, particularly when an opportunity arose to go to Italy, I would make inquiries about the Volpi family and possible ancestors. On a few occasions I made cold calls when traveling in Italy, hoping that whoever I called spoke English or could communicate with my limited Italian language "skill." I often found it difficult. Once, when trying to get to my sister's house near Milan, I had to stop a couple of times and call again. (It's not like they lived on main street in some identifiable village. No, it was small suburb, not on the beaten track.)

I've already published a full-sized book (appropriately titled *Lover, Soldier, Reprobate*), tracking my father's career, life and shenanigans; so only some fundamental information about the surname Volpi will be repeated (below) in this book.

The Family Name "De Volpi" in the United States (1892)

Originally, when my father joined the U.S. Army in 1892, he enlisted at a military installation on Davids Island, just off New York City, as Bonaventura Weiss, initially going by his mother's family name Weiss.

Here's an entry taken from his enlistment record found in Washington, DC, archives:

Figure 26. Bonaventura Enlistment in U.S. Army at Davids Island.

Item 470: **Weiss, Bonaventura**; Nov. 21 [1892]; New York, NY; enlisted by Burke; born Venice, Italy; age 21; occupation Sailor; Blue eyes; Brown hair; Dark complexion; 5'7" height.

That all seems to have been valid, including him having been a sailor because when he first arrived in the United States from Italy, he was evidently shanghaied in New York City to serve on board a ship headed to Chile. (His Army enlistment medical exam confirmed bumps on his head, such as those obtained when knocked out by bean bags.)

I've never been able to find any records of his immigration into the United States, although there's still not much info available on ship's crews those days. Immigration records posted online are not complete, by any means.

However, when he signed up in the Army, he underwent a thorough medical "short arm" inspection, resulting in the medical indications described in Figures 27 and 28. Note the scars on his arms and head, quite possibly due to his having been shanghaied when he first arrived in the States.

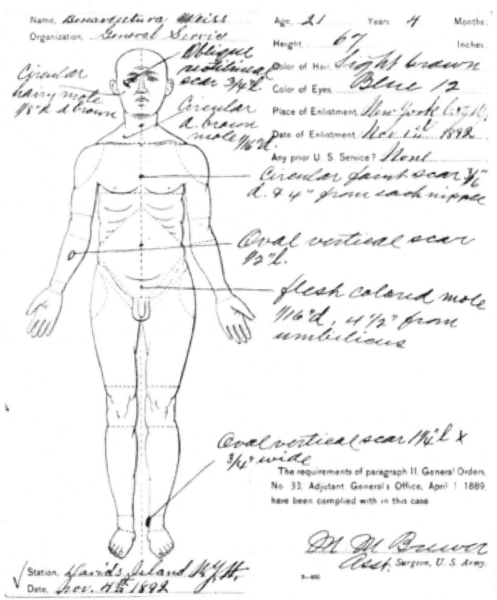

Figure 27. Bonaventura Medical Profile on Enlistment in U.S. Army (front view) .
Note scars.

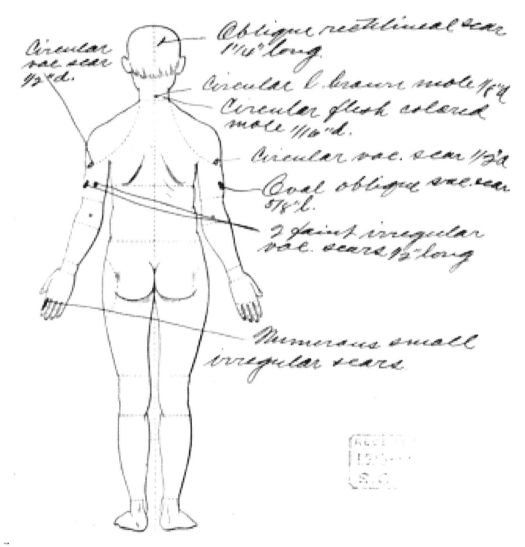

Figure 28. Bonaventura Medical Profile on Enlistment in U.S. Army (back view). Note scars.

A "How-To" On Getting Shanghaied. The Thirteenth U.S. Constitutional Amendment outlawed slavery in 1865, but men were routinely drugged, beaten, and kidnaped long into the 20th Century for involuntary service on ships. No seafaring experience or knowledge was required for the menial jobs aboard a sailing ship; any able body would do.

An unaware teenager might have passed out from liquor, a drug, or a blackjack – only to be awakened aboard a ship bound for Chile, going around Cape Horn. Thousands of victims fell prey to crimps along the waterfronts of port cities on both coasts. One guy thought the stranger he met on New York's Canal Street was hiring him to help whitewash a ship anchored offshore. Instead he scraped masts and decks all the way around Cape Horn to California. Two guys sightseeing in Baltimore in 1888 were befriended by a man who, after several drinks, invited them to visit his yacht. It turned out to be a commercial oystering sloop.

The crimp's primary targets were seamen, abducted from boardinghouses and bars or off the streets, and shuttled to waiting ships. Any reluctance to sign shipping articles specifying wages and duties could be overcome by force or forgery, often just a witnessed X. Some crimps were legitimate middlemen. But most, despised by sailors and shipowners alike, just supplied bodies for sailing crews. As one victim observed, it "reduced the value of a sailor to the price of a knockout drop."

At or about the time, cholera was rampant around the world. In view of the 2020 Covid-19 pandemic, it is worthwhile to be reminded of the 1892 cholera epidemic (note: pandemics are widespread, while an epidemic is confined to a smaller accumulation of people, such as the passengers in steerage aboard a ship):

Cholera is an infection of the small intestine that causes a large amount of watery diarrhea. The main symptoms are profuse watery diarrhea, vomiting, and abdominal pain. Transmission is primarily through contaminated drinking water or food. The severity of the diarrhea and vomiting can lead to rapid dehydration and electrolyte imbalance. Primary treatment now is with oral or intravenous rehydration solutions. Nowadays, antibiotics may in certain cases be used. Cholera is a major cause of death in the world. It was one of the earliest infections to be studied by epidemiological methods.
Cholera likely has its origins in and is endemic to the Indian subcontinent. The disease originally spread by trade routes (land and sea) to Russia, then to Western Europe, and from Europe to North America.

Cholera is now no longer considered a pressing health threat in Europe and North America due to filtering and chlorination of water supplies, but it still heavily affects populations in developing countries. For example, in late 2010, long after a disastrous earthquake in Haiti, a cholera outbreak in the capital, Port-Au-Prince, had already killed over 200 people.

Because Cholera is waterborne, chlorine can be added to the drinking water to help contain the bacterial infection. Washing hands with soap and disinfecting water are also important preventative measures.

Yeah, Bonaventura immigrated to the States around 1890, when still a teenager, and joined the army, the U.S. Army, around 1892. Enlisted in New York. Guess that was the best thing going then; the Army was eager to accept anyone, even non-citizens.

Incidentally, about that time, there was a lot of turmoil going on in the "Wild West" of the United States.

Steerage is the lower deck of a ship, where the cargo is stored above the closed hold. In the late 19th and early 20th century, steamship steerage decks were used to provide the lowest cost and lowest class of travel, often for European and Chinese immigrants to North America.

Cholera Arrives in New York Bay. In August 1892, cholera was affecting Russian Jews who arrived in New York harbor from Hamburg, Germany. According to *Harper's Weekly*, September 17, 1892:

On the 17th of August, the *Moravia*, a two-masted steamer of the Hamburg line, sailed from that city with 385 steerage passengers, bringing [to New York] a clean bill of health from the American consul, who certified that when the ship sailed there were no infectious or contagious disease prevailing in Hamburg. The American consul was deceived, like the rest of the world....

An evaluation of the surgeon's report showed that there had been twenty-four cases of "cholerine" and twenty-two deaths during the voyage. The health office ordered that the *Moravia* should steam to lower Quarantine, in the outer bay [of New York harbor]. Examination showed that the "cholerine" on the *Moravia* was Asiatic cholera of the most fatal type.

The announcement of cholera on the ship caused a great deal of excitement in New York and in the country in general. All ships coming from Europe were detained longer than usual while health officials tried to determine the gravity of the threat. Inspections of other ships showed that there was Cholera on the *Rugia* which sailed from Hamburg on August 21 and the *Normannia* which had sailed from Hamburg on the 27. Both ships had made other stops before leaving Europe. All deaths on these ships were in steerage.

Steerage passengers from these ships were taken to Hoffman Island and bathed while the ships were disinfected. All passengers regardless of class were detained on board.

As for his first name, Bonaventura explained to someone else, it was his given name: translates roughly to "good luck."

Wounded Knee Massacre. On 29 December 1890, the Wounded Knee massacre of native-Americans took place in South Dakota. Between 150 and 300 Sioux Indians were killed by U.S. troops sent to disarm them. Up to 30 U.S. soldiers died in the action. The massacre happened near Wounded Knee Creek on the Lakota Pine Ridge Indian Reservation. Chiefs Sitting Bull and Big Foot had been killed just before and at the massacre. Sitting Bull was famous for his major victory in 1876 against Col. George Armstrong Custer at the Battle of the Little Bighorn.

Figure 29. Map of Oklahoma in 1890s, with Indian Territory upper left, marked in red. (Bordered [clockwise] to the East by Nebraska, South and West by Texas, and North by Kansas.)

When he first signed up in 1892 in the U.S. Army, Bonaventua was sent off with a regiment assembled to manage the forthcoming Cherokee Strip land rush in September 1893 (see Figures 29-31). The Army was eager to accept anyone, even non-citizens. Although at the time there was a lot of turmoil going on in the "Wild West" of the United States, the infamous Wounded Knee Massacre was already a matter of history.

Altogether, Bonaventura served in the U.S. Army for something like 25 years with distinction and medals awarded, reaching the lofty enlisted rating of Chief Master Sargent.

Shipboard Cholera Quarantine and Passenger Consequences. The 1892 *Harpers* article goes on to say:

Here were nearly six hundred people shut up in infected ships on which deaths from the infection were of daily occurrence, with the only water aboard that from the polluted Elbe [A river in Germany, its original source of water before departing].

For many more days there was no practical solution of this problem, and from the ships came daily pathetic appeals for help and indignant protests against what the imprisoned passengers thought to be official heartlessness and incompetency. Both appeal and protest were natural. Among the passengers were United States Senator McPherson, of New Jersey; Mr. E. L. Godkin, editor of the New York Evening Post; the Rev. Richard D Harlan, of New York; and Mr. A. M. Palmer, the well-known theater manager.... [Also] Lottie Collins, the dancer and singer who made famous the song "Ta-ra-ra-boom-de-ay," was also among the *Normannia's* passengers.

Letters sent from the ships were fumigated before being delivered. In following days there were continued deaths on these three ships but only two new infected ships arrived. All of the people who worked with the passengers on the ships and on the two islands were cut off from "their family and loved ones" as long as there were cholera cases on the islands.

The big question was "What to do with the healthy passengers?" This turned into a first-degree farce as first-class passengers were moved from one boat to another. Later they were taken to a quarantine camp on Fire Island where they were opposed by locals before finally allowed to land and then transported back to the New York Harbor. They were finally permitted on September 17th to disembark at Hoboken piers.

In the end: There were a total of 110 deaths, 66 on board the ships and 44 in the Quarantine Station. Something in the neighborhood of 5,300 immigrants were bathed and disinfected on Hoffman Island.

Cholera was not the only infectious disease present on these ships. The *Scandia* also had a measles epidemic among the children in steerage.

The twenty-day quarantine period subsequently imposed on all incoming vessels greatly slowed immigration until the embargo was lifted a half-year later.

The 1892 outbreak in Hamburg killed 8,600 people. The incident also had the unfortunate repercussion of instilling prejudice against Russian Jewish immigrants in New York City.

Some Native Americans in the United States have had heightened difficulty with the abuse of **alcohol**. Among contemporary Native Americans and Alaska Natives, about 12% of all deaths are alcohol-related. A survey of death certificates from 2006-2010 showed that deaths among Native Americans due to alcohol are roughly four times as common as in the general US population.

Historically, those Native American tribes who manufactured alcoholic drinks used them and other mind-altering substances in ritual settings and rarely for personal enjoyment. Alcohol dependence was largely unknown when European contact was made. The use of alcohol as a trade item and the practice of intoxication for entertainment gradually undermined traditional Native American culture. By the late 18th century, alcoholism was recognized as a serious problem in many Native-American communities.

Figure 30. Old Photograph of Boomers Camp in Kansas, waiting for the Cherokee Strip to be opened to settlers.

Hot off the press: U.S. Supreme Court rules **nearly half of Oklahoma is tribal land**. A 5-4 decision declaring that much of eastern Oklahoma is an Indian reservation (See Figure 30) could reshape criminal justice in the area by preventing state authorities from prosecuting Native Americans. The July 2020 decision was steeped in the United States government's long history of brutal removals and broken treaties with Indigenous tribes, and grappled with whether lands of the Muscogee (Creek) Nation had remained a reservation after Oklahoma became a state.

Fort Supply, Indian Territory. In the Oklahoma Indian Territory, Fort Supply, was originally established as "Camp of Supply" on November 18, 1868, in support of General Philip Sheridan's winter campaign against the Southern Plains Indians.

The Cherokee Nation was a legal, autonomous, tribal government in North America existing from 1794–1906. Often referred to simply as The Nation by its inhabitants, it should not be confused with what is known today as the "modern" Cherokee Nation.

Other native-American tribes in the boundary at the time (shown in Figure 31) included the Creek, Chickasaw, Choctow, and Seminole Nations.

Fort Supply was near the center of the Indian Territory. The historic site of Ft. Supply is now north and west of Oklahoma City.

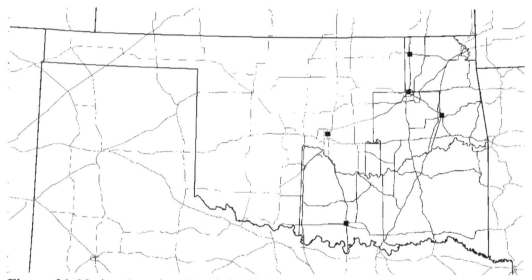

Figure 31. Native-American Lands in Oklahoma Affected by U.S. Supreme Court 2020 Decision. The dots indicate locations of major cities now situated near or on Indian tribal reservations.

The original Nation consisted of many indigenous peoples: the Cherokee of the Qualla Boundary; those who relocated voluntarily from the southeastern United States to the Indian erritory (circa 1820); those who were forced by the United States government to relocate by way of the Trail of Tears (1830s); Cherokee Freedmen (freed slaves); and many descendants of the Natchez, the Delaware and the Shawnee peoples.

Fort Supply had three roles in its 25-year history: (1) its first ten years (1868-78) helping to protect the Cheyennes and Arapahoes from other Indian tribes (mainly the raiding Kiowas) as well as from exploitation by "Whites," especially whiskey traders from Kansas who used the supply routes to ply their illegal trade in the nearby Indian villages; (2) the following dozen years protecting the cattle business along quickly developing cattle trails (the Chisholm Trail to the east and the Dodge City Road to the west); and (3) after 1890, serving as headquarters for the opening of the Cherokee Outlet to homesteaders.

Figure 32. Preserved postcard-style photos depicting opening of third Cherokee Strip land run on 16 September 1893 in Oklahoma; top photo is annotated "one minute before the start."

According to a letter from his mother, Bonaventura wrote to her that he had married an Indian (Native-American) girl and sired a son Henry. I've been utterly unable to confirm either of his assertions. In any event, it appears that around 1895 he was shipped by train, presumably with his regiment, to Fort Eire in New York State, near Niagara Falls and across from Canada. This information is contained within a letter preserved by what I distinguish as the "Michigan branch" of the De Volpi family, which had moved there from Lockport, NY.

Here's a tabulation of Bonaventura's likely and possible wives and children:

Wives and Children of Bonaventura

Wives	Where Married	Year of Marriage	Children	Year of Child's Birth
Virginia	Oklahoma Indian Territory	~1893	Henry?	~1893
Bessie Repass	Lockport, New York	1895	Paul Charles Harold (Carl Francis)	1897 1898
Kate Howe	New York City	1899	Charles Patrick Charlotte David	1910 1910 1912
?	Philippines or Orient	1902-1908	?	
[Agatha Allison]	Philadelphia	~1920	Ventura	~1920
[Annette Meus]	London, Naples, or shipboard	late 1920s?	Loreta	1929
Bertha Gaber	New York City	1930	Alexander	1931 (last child)
Romana Mischi	Milan	1934	Irène	1926

Indeed, that's at least four and up to eight wives, with at least seven maybe up to eleven children.

Notice the gap of about a half-dozen years from 1902 through 1908, or so, at which time Bonaventura might very well have had a wife and family in the Philippines, although no documents to that effect have surfaced.

According to military records, Bonaventura had first served with the U.S. Army in the American West, in particular at the opening of the Cherokee Strip in Oklahoma to settlers in 1892. He was then shipped to a "Fort Niagara" in northern New York state.

Documented later as his first wife was Bessie, of the Lockport DeVolpi-family branch — the kinfolk of Pete, Paul, and Jeannette whom I met decades later in Michigan.

The Family Name "De Volpi" in Upper New York State (1895)

In 1895 Bonaventura married Bessie Repass in upstate New York, and had two children by her, all under his original surname of Weiss. On the way East from Chicago once, I drove from Chicago to Lockport, New York, but no members of the De Volpi or Repass family still lived there.

It was children of this family and their progeny, particularly Pete De Volpi, that I met in the course of time and compared family-history notes. Much of this family had moved from Lockport, New York, to Michigan, although Pete was living in Harrisburg, Pennsylvania, when I first visited him at his home.

Fort Niagara is a fortification originally built to protect the interests of New France in North America. It is located near Youngstown, New York, on the eastern bank of the Niagara River at its mouth, on Lake Ontario.

Beginning in 1756, the main entrance to Fort Niagara was established at the southern bastion, on the bank of the Niagara River. The French named this gate the *Porte des Cinq Nations*, that is the Gate of the Five Nations, in honor of the Iroquois Confederacy.

In 1726, a two-story "Maison a Machicoulis" or "Machicolated House" was constructed on the same site. The fort was expanded in 1755 due to increased tensions between French and British colonial interests.

The newer Fort Niagara contained a thousand-yard rifle range, access to rail lines, and access to the industrial areas of Niagara Falls and Buffalo. Fort Niagara trained troops for the Spanish–American War.

Lockport, NY, is about 20 or so miles from Fort Niagara.

The Family Name "De Volpi" in Canada (1899)

On 22 May 1899, about five months after he was discharged from the his military unit (the Rhode Island Volunteers), Bonaventura in New York City married Katherine Howe, a woman from Montreal, Canada. Bonaventura used the name Paul B. De Volpi for the obvious purpose of skirting the laws of New York State regarding bigamy. (He was still married to Bessie Repass.)

Much of the story about this marriage to Kate is narrated in *Lover, Soldier, Reprobate*. Bonaventura managed to keep the New York and Canadian families from knowing about each other, probably until the 1920s when a multiple ex-wife scramble to get a share of his pension came about.

Eventually, having started my own inquires, I decided to call her son Charles in Canada at about a month after Pete called him. That coincidence ended up with Pete and I getting in touch with each other and finding out about our common paternal origin.

The Family Name "De Volpi" with the US Army in the Philippines (1899)

A few months after his 1899 marriage to Kate, Bonaventura sailed for the Philippines with the 47th U.S. Volunteers, having been designated Regimental Sergeant Major. That's a rather high noncom rating, as anyone who has served in the military will tell you.

It was nearly a decade before he reappeared stateside; so, in retrospect, based on his subsequent rather free-handed practice regarding monogamy in marriage, we can assume he might have had other wedded or non-wedded arrangements with women in the Philippines.

At a point in time when I was conducting family-history research, it included a visit to the Philippine Embassy in Washington, DC, where I scoured the telephone directories they had available. No luck. No one with any relevant name permutation.

Recommendation for Field Commission. There were several letters on file recommending 1ˢᵗ Sgt. B.P. Weiss be commissioned as an officer for "conspicuous service... exceptional influence and control over men in quarters and in the field... and repeatedly displayed in action exceptional daring and good judgment." (18 Jul 1900). Curiously, no specifics are provided for the military "action."

Months later, he was again recommended, this time for "marked judgement, courage and capability", this time with accompanying specifics about his combat experience in expeditions and battles in the Philippines.

Another letter in his file says, "It is his desire to be recommended for Lieut. of Native Scouts. He is well fitted for this position by his knowledge of the spanish language and past experience with native guides and scouts, besides being a man of undoubted courage and an excellent soldier...." (26 Feb. 1901)

Because Bonaventura was not an American citizen, he couldn't be advanced to commissioned rank. (Born in Italy but did not need to be a citizen to serve in the U.S. armed forces).

The Family Name "De Volpi" elsewhere in the United States and Canada

That search of Philippine records reminds me of a comment made I think by Harold (Repass) to the effect that, wherever he went in the United States, he examined phone directories and whenever he could, looked for like-named relatives.

Medical Report on an Invalid.

Station Shorncliffe.

Date 31/3/15.

P.P.C.L.I.

1. Unit

2. Regimental No.   1224.

3. Rank   Sergt.

4. Name   De Volpi, Paul B.W.

5. Age last birthday   44 years.

6. Enlisted { on 12/8/1914.
            { at Montreal

7. Former Trade { Soldier.
   or Occupation {

8. Disability.

Malaria and Gastro Enteritis.

Statement of Case.

Note.—The answers to the following questions are to be filled in by the Officer in medical charge of the case. In answering them he will carefully discriminate between the man's unsupported statements and evidence recorded in his military and medical documents. He will also carefully distinguish cases entirely due to venereal disease.

9. Date of origin of disability.   1900.

10. Place of origin of disability.   Phillipines Islands.

11. Give concisely the essential facts of the history of the disability, noting entries on the Medical History Sheet bearing on the case.

   1. History of 40 years active service, mostly in tropical and semi tropical countrys, never in Brittish forces.

   2.—Contracted Amoe Dysentry in China.

   3.—At present recurrent attacks of fever and ague.

   4.—At present chronica Cyrtitis and prostatis in addition to the above.

12. (a) Give your opinion as to the causation of the disability.

    Infection with- a. Plarmodium.Malaria.
                    b. Amoe dysentry.

   (b) If you consider it to have been caused by active service, climate, or ordinary military service, explain the specific conditions to which you attribute it (*See notes on page* 3).

   Active service and climatic conditions.

Figure 33. 1915 Canadian Army disability record for Bonaventura (Paul B. W. De Volpi), which was filed in Shorncliff, England, when he was serving with the Canadian Army in World War I.

During the time gap between late 1901 and later in the decade, a couple of DeVolpi-family-related things were happening elsewhere in the world. On 11 April 1904, some formal photos were taken in Munich depicting Bonaventura's mother Fanny in one photograph, and others with his sister Anita. In this book I've not previously mentioned anything about Anita (Figure 36, next page).

In 1908, or maybe a year later, Bonaventura's sister got married, probably in Montreal. It's a story included with considerable detail in *Lover, Soldier, Reprobate*, but left out here because of its many distracting twists and turns.

And, for the record, another of Bonaventura's future wives, Romana, was born in Italy, 6 March 1905.

The Family Name "De Volpi" in Canada Before and During World War I (1914)

Immediately after World War I broke out in Europe, Canada mobilized a volunteer regiment, the "Princess Pats" to go to the aid of England. Bonaventura enlisted too, but by December 1914 either he had a new disablement or his old injuries caught up with him His medical report of March 31, 1915 [Figure 35] indicates a number of disabilities that he did indeed acquire in the Phillippines.

Not surprisingly, Bonaventura had been assigned a cushy job as supply sergeant for the Canadian contingent fighting in France.

Bonaventura Imprisoned in England (1917-1921)

Because of his deteriorated physical condition (Figure 35), and thus officially unable to fight any longer on the front lines during World War I, Bonaventura had been assigned to a cushy job in Britain, still working for the Princess Pats Canadian regiment. That reassignment turned out to his downfall, getting caught stealing Canadian army checks sent routinely to England for payments to what turned out to be dead soldiers. He and another co-conspirator had been cashing the checks for themselves.

His offense was so egregious that it even made the newspaper in far away Australia.

Bonaventura was discharged for "Misconduct" on 19 November 1918, reduced in rank to private, and stripped of his medals and decorations. Up through August 1917, things seem to be going alright for Bonaventura. That month he was written up in the London Gazetteer for valiant war services with the Princess Pats in France. A month later he was appointed what appears to be "Supply Clerk." Even as late as May 1918, he was still receiving commendations for "valuable services rendered in connection with the war."

Bonaventura was sentenced to prison in England, and he didn't return to Montreal until about 1921, apparently serving about a five- or six-year term. I say "about" because it is unclear just when he returned to Canada and whether he might have been furloughed from prison to join the Canadian contingent fighting in Russia (see tabulation later of 13 Bonaventura Enlistment and Military Combat Claims and Events).

The Family Name "De Volpi" in Montreal (1899 and after 1921)

Starting October 1899, while he was in the Philippines, Bonaventura designated his military family pay share to be allotted to Mrs. Katherine De Volpi, of 331 Ontario St., Montreal, Canada.

His U.S. Army pay in the amount of $30/month was allotted to Katherine. At first, on the enrollment papers, he had filled in "single," but listed "Mrs. P. De Volpi" of 51 W. 9th Street, in Greenwich Village, as his emergency contact. That would be Kate, the second Mrs. P. DeVolpi; by then he had abandoned his first wife, Bessie, who lived upstate New York.

It was to Montreal and to Katherine that he returned in 1921 after his imprisonment in England. Sometime before, his sister Anita (Fig. 34) had moved to Montreal.

Figure 34. Anita, Bonaventura's sister.

The Family Name "De Volpi" in Lockport, New York (1950s or 60s)

When I passed through Lockport sometime in the 1960s or 70s, I could find no sign of any De Volpi's having lived in the town. (They had long ago relocated the family to Michigan.)

The Family Name "De Volpi" in New York City (1930-)
In 1904, my mother arrived in New York City as a child with six members of her family, the Gabers. When she married Bonaventura in 1930, she took on the name De Volpi.

For a while his service records reflect a dual identity, and then a transition from Bonaventura P. Weiss to Bonaventura P. W. De Volpi. It's hard to figure out just how he pulled this off with the Army.

Somewhere along the way, according to his U.S. Army military records, Bonaventua had changed his last name to reflect his father's family origins: Volpi and De Volpi, the latter meaning "from or of the Volpi" family (of Trento).

There are some very vague indications in Bonaventura's correspondence with his mother that while he was in the Army in Oklahoma he might have gotten married or had an "affair" or simply knocked up a "squaw," and that she bore him a son, possibly named Henry. I've been unable to verify this conjecture, which only derives quite indirectly from a long letter written to him in Italian by his mother.

Ice Cream, Anyone? The ice cream sundae originated in the late 19th century. Some sources say that the sundae was invented to circumvent blue laws, which forbade serving sodas on Sunday.

Buffalo, New York (not far from Lockport) is one of the cities claiming to be the birthplace of the sundae. The ice cream cone and banana split both became popular in the early 20th century. Several food vendors claimed to have invented the ice cream cone at the 1904 World's Fair in St. Louis, but Europeans were enjoying cones long before 1904.

In the early 20th century of the United States, the ice cream soda became a popular treat at the soda shop, the soda fountain, and the ice cream parlor. During American Prohibition, the soda fountain to some extent substituted for outlawed alcohol establishments such as bars and saloons.

The introduction of soft ice cream came about in the 20th century.

The Spanish-American War and the Philippine Insurrection.

According to his service file, after training in upstate New York, Bonaventura remained in the U.S. Army as a career soldier. When the Spanish-American War broke out, his regiment prepared for military action, but the war ended quickly. However, the Philippine Insurrection ensued, and the Army sent his unit over to the Philippine Islands, where he fought (valiantly, according to his military records) for the duration of the conflict. As best I can tell, he probably remained in the Philippines in some sort of irregular status for at least a half-dozen unaccountable years.

At the time, the Philippines was a major producer of hemp, a type of manila-cord plant, then widely used for clothing and animal feed. There is a notable history of the U.S. Army's efforts to open up the hemp ports. According to his service file, Bonaventura was commended for distinguished action in armed combat during the Philippine Insurrection, especially with what was called Major Kobbè's expedition to open up the ports.

The "First Vietnam." The Philippine-American War (Insurrection) has become a forgotten war in the U.S. annals. The civil war in the Philippines was ugly, ruthless, and brutal, considered among the cruelest conflicts, sometimes referred to as the "first Vietnam" for the United States.

American textbooks might contain several pages on the Spanish-American War but usually only devote a paragraph on the Philippine-American War, despite the fact that the latter was more pronounced in terms of duration, scale, and number of casualties.

As many as 126,000 American soldiers, or three-fourths of the U.S. Army, were shipped to the Philippines, and at least 600,000 Filipinos died during the decade-long war. Tropical diseases took their toll of the Americans, with nearly one-third of the U.S. troops on sick lists at times. Filipino casualties altogether may have been close to one million or the equivalent of one-sixth of the country's population.

Bonaventura did not return stateside until about 1909. There's nothing in his military records to indicate what he was doing for the intervening 7 or 8 years in or around the Philippines. Evidently Bonaventura stayed until then in the Islands, accumulating some cash which he splashed about when he showed up in the States.

Before the Farm Bill of 2018 passed, **cannabidiol** or "CBD" and the psychoactive THC had no legal differentiation. The 2018 Farm Bill was more expansive. It allowed hemp cultivation broadly, not simply pilot programs for studying market interest in hemp-derived products. It also put no restrictions on the sale, transport, or possession of hemp-derived products, so long as those items are produced in a manner consistent with the law.

Upon his return from the Philippines, he bypassed Katherine Howe whom he had married in 1899 in New York City, where he used the name Paul B. De Volpi for the obvious purpose of skirting the laws of New York State regarding bigamy. Katherine, however, was from Canada.

Hemp in the United States. In the 18th and 19th centuries hemp was a legal agricultural crop. However, in the 20th century bans were issued on the substance, but in the 21st century hemp returned as a legal U.S. crop. By 2019, the United States had become the world's third largest producer, behind China and Canada.

Federal policies, tightened by the Controlled Substances Act of 1970, virtually banned the production of industrial hemp during the U.S. war on drugs. According to an industry group, "the 1970 Act abolished the taxation approach [of the 1937 Marijuana Tax Act] and effectively made all cannabis cultivation illegal." The Drug Enforcement Administration refused to issue permits for legal hemp cultivation and held that, since industrial hemp (despite being of lower THC yield) is from the same species plant as prohibited cannabis, both were forbidden under the Controlled Substances Act.

However, the Agricultural Act of 2014 (farm bill) allowed agricultural hemp on an experimental basis. Moreover, under the 2018 U.S. farm bill, commodity-hemp production was federally legalized. The 2028 Act removed hemp, defined as cannabis (*Cannabis sativa L.*) and derivatives of cannabis with extremely low concentrations of the psychoactive compound delta-9-tetrahydrocannabinol (THC) (no more than 0.3 percent THC on a dry-weight basis), from the definition of marijuana.

When Bonaventura returned around 1909 to North America (through San Francisco, apparently) he initially reunited with his first wife Bessie (and children) in northern New York state. He had married Bessie Repass in 1895, and had two children by her (under his original surname of Weiss) before he was shipped to the Philippines.

The Family Name "De Volpi" in Canada: Kate

Somewhere along the way, in Canada near Montreal, he had met Kate (Katherine Howe) who became his second wife in 1899. A son of theirs, Charles De Volpi (or de Volpi), was likely conceived around November 1910, at most a year after Bonaventura returned from the Philippines. Charles became a well-published author living in Montreal, a clue which led me and Pete (of the New York State DeVolpi clan) to realize at about the same time that three of us had the same father.

About 2 decades later I was conceived in New York City. Sometime in the 1980s or 90s, Pete and I, and then all three of us — Pete, Charles and I — got on the phone together sharing our connection, relationship and amazement.

Kate had two other children (evidently with Bonaventura): Charles's twin sister, Charlotte, and a son, David. My Canadian half-brother Charles and his wife Margaret became parents of two sons, David and Thomas, whom I have visited and met; they live now in retirement north of Montreal.

The Hemp plant is a variety of the *Cannabis sativa* plant species grown specifically for industrial uses of its derived products. It is one of the fastest growing plants and was one of the first to be spun into usable fiber 50,000 years ago. Hemp can be refined into a variety of commercial items, including paper, textiles, clothing, biodegradable plastics, paint, insulation, biofuel, food, and animal feed.

Although cannabis as a drug and industrial hemp both derive from the species *Cannabis sativa* and contain the psychoactive component tetrahydrocannabinol (THC), they are distinct look-alike strains with unique phytochemical compositions and uses. Industrial hemp has lower concentrations of THC and higher concentrations of cannabidiol, which might decrease or eliminate

Figure 35. Classic symbol for hemp plant.

its psychoactive effects. The legality of industrial hemp varies widely between countries. Some governments regulate the concentration of THC and permit only hemp that is bred with an especially low THC content.

A type of fiber obtained from the leaves of the abacá plan is called Manila hemp. It is not actually hemp, but named so because hemp was long a major source of fiber, and other fibers were sometimes named after it. The name Manila also refers to the capital of the Philippines, once one of the main producers of abacá.

Manila rope is very durable, flexible, and resistant to salt water damage, allowing its use in rope, hawsers, ships' lines, and fishing nets] It can be used to make handcrafts like bags, carpets, clothing, furniture, and hangings.

Manila ropes shrink when they become wet. This effect can be advantageous under certain circumstances, but if it is not a wanted feature, it should be taken into account. Since shrinkage is more pronounced the first time the rope becomes wet, new rope is usually immersed into water and dried before use so that the shrinkage is less. A major disadvantage in this shrinkage is that many knots made with manila rope became harder and more difficult to untie when wet, thus becoming subject of increased stress. Manila rope will rot after a period of time when exposed to saltwater.

Manila hemp rope was previously the favored variety of rope used for executions by hanging, both in the UK and USA. Usually 3/4 to 1 inch diameter, boiled prior to use to take out any over elasticity. It was also used in the 19th century as whaling line.

Tabulation of 13 Bonaventura Enlistment and Military Combat Claims and Events

Event No.	Event/Claim	Begin	End	Where	What Claimed	How
1	Chilean Navy	1890	1892	Chile	Conscripted in Chilean Navy during 1891 Chilean Civil War	Voluntarily enlisted or possibly shanghaied
2a	1st U.S Enlistment (Indian Wars)	1892	1894	Ft. Supply, Oklahoma Indian Territory	Indian Wars and opening of Cherokee Outlet	Deployed with 13th Rgt, U.S. Infantry, after enlisting in New York City
2b	2nd U.S. Enlistment (Ft. Niagara)	1894	1897	Ft. Niagara, New York	Detachment reassigned to Ft. Niagara at end of Oklahoma tour	Part of 1st enlistment
3	Italo-Ethiopian War	1895	1896	Abyssinia	With Italian Army in 4-month war	Would have had to get leave of absence
4	3rd U.S Enlistment, Spanish-American War	1898	1898	Camp Alger, Virginia; Thorough-fare Gap, Virginia; Camp Meade, Pennsylvania	Rhode Island Volunteers	Enlisted at Quonset Pt., RI, 1st Rhode Island Infantry
5	4th U.S. Enlistment, Philippine Insurrection	1899	1901	Philippine Islands	Combat on Luzon	Deployed with 47th Rgt., U.S. Volunteer Infantry
6	Boxer Rebellion	June 1900	Aug. 1900	China	Part of U.S. Boxer Relief Expedition	Special Duty assignment from 47th Rgt.
7	Russian-	1904	1905	Manchuria		Mercenary

	Japanese War					
8	Mexican Revolution	1910	1910	Mexico	Fought for *Federales* under President Diaz	Mercenary
9	Italo-Turkish War	1911	1912	Libya	Fought for Italian Army, possibly *Alpini*	Mercenary
10	First Balkan War	1912	1913	Balkans	Fought with Italian or Greek Army	Mercenary
11	Mexico	early 1914	mid 1914	Mexico	U.S. invasion of Veracruz	Mercenary
12a	First World War	late 1914	1915	France	In combat with Canadian Army, Princess Pats Rgt.	Sent back to London for hospitalization
12b	2nd part of enlistment with Princess Pats Regiment	1915	1918	London, England	Assigned to Regimental Pay Office and later convicted of felony	Sentenced to 3 years penal servitude
13	Russian Revolution	1917?	1919?	Siberia?	Canadian troops with Allied Army in Siberia during Bolshevik revolution	Would have had to be paroled from prison to fight with Canadian regiment in Siberia

In the table above, the 13th and final event of Bonaventura's known enlistments and military combat events includes a hint that he might have been paroled along with other Canadians in order to join a Canadian-army regiment fighting in Russia during the Bolshevik revolution.

Bonaventura's Military Adventures — Purported and Real

For my book *Lover, Soldier, Reprobate*, I did considerable research sorting out verifiable fact from Bonaventura's fiction. There was an (Undated [November 1928]) article in Irène's collection of newspaper clippings: Here's what she found he had asserted about his military service:

> **Havana, Cuba.** The Lions Club will hold its weekly luncheon today... Col.... Paul de Volpi, as the speaker of the day, will give a talk on fascism as it exists today. Col. De Volpi has a most interesting record, having served 20 years in the American Army. He enlisted in 1892, and was sent into the western portion of the States to fight against the Indians. During the

Spanish-American war he came to Cuba, and after was sent to the Philippines where he served for five years. During the World war he enlisted in the Italian army against the central powers. Later he served with the allied army with the White Russians against the Reds.

Col. De Volpi at present represents the fascisti government. His talk will tend to eliminate certain misunderstandings that have arisen in foreign countries concerning the Mussolini dictatorship....

In the 1920s Bonaventura was apparently living in Canada, and in 1925 there's reason to believe he was in Italy. Also, in the 20s, he had some business shenanigans going on in the States, in which he might have been involved.

In a notarized letter written in 1938, Kate says that Bonaventura deserted her in March of 1927. Their daughter Charlotte attempted to find her father by writing to the U.S. Pension Board In 1935.

Let's see: His actual service in the U.S. Army totaled about eight years, not 20 years. So much for that claim of his. But he did enlist in the U.S. Army in 1892 and indeed "was sent into the western portion of the States to fight against the Indians." That corresponds to my findings about his service with the 13th Infantry Regiment at Ft. Supply, Oklahoma Indian Territory.

Figure 36. Medal that my father carried about.

He did ***not***, however, get sent to Cuba during the Spanish-American War. His military records are quite detailed to the contrary, accounting for him training entirely in the Eastern Atlantic States with the Rhode Island Volunteers during that very short war. So the medal shown in Figure 36 is of questionable (Army-Navy surplus store) origin.

As for the Philippines, Bonaventura officially served in the U.S. Army for two, not five years. However, he might have stayed in the Philippines in some paramilitary capacity for as much as five more years. But I don't know when or how he could have acquired any real rank of colonel.

It looks like just before the first World War broke out, he did enlist in the Italian army, but he was then fighting against the Ottoman Empire (Turkey), not against the central European powers. There were indeed a number of military actions in which he might have participated in the Mediterranean during the runup to the first World War. He

Figure 37. Insignia of Princess Pats Regiment. Bonaventura signed up with the regiment in Canada at beginning of World War I.

later fought against the "central powers"during World War I, but it was in a Canadian uniform with the Princess Pats Regiment (Figure 37) in France. The regiment (including Bonaventura) had been one of the first shipped off to Europe. They fought valiantly during the trench-style, poison-gas episodes of the war, suffering considerable casualties.

The adjacent map, Figure 38, indicates the ethnic regions claimed by the Fascists to be within the Kingdom of Italy in the 1930s.

No matter what, Bonabentura must have survived a lot of military combat during his military career, although it gradually took a debilitating toll on his health, and he was shipped back from the World War I front lines in France to a hospital in England to recover.

Figure 38. Italian (Kingdom of Italy) ethnic regions claimed by the Fascists in the 1930s: Green: Nice, Ticino and Dalmatia; Red: Malta; Violet: Corsica. Later the Duchy of Savoy was included, along with Turin and other territories in Piedmont, a region in northwestern Italy.

You can find many more details about Bonaventura's military and personal adventures in the biographical book *Lover, Soldier, Reprobate,* available on-line from Amazon.com. In preparing that book, I did a considerable amount of research involving American military, Italian regional, and Canadian government files, as well as delving into genealogical records.

Figure 39 is a photo of him in full regalia, taken by the De Volpi family branch that had relocated from Lockport, New York, to Michigan. The photo might have been taken when he was in the Phillippines, sometime before he returned to the States, to the Lockport branch of the family, probably bypassing the Canadian branch.

Barely visible, marked on top of the photo, seems to be the year 1898, but it is most likely taken in 1899 or 1900.

Figure 39. Master Sergeant Bonaventura in uniform.

Reprobate

That's what my half-brother, Charles (Bonaventura's son of the Canadian branch), called him – with good reason. A reprobate is a person of bad character, without moral principles, unprincipled. Many of Bonaventura's duplicities had been tracked by Charles.

According to Ancestry.com, a "Mrs. de Volpi," traveled from Montreal to England in November 1911 with "2 infants" listed as John and Jane (deVolpi). The line filled in above Mrs. de Volpi, listed a "Miss Howe" as "*dom.*" which suggests that she was a domestic servant. Now, that's odd, because Howe was the family name of Bonaventura's Canadian wife, Kate. Here's what I figure:

Katherine Howe De Volpi, with a pair of two as-yet-unnamed twins, was off to London to join Bonaventura, with the help of her sister, who was listed as the "domestic" — a maid. The twins – not yet named – were later called Charles and Charlotte, possibly after Kate conferred with their dad.

Figure 40. Photo of Bonaventura wearing coat and tie, undated (probably the 1930s).

At about that time Bonaventura says he was soldering in the Balkans, in a war in which the Italian army was pitted against the Turks. Presumably Katherine got a letter, inviting her and the twins to England, or maybe on to the European continent, to join him. He might have been granted temporary leave from his military duties.

Just how long Katherine stayed in Europe is a matter of speculation. Since their second son, David, was born in December 1912, we can guess that she and Bonaventura were together, either in Europe or Canada, sometime around March 1912. The Italo-Turkish War, which started in September 1911, ended in October 1912. Immediately after, the first of two wars in the Balkans began.

At some point in the 1920s Bonaventura apparently moved to New York City (without informing his Canadian wife Kate). Taking a train or trains presumably was the easiest and quickest way to New York City from Montreal.

The Family Name "De Volpi" in New York City (1920s-30s)

For several decades in the 20s and 30s Bonaventura operated a shady export-import business out of an office in Greewich Village (as detailed in *Lover, Soldier, Reprobate*). The business and his dealings had the air of legitimacy; I think it focused on wines and cultural relics, although some of the latter were found to be of questionable legality. In fact, as described in that book, it seems like he might have been involved in a mysterious art scandal, although never legally implicated.

My father's third wife of record, my mother, lived in New York City's Greenwich Village (pronounced Grenwich, not Greenwich), where they met and married; so my 1931 birth-certificate surname is De Volpi with a space between the De and V.

In those days, international travel was mostly by passenger ships, which took nearly a week to cross the Atlantic, and afforded a number of social opportunities aboard.

On May 21, 1927, Charles A. **Lindbergh** completed the first solo, nonstop transatlantic flight in history, flying his *Spirit of St. Louis* from Long Island, New York, to Paris, France. Commercial transatlantic airflights started in 1939.

As you can tell, whether for religious reasons or convenience, Bonaventura never disentangled his marital relationships with legal divorces or formal separations. Nor did he disclose these prior entanglements to my mother (who discovered that he had a neck chain having a locket with photos of several women).

It was many, many decades later before I found out about his duplicity — in fact, not until my mother passed away, although she had uncovered reasons to be concerned about his marital past when seeking during the economic depression to obtain her share of his U.S. military pension.

The Family Name "DeVolpi" in Los Angeles — 2002)

This one is really "iffy." On 15 July 2002 it was reported in The LA Times that Evelyn R. Devolpi (*sic*) died in Los Angeles, California, giving her birth date as November 7, 1917. Because the surname is so unique, I've paid some attention. There's no mention in the obit of any relatives or any other supplemental information. My followup inquiries yielded no indications of Evelyn's family heritage or of any relatives or of any life-span or occupational activities in LA.

In November 1917 Bonaventura was likely (but not for sure) in prison in England. I suppose hypothetically it's possible that Evelyn's mother got together with him in England early in 1917. It seems unlikely, although I can't rule any connection out.

According to sparse published death records, we are informed that Evelyn R. Devolpi was born November 7, 1917, living 84 years old, and had been residing in Los Angeles, California. I didn't find out about her until after she passed away, nor could I uncover any kin of hers anywhere.

Evelyn's birth conception would have been around early February 1917 at about that time — and a couple of years before and afterward — that Bonaventura was probably imprisoned in England. But it is not entirely clear just when he was released and exactly where he went. There's a gap of a couple of years for which speculatively (like in the movie *Dirty Dozen)*, he might have been paroled early in 1917 to fight in the Bolshevik Revolution. Indeed! So, having searched many records, it would be quite a stretch for Evelyn's mother to have been one of his wives or trip encounters.

The Dirty Dozen is a British-American Academy-Award war film released in 1967, which caused controversy with its extreme violence but became one of the highest-grossing movies of the decade. The movie is noted for its taut action, dark humor, and stellar cast.

According to the movie script, in March 1944, an OSS officer is ordered to undertake a top-secret assignment transforming 12 prisoners into commandos and sending them on a suicide mission in France. As an incentive, survivors of the mission would have their sentences commuted and be restored to active duty. The plan is not carried out perfectly, but the chateau is destroyed and many German officers are killed

What's relevant here is the movie's underlying premise: that leading up to the Russian Revolution, soldiers of fortune might have been released from prisons to form a cadre that fought for or against the Bolsheviks in military skirmishes. In fact, Bonaventura at one time suggested exactly that to my mother and her brother (although Bonaventura had a lot of war stories).

Because Evelyn Devolpi had traveled by ship to England, and Bonaventura on business often crossed the Atlantic by passenger ship, it's not entirely possible to rule out some encounter with Evelyn's mother. No other records have surfaced of Evelyn's familial origins. Because the name Devolpi is concocted and unusual, it's still rather mysterious how she came by that surname.

Another outside possibility is that Bonaventura's sister Anita was Evelyn's mother and gave birth to Evelyn in England or Canada. At about the time Evelyn was born, Anita was married to an Italian diplomat in 1908, and living in Montreal in 1917. Traveling from Canada to the United States often left no written record.

Here's another set of information below, about "Devolpi Mens," which looks like a false lead. I realize that Ancestry.com's rendition of Mens could have been Meus, but neither spelling — Mens or Meus — cross-checks as an offspring of Bonventura.

Ship Manifest Family Name "Devolpi Mens" (According to Ancestry.com).
Name: Annette Maud Devolpi Mens [Meus]
Arrival Date: 4 Mar 1937
Birth Date: abt 1893
Last Permanent Address: Manciano, Italy
Age: 44
Gender: Female
Ethnicity/Nationality: Italian (South)
Place of Origin: Italy
Port of Departure: Villefranche-sur-Mer, France
Port of Arrival: New York, New York, USA
Ship Name: *Conte Di Savoia*

The Family Name "De Volpi" in Contemporary Italy

Bonaventura's last (known) wife was Romana Mischi, and they were married (see the following Figure 41) in Italy back in 1934 — unbeknownst to any of his other wives in North America. This was three years after I was born.

Irene was their only daughter, born a year or two before me, and she has a family (with Emilio Valiati) that now lives on in contemporary northern Italy. I've been in occasional communication through email with her son Paulo.

I have met and been hosted by the Valiati family in Brugherio, in the outskirts of Milano.

Paulo Valiati, at the University of Milano, has specialized in the history and breeding of horses, and I met some of other Valiati offspring on various trips to Italy.

Just this past week (mid-2020) Paolo and I exchanged greetings by email.

The Volpi Clan Currently Elsewhere in the World

T R A N S L A T I O N

DE VOLPI

IN re: Bonaventura DE VOLPI
        C 2 361 267

TOWN OF MILANO

CIVIL REGISTRY OFFICE

EXTRACT FROM THE REGISTER OF MARRIAGES FOR THE YEAR
1934
No. 2130 - Register No. 1
Part II A

On November 30, 1934, there contracted marriage at Milano, BONAVENTURA VOLPI, age 61, occupation merchant, born in Venice, residing in Venice, son of the late Alessandro and of Francesca Weiss, and; ROMANA MISCHI, age 29, occupation employee, born at Milano and residing at Milano, the daughter of Elisa Mischi.

January 15, 1951.

A true copy of its original issued on tax free paper for war pension purposes.

The Clerk in Charge   The Civil Registrar

(Initials illegible)   (Sgd) B. Agostinelli

(SEAL)(Stamps)

On the reverse appears certification of the above signature, signed by the Court Clerk of Milano, dated January 16, 1951.

Attached: Certification of the Vice Consul of the United States of America, at Milan, dated January 26, 1951. Service No. 2202.

(SEAL)

VERIFIED TRANSLATION

AUG 28 1951

TRANSLATION SECTION
MAIL AND DISTRIBUTION DIV
VETS ADMIN

Translated from Italian
Bothwell/tbt

Figure 41. Register of Marriage for Bonaventura and Romana Mischi in Milano, 1934. (Official copy obtained in 1951).

Because many Italians have migrated to South America, it's not unusual to find the name Volpi or a variant in that continent, especially in Argentina and Brazil.

Sometimes it helps to have a distinctive name, sometimes not. Traveling in Europe on business, I was booked for trains, hotels, and conferences under either Volpi — or DeVolpi — at times with a De and occasionally with a Di, and once in a while with a space between the e and V. When computerized name-sorting programs eventually became less rigid, it mattered less.

While doing Italian genealogical research in terms of family origins, I often had to sort out my specific Volpi clan from the many others who might have been related. The name Volpi was and is fairly common in contemporary Italy. Sorting records about potential ancestors and relatives usually required knowledge about their geographical origins or setting. On several occasions when reaching out in Italy, I was politely set straight, although sometimes not until substantive but patient depth of inquiry.

"De Volpi" Wild-Goose Chases

In the 1980s and 90s, after my mother passed away and based on some records she kept, some in her safety-deposit boxI tried to track my father's worldwide peregrinations. My last available photo with him was as a child of maybe six. That would mean he was in New York City at around 1937, about 3 years after he had married Romana Mischi in Italy (without divorces from prior wives, of course).

Most of my genealogical record searches (primarily at the LDS library in Salt Lake City) led to dead ends, until the matchups with Pete and Charles, which thereupon unexpectedly opened up the gates for subsequent Volpi family reunions and revelations.

But how did Bonaventura originally get to the States? My best guess is that he came in on ship through New York harbor, probably around 1890. In his case, getting here involved either paying for steerage class or signing up as an able seaman – probably the latter: can't imagine he had much money when he left Europe. There's nothing in U.S. immigration records or ship manifests.

On 22 May 1899, about five months after he was discharged from his military unit, the Rhode Island Volunteers, Bonaventura married Katherine Howe in New York City. He used the name Paul B. De Volpi for the obvious purpose of skirting the laws of New York State regarding bigamy.

Timeline of Events Regarding Bonaventura's Whereabouts.
born 1873 in Venice, Italy, as Bonaventura Weiss (full name uncertain)
enlisted Nov. 21 1892 in New York, NY (at US Army base Fort Slocum on Davids' Island) by "Burke")
(Fort Slocum, New York was a US military post which occupied Davids' Island at the western end of Long Island Sound.)
occupation Sailor; Blue eyes; Brown hair; Dark complexion; and height 5'7"
transported by Army to wild west
shipped 1894 by Army to upstate New York: U.S. Army camp Ft. Niagara
married 1895 Bessie Repass in northern New York State under original name of Weiss: (had 2 children by her)
trained in Rhode Island, Quonset Point, with U.S. Army volunteers
married 1899 Katherine Howe in New York City (using the name Paul B. DeVolpi for the apparent purpose of skirting the laws of New York State regarding bigamy)
shipped 1899 by U.S. Army to Philippines
started ~1900 to sign his name as De Volpi
returned 1909 to the United State (apparently from Philippines)
showed up by 1910 in Montreal
in Europe 1915-1920 serving in Canadian Army during World War I
In Canadian Army prison in England (1917-1920?) during and after World War I
married my mother (May, 1930) in New York City
approximate date (~1 June 1930) of my conception in New York City (my birthdate: 28 Feb 1931)
his death in Milan: 1951 (age 78)

As detained in *Lover, Soldier, Reprobate*, shanghaiing took place only at waterfront locations frequented by a tiny, boisterous segment of citizenry. Politicians and law officers could easily ignore the problem or benefit from it. The relevant laws served more to protect shipowners and captains from mutiny than to safeguard the rights of seamen. And most victims were not literate enough to record their plights and few non-seamen even cared about their fate.

The shipping master, charged with producing a crew, depended primarily on the boarding master, or boardinghouse keeper, for his supply of sailors. The boarding master provided food, shelter, liquor, and entertainment for men awaiting berths. In addition, the ship's captain had to pay the crimp a commission per man.

Following are descriptions of some perils Bonaventura would have faced around the time he immigrated to the States.

Like today's high-level drug traffickers, crimps defied law enforcement, bribing city officials and threatening captains, who accepted the system partly from fear. Exact numbers are of course impossible to pin down, but it is likely that crimps used various forms of shanghaiing to fill perhaps as much as 20 percent of merchant-ship berths. In 1890 The *New York Times* reported that shipping masters still had "a complete monopoly" on supplying sailors for outgoing ships.

Sailing masters clubbed and flogged men, sometimes to death, for misreading a compass, responding too slowly to an order, or simply getting sick. Shanghaied landlubbers, knowing nothing of halyards, jackstays, and jib booms, suffered most of all.

Shanghaiing was the practice of conscripting men as sailors by coercive techniques such as trickery, intimidation, or violence. Those engaged in this form of kidnaping were known as "crimps." Forced labor was widely used aboard American merchant ships until 1915.

The role of crimps and the spread of the practice of shanghaiing resulted from a combination of laws, economic conditions, and the shortage of experienced sailors.

Along with the terms "crimping" and "sailor thieves," the verb "to shanghai" joined the lexicon in the 1850s. The most widely accepted theory is that the term came from the Chinese port city of Shanghai, then a common destination of ships with abducted crews. The term has since expanded to mean "kidnaped" or "induced to do something by means of fraud."

Crimps flourished in American West Coast port cities like San Francisco, Portland (Oregon), and Seattle. Portland eventually surpassed San Francisco for shanghaiing. On the East Coast, New York easily led the way, followed by Boston, Philadelphia and Baltimore.

The practice was driven by a shortage of labor, particularly on West Coast ships. When the California Gold Rush began in the mid-1800s, crews abandoned ships *en masse*; so a healthy body on board ship was a boon.

Shanghaiing was sustained by boarding masters, whose job it was to find crews for ships. Paid "by the body," boarding masters had a strong incentive to place as many seamen on ships as possible. This pay was called "blood money."

The most straightforward method for a crimp to shanghai a sailor was to render him unconscious, then forge his signature on the ship's articles and pick up the "blood money." Per year, some crimps made as much as $9,500 in 1890s currency, equivalent to about $220,000 in 2007.

Crimps positioned themselves politically to protect their lucrative trade. Boarding-house keepers supplied men on Election Day to go from one polling place to another, "voting early and often" for their candidate. In San Francisco, men such as Joseph "Frenchy" Franklin and George Lewis, long-time crimps, were elected to the California state legislature, an ideal spot to assure that no legislation was passed that would have a negative impact on their shanghaiing business.

With no recourse and very little money, escape was difficult even when the ship was in port. Sailors knew they could be arrested as deserters even if their service had been involuntary. Considered riffraff, few people cared.

As the crimps' network expanded through the late 1800s, menacing neighborhoods grew even more perilous. In New York crimps mostly employed contact men called runners, whose strong arms and weak principles might find a likely candidate in any wanderer making his way through the swarms of streetwalkers, procurers, panhandlers, thieves, gang members, seamen, and drunks at the lower end of the Bowery. No fewer than two hundred boardinghouses were interspersed among the rough-and-tumble bars and brothels in lower Manhattan.

An article in the *Coast Seamen's Journal* in 1908 reported: "The more ignorant or complaisant man they found, the better the blood-money-hungry crimps liked him. All sorts and conditions of humanity were regularly shanghaied on board outward bound windjammers and turned over to the bucko mates to be 'combed out' and remodeled into a sailor. If his alternative was being bloodied by a belaying pin, he became a willing deck hand." The seaman writer had himself once been shanghaied in Norfolk, Virginia.

Women, too, took part in aiding the crimping. In San Francisco a Mother Bronson ran a boardinghouse and bar on Steuart Street, and a Miss Piggott owned a similar establishment on Davis Street. Perhaps following the example of Shanghai Kelly, their drugged victims were sent by trapdoor to waiting boats. Mother Bronson was capable, according to a reporter, of "lifting a customer from the floor to the top of the bar with one kick."

One boardinghouse keeper of low repute was convicted and sent to prison in 1894 for murdering a man while attempting to shanghai him.

Some successful crimps never resorted to force. The San Francisco boardinghouse keeper Mike Conner trained greenhorns briefly at a back-yard contrivance consisting of a ship's wheel, mast, jib, and rigging and then passed them off on captains as experienced hands.

Seasoned crimps did not always wait for victims to come ashore; they might send runners to meet vessels just entering the harbor. The runners gathered seamen with promises of good times and bribes of liquor, loaded them into boats, and delivered them to the docks. From there, draymen carted them on to boardinghouses.

[This preceding "How-to" episode was adapted from a copyrighted on-line article SHANGHAIED! by David Neal Keller, a freelance writer and independent documentary film-maker, in the September 1995 issue of *American Heritage Magazine*.]

Judging by the scars on my father's head and body, I'd say he went the hard way.

Ending the Practice of Shanghaiing. In 1884 Congress passed a law banning all advance payments of sailor wages except when made voluntarily to dependent relatives. The Supreme Court had previously ruled that the 13th Amendment freeing slaves did not refer to seamen.

The American Seamen's Friend Society planned in 1904 to build "the world's largest and best equipped sailors' home" in New York. Two years later Congress made shanghaiing punishable by a fine or imprisonment. The Seamen's Act of 1915 abolished all wage prepayments to "original creditors," namely the crimps. It made crimping a federal crime, and finally put an end to it.

This legislation was successful primarily because of the widespread encroachment of steam-powered vessels in the world's merchant marine services. Without acres of canvas to be furled and unfurled, the demand for unskilled labor greatly diminished. Steamships gradually replaced sailing vessels on the open seas. While a landlubber could pull a rope, he would not be expected to tend an engine.

Even though the practice passed into history, many wealthy or "proper" families were not eager to have the world discover that their ancestral fortune began with a blow to somebody's head.

Discovery of Volpi and DeVolpi Roots and Contemporary Kin

Eventually, persevering in family-history research, I found that my biological half-sister (Irene) was living in Italy. Three-years older than me, she was born in 1934 in Italy. Up to then we had no knowledge or connection with each other.

Finding Irene. This was quite a quest, beginning with many searches in American libraries, such as the University of Chicago, Harvard University and Dumbarton Oaks. Clues from the research eventually panned out after sending an inquiry to the mayor (*sindaco*) of Milan, who (a half-year later) responded (Figure 41) with Irene's then-current address in Brugherio, a suburb of Milan.

Even though Irene had married and moved from Milan to a suburb, the *sindaco* (mayor) of Milan returned my inquiry with her new address. I didn't even know that she was a blood-related sister (half-sister, as it was) until then and not for sure until we met and compared notes, records, and photos of Bonaventura. It even turned out that Irene had come across some newspaper clippings similar to those that I had collected.

I've often remarked that if the same type of inquiry were made to the mayor of Chicago, it would have been either laughed at or ignored, there being no official census records connecting the city with the suburbs.

Here's an undated handwritten draft translation of the letter I sent to the *Sindaco* (mayor) of Milano, in my best Italian which I had been trying to improve through evening classes. Figure 41 contains their formal response.

Translating back to English, my draft letter to the *Sindaco* went as follows:

> Dear Mayor,
> I seek information of a sister-in law, Irene, daughter of Romana Mischi De Volpi, who was married to my father, Paulo Bonaventura De Volpi in 1934.
> The mother Romana Mischi was born in Milano 6 March 1905. She died 9 October 1973 in Milano.
> My father was born in Venice in 1873; he died in Milano on 9 January 1951.
> The daughter, Irene, was born 27 October 1925.
> The last address of the family was Via Castel Morrone 1, Milano, in 1973.
> I would appreciate some information about Irene Mischi (De Volpi).

I later found out that Irene had a husband and family near Milano, and subsequently many opportunities came up for me to visit them in their home. Here's what I wrote *in Lover, Soldier, Reprobate*:

What do you mean "went under the name De Volpi"? *Thought that was your name. What* **is** *your name?*

It's Alexander DeVolpi, but the surname combination is really concocted, created by my father! That's why any person with the family name "DeVolpi" is probably related, because Bonaventura fabricated the surname. In Italy the "De" literally means "of the family," and generally represents a titled or long-established family. But my father wasn't really authorized to use the "De" prefix because his mother couldn't get legally married to Bonaventura's father.

His birth father (Alessandro Volpi) was from a noble family in Trento, in the northern Trentino province. However, Alessandro couldn't get divorced from his lawful wife despite trying all over Europe. Alessandro (who was wealthy and well-connected) even attempted to get the Emperor of Austria-Hungary to give him a divorce, and he also tried in other countries without success. Anyway, Fanny Weiss bore him a son, a daughter and maybe another child. Not sure now about the third one. (Northern Italy was then under the control of the Austrian-Hungarian Empire.)

It was a sad and deplorable saga: A letter from Bonaventura's mother, Fanny Weiss, to Bonaventura in the 1890s, and translated from Italian, revealed the full heart-rending story. Someone, somebody, in the American side of family preserved and translated the original letter, and it provides the sordid details.

So, anyway, long-story-short, Bonaventura originally went under the surname Weiss, his mother's maiden name, even though the baptismal certificate said Volpi. (A baptismal document in Italy differed from an official birth certificate, which I couldn't find after searching in Venice. For one thing, many records got destroyed in wars and other catastrophes. Besides, from what I understand, under Italian law he would not have been allowed to use his father's surname.)

It was much later – maybe 25 years later – that he started identifying himself as De Volpi (with the space between the e and V). Up to then he carried on as Bonaventura Weiss (really Bonaventura Paulo Alessandro Weiss), but about 1900 or so changed his signed last name to De Volpi. Most likely, he had something or someone to dodge.

The name Bonaventura, by the way, is probably derived from St. Bonaventura, one of many patron saints in the Catholic Church. (It translates literally to "good luck." or "good fortune"). To my mother, he was Paul. During her marriage to Bonaventura, our family name was De Volpi with or without a space between the e and V.

Quarantine and Consequences. The 1892 *Harpers* article goes on to say:
Here were nearly six hundred people shut up in infected ships on which deaths from the infection were of daily occurrence, with the only water aboard that from the polluted Elbe [A river in Germany, its original source of drinking water].

For many more days there was no practical solution of this problem, and from the ships came daily pathetic appeals for help and indignant protests against what the imprisoned passengers thought to be official heartlessness and incompetency. Both appeal and protest were natural. Among the passengers were United States Senator McPherson, of New Jersey; Mr. E. L. Godkin, editor of the New York Evening Post; the Rev. Richard D Harlan, of New York; and Mr. A. M. Palmer, the well-known theater manager.... Lottie Collins, the dancer and singer who made famous the song "Ta-ra-ra-boom-de-ay," was also among the *Normannia's* passengers.

Letters sent from the ships were fumigated before being delivered. In following days there were co
ntinued deaths on these three ships but only two new infected ships arrived. All of the people who worked with the passengers on the ships and on the two islands were cut off from "their family and loved ones" as long as there were cholera cases on the islands.

The big question was "What to do with the healthy passengers?" This turned into a first-degree farce as first-class passengers were moved from one boat to another. Later they were taken to a quarantine camp on Fire Island where they were opposed by locals before finally allowed to land and then transported back to the New York Harbor. They were finally permitted on September 17th to disembark at Hoboken piers.

In the end: There were a total of 110 deaths, 66 on board the ships and 44 in the Quarantine Station. Something in the neighborhood of 5,300 immigrants were bathed and disinfected on Hoffman Island.

Cholera was not the only infectious disease present on these ships. The *Scandia* also had a measles epidemic among the children in steerage.

The twenty-day quarantine period subsequently imposed on all incoming vessels greatly slowed immigration until the embargo was lifted a half-year later.

The 1892 outbreak in Hamburg killed 8,600 people. The incident also had the unfortunate repercussion of instilling prejudice against Russian Jewish immigrants in New York City.

With the extensive help of professional genealogist Trafford Cole, who resided with his Italian-born family near Padua, I was able to construct a Volpi family tree for the Trento branch, as shown in the following Figure 42.

Unbeknownst to those Volpi's who lived in the Trentino region were their historic genealogical connection to both the originating Como branch and the breakaway Bari branch many centuries before. At the time when the Bari branch took root, the hundreds of miles between Como (and Trento) and Bari were effective as information partitions (as they were far enough apart to avoid epidemic transmission).

Alessandro

It appears from the following Figure 42 family tree that the ancestor that I was named after was scion (primary descendent) of the Volpi family line in Trento at the time (1820-1873).

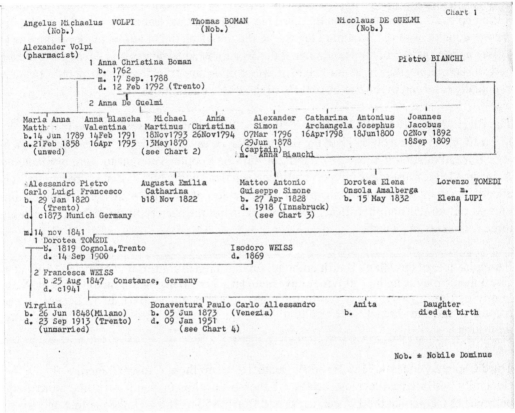

Figure 42. Volpi family tree for Trento family originating in northern Italy. The abbreviation (Nob.) stands for being born (male) in a heraldry-recognized noble family. This tree extends down all the way to my father, Bonaventura, born 5 June 1873.

Surprise! Judging from the Volpi family tree, it looks like Bonaventura lied about his age when joined the Canadian army (in 1915), claiming to have been born in 1871 (but as the genealogical chart indicates, he was born in 1873).

A History of Plagues

Looking back two thousand years, here are the major medical scourges of ancient times:

Antonine Plague (165 AD): Death Toll: 5 million; Cause: Unknown
Also known as the Plague of Galen, the Antonine Plague was an ancient pandemic that affected Asia Minor, Egypt, Greece, and Italy and is thought to have been either Smallpox or Measles, though the true cause and agent is still unknown. This unknown plague was brought back to Rome by soldiers returning from Mesopotamia around 165 AD.

Unknowingly, they spread the disease, killing over 5 million people and decimating the Roman army.

Plague of Justinian (541-542 AD): Death Toll: 25 million; Cause: Bubonic Plague
Thought to have killed perhaps half the population of Europe, the Plague of Justinian was an outbreak of bubonic plague that afflicted the Byzantine Empire and Mediterranean port cities, killing up to 25 million people in its year-long reign of terror. Generally regarded as the first recorded incident of the Bubonic Plague, the Plague of Justinian left its mark on the world, killing up to a quarter of the population of the Eastern Mediterranean and devastating the city of Constantinople, where at its height it was killing an estimated 5,000 people per day, eventually resulting in the deaths of 40% of the city's population.

The Black Death (1346-1353): Death Toll: 75 – 200 million; Cause: Bubonic Plague
From 1346 to 1353 an outbreak of the Bubonic Plague ravaged Europe, Africa and Asia, with an estimated death toll between 75 and 200 million people. Thought to have originated in Asia, the Plague most likely jumped continents via fleas living on rats that so frequently lived aboard merchant ships. Ports being major urban centers at the time, were the perfect breeding ground for the rats and their fleas, and thus the insidious bacterium flourished, devastating three continents in its wake.

Particular note of this **Black Death** outbreak can be taken in context regarding the Volpi clan. The bubonic plague in the 1300s may have been largely responsible for members of the Volpi family of Como moving way north to Trento and/or south to Bari. In fact, genealogical records of the Bari branch specifically refer to this period of pestilence and consequential relocation.

Third Cholera Pandemic (1852–1860): Death Toll: 1 million; Cause: Cholera
Generally considered the most deadly of the seven cholera pandemics, the third major outbreak of Cholera in the 19th century lasted from 1852 to 1860. Unike the first and second pandemics, the Third Cholera Pandemic originated in India, spreading from the Ganges River Delta before tearing through Asia, Europe, North America and Africa and ending the lives of over a million people. British physician John Snow, while working in a poor area of London, tracked cases of cholera and eventually succeeded in identifying contaminated water as the means of transmission for the disease. Unfortunately the year of his discovery (1854) went down as the worst year of the pandemic, in which 23,000 people died in Great Britain.

19th-Century Flu Pandemic (1889-1890): Death Toll: 1 million; Cause: Influenza
Originally called the "Asiatic Flu" or "Russian Flu," this strain was thought to be an outbreak of the Influenza A virus subtype H2N2, though recent discoveries have instead found the cause to be the Influenza A virus subtype H3N8. The first cases were observed in May 1889 in three separate and distant locations: Bukhara in Central Asia (Turkestan), Athabasca in northwestern Canada, and Greenland. Rapid population growth of the 19th century, specifically in urban areas, helped the flu spread, and — before long — the outbreak spread across the globe. It was the first true epidemic in the era of bacteriology, and much was learned from it. In the end, the 1889-1890 Flu Pandemic claimed the lives of over a million.

Influenza, commonly known as "the flu," is an infectious disease caused by a virus. The most common symptoms include high fever, runny nose, sore throat, muscle and joint pain, headache, coughing, and feeling tired.

Usually, the virus is spread through the air from coughs or sneezes, believed to occur mostly over relatively short distances. It can also be spread by touching surfaces contaminated by the virus and then touching the eyes, nose or mouth. A person may be infectious to others both before and during the time they are showing symptoms.

Influenza currently spreads around in yearly outbreaks, resulting in many cases of severe illness and deaths. In the northern and southern parts of the world, outbreaks occur mainly in the winter, while around the equator, outbreaks may occur at any time of the year. Death occurs mostly in high risk groups — the young, the old, and those with other health problems. Influenza may also affect other animals, including pigs, horses and birds.

Larger outbreaks known as pandemics are less frequent. In the 20th century, three influenza pandemics occurred: Spanish influenza in 1918 (17–100 million deaths), Asian influenza in 1957 (2 million deaths), and Hong Kong influenza in 1968 (1 million deaths). In June 2009 the World Health Organization declared an outbreak of a new type of influenza A/H1N1 to be a pandemic.

Seven **cholera pandemics** have occurred in the past 200 years, the first originating in India in 1817. Additionally, there have been many lesser documented cholera outbreaks, such as 1991–1994 in South America and, more recently, Yemen.

Although much is known about the mechanisms behind the spread of cholera, this has been no full understanding of what makes cholera outbreaks happen. Lack of treatment of human feces and drinking water greatly facilitate its spread. Bodies of water serve as a reservoir, and seafood shipped long distances can spread the disease.

Between 1816 and 1923, the first six cholera pandemics occurred consecutively and continuously over time. Increased commerce, migration and pilgrimage are credited for its transmission. Late in this period (particularly 1879-1883), major scientific breakthroughs towards the treatment of cholera developed: the first immunization by Pasteur, the development of the first cholera vaccine, and identification of the bacterium.

Deaths in India between 1817 and 1860, in the first three pandemics of the nineteenth century, are estimated to have exceeded 15 million people. Another 23 million died between 1865 and 1917, during the next three pandemics. Cholera fatalities in the Russian Empire during a similar time period exceeded 2 million.

Like its five previous incarnations, the Sixth Cholera Pandemic originated in India where it killed over 800,000, before spreading to the Middle East, North Africa, Eastern Europe and Russia. The Sixth Cholera Pandemic was also the source of the last American outbreak of Cholera (1910–1911). American health authorities, having learned from the past, quickly sought to isolate the infected, and in the end only 11 deaths occurred in the U.S. By 1923 Cholera cases had been cut down dramatically, although it was still a constant in India.

The seventh cholera pandemic spread in 1961. The pandemics subsided in 1970s, but continued on a smaller scale, with outbreaks across the developing world to the current day. Epidemics occurred after wars, civil unrest, or natural disasters, when water and food supplies become contaminated, and also due to crowded living conditions and poor sanitation.

The influenza epidemic, also known as the "**Spanish Flu** or "La Grippe" of 1918-1919, was a global health disaster. In the two years that this scourge ravaged the earth, a fifth of the world's population was infected. The flu was most deadly for people ages 20 to 40. This pattern of morbidity was unusual for influenza which is usually a killer of the elderly and young children.

It infected about 28% of all Americans. An estimated 675,000 Americans died of influenza during the pandemic, ten times as many as in the world war. Of the U.S. soldiers who died in Europe, half of them fell to the influenza virus and not to the enemy. Approximately 43,000 servicemen mobilized for WWI died of influenza. 1918 would go down as unforgettable year of suffering and death and yet of peace.

Spanish-Flu Pandemic (1918); Death Toll: 20 -50 million; Cause: Influenza
Between 1918 and 1920 a disturbingly deadly outbreak of influenza tore across the globe, infecting over a third of the world's population and ending the lives of 20 – 50 million people. Of the 500 million people infected in the pandemic, the mortality rate was estimated at 10% to 20%, with up to 25 million deaths in the first 25 weeks alone.

What separated the 1918 flu pandemic from other influenza outbreaks was the victims; where influenza had always previously only killed juveniles and the elderly or already weakened patients, it struck down hardy and completely healthy young adults, while leaving children and those with weaker immune systems still alive. The lower range of death toll in World War I was about 10 million military personnel and about 10 million civilians. The 1918 Spanish flu pandemic was unusually deadly, and traced to the H1N1 influenza A virus.

Asian Flu (1956-1958); Death Toll: 2 million; Cause: Influenza
Asian Flu was a pandemic outbreak of Influenza A of the H2N2 subtype, that originated in China in 1956 and lasted until 1958. In its two-year spree, Asian Flu traveled from the Chinese province of Guizhou to Singapore, Hong Kong, and the United States. Estimates for the death toll of the Asian Flu vary depending on the source, but the World Health Organization places the final tally at approximately 2 million deaths, 69,800 of those in the US alone. (I'm old enough to remember and lived through this epidemic.)
Hong Kong Flu Pandemic (1968); Death Toll: 1 million; Cause: Influenza
A category 2 Flu pandemic sometimes referred to as "the Hong Kong Flu," the 1968 flu pandemic was caused by the H3N2 strain of the Influenza A virus, a genetic offshoot of the H2N2 subtype. From the first reported case on July 13, 1968 in Hong Kong, it took only 17 days before outbreaks of the virus were reported in Singapore and Vietnam, and within three months had spread to The Philippines, India, Australia, Europe, and the United States. While the 1968 pandemic had a comparatively low mortality rate (.5%) it still resulted in the deaths of more than a million people, including 500,000 residents of Hong Kong, approximately 15% of its population at the time. (This was another I was fortunate to avoid too; probably had a preventive flu shot.)

Domestication is a sustained multi-generational relationship in which one group of organisms assumes a significant degree of influence over the reproduction and care of another group to secure a more predictable supply of resources from that second group. Dogs and sheep were among the first animals to be domesticated.

Charles Darwin recognized the small number of traits that made domestic species different from their wild ancestors. He was also the first to recognize the difference between conscious selective breeding in which humans directly select for desirable traits, and unconscious selection where traits evolve as a by-product of natural selection or from selection on other traits. There is a genetic difference between domestic and wild populations. There is also such a difference between the domestication traits that researchers believe to have been essential at the early stages of domestication, and the improvement traits that have appeared since the split between wild and domestic populations. Domestication traits are generally fixed within all domesticates, and were selected during the initial episode of domestication of that animal or plant, whereas improvement traits are present only in a proportion of domesticates, though they may be fixed in individual breeds or regional populations.

The dog was the first domesticated vertebrate, and was established across Eurasia before the end of the Late Pleistocene era, well before cultivation and before the domestication of other animals. The archaeological and genetic data suggest that long-term bidirectional gene flow was common between wild and domestic stocks — including donkeys, horses, New World and Old World camelids, goats, sheep, and pigs. Given its importance to humans and its value as a model of evolutionary and demographic change, domestication studies have attracted scientists from archaeology, paleontology, anthropology, botany, zoology, genetics, and the environmental sciences.

Among birds, the major domestic species today is the chicken, important for meat and eggs, although there are other economically valuable poultry such as the turkey and guineafowl. Birds are also widely kept as cagebirds, from songbirds to parrots. The longest established invertebrate domesticates are the honey bee and the silkworm. Land snails are raised for food, while species from several *phyla* are kept for research, and others are bred for biological control.

The domestication of plants began at least 12,000 years ago with cereals in the Middle East, and the bottle gourd in Asia. Agriculture developed in at least 11 different geographic areas around the world, domesticating different crops and animals.

HIV/AIDS Pandemic (At its peak, 2005-2012); Death Toll: 36 million; Cause: HIV/AIDS
First identified in Democratic Republic of the Congo in 1976, HIV/AIDS has truly proven itself as a global pandemic, killing more than 36 million people since 1981, primarily due to unprotected sexual contact. Currently there are between 31 and 35 million people living with HIV, the vast majority of those are in Sub-Saharan Africa, where 5% of the population is infected, roughly 21 million people. As awareness has grown, new treatments have been developed that make HIV far more manageable, and many of those infected go on to lead productive lives. Between 2005 and 2012 the annual global deaths from HIV/AIDS dropped from 2.2 million to 1.6 million.

My Current-Day Post-Retirement

Skipping many decades for the moment, this personal saga now surfaces — in order to summarize my present situation: as a long-retired nuclear physicist who served in the Navy during the final years of the Korean War commissioned military officer. During my subsequent professional technical career, I found it necessary to become, reluctantly — what turned out to inescapably — a rational leader of group of independent American scientists rightfully fearful of Cold War nuclear extremes, East West of the Iron Curtain.

My professional and semi-professional obligations, capabilities and experiences as a nuclear physicist and engineer, occupying some of those dicey periods, have been amply reported in several of my books, particularly the coauthored *Nuclear Shadowboxing* series, as well my subsequent *Nuclear Insights* series.

While proud of my family heritage, having found appropriate documentation not only matters, it reinforces the narrative. Indeed, many families nowadays have well-corroborated heritages. Although my research findings pale in comparison to some legacies, you'll see that this one you are reading is explicit throughout in terms of genealogical and historical-context tracing. I have no reason to proceed any further in reporting on my family heritage or my own endeavors.

Just today I received notice from Family Tree DNA that reaffirms inexplicable family matches to only three relatives with names in an arabic script and listing those arabic names as the only "known ancestors." Family Tree DNA has no matches for me listed with anyone from Italy or elsewhere. It would be pure speculation as to how those arabic individuals could be related. I'm going to submit a sample to a different analysis company, Ancestry.com

Ironically, now — during the Covid-10 corona-virus epidemic — I'm engaged consciously in daily measures and voluntarily imposed restraints to stay at home and avoid interaction with others, especially those outside of the household (now just consisting of my wife Bobbi, her son Greg, and her dog Diego — and once in a while a rare pair of visitors — such as her sister and home partner).

We just found out that the owners of the house we're renting, on the outer fringes of Oceanside, will be returning in a half year, necessitating this book be finished before then.

Having read this far into the book, you might very well be interested in a reminder of our constitutional protections, tabulated in full on the next page.

Ratified Amendments to U.S. Constitution

1st Protects freedom of religion, freedom of speech, freedom of the press, freedom of assembly and the right to petition the government.

2nd Protects the right to keep and bear arms.

3rd Restricts the quartering of soldiers in private homes.

4th Prohibits unreasonable searches and seizures and sets out requirements for search warrants based on probable cause.

5th Sets out rules for indictment by grand jury and eminent domain, protects the right to due process, and prohibits self-incrimination and double jeopardy.

6th Protects the right to a speedy public trial by jury, to notification of criminal accusations, to confront the accuser, to obtain witnesses and to retain counsel.

7th Provides for the right to a jury trial in civil lawsuits.

8th Prohibits excessive fines and excessive bail, as well as cruel and unusual punishment.

9th States that rights not enumerated in the Constitution are retained by the people.

10th States that the federal government possesses only those powers delegated, or enumerated, to it through the Constitution.

11th Makes states immune from suits from out-of-state citizens and foreigners not living within the state borders; lays the foundation for state sovereign immunity.

12th Revises presidential election procedures by having the president and vice president elected together as opposed to the vice president being the runner up in the presidential election.

13th Abolishes slavery, and involuntary servitude, except as punishment for a crime.

14th Defines citizenship, contains the Privileges or Immunities Clause, the Due Process Clause, and the Equal Protection Clause, and deals with post–Civil War issue.

15th Prohibits the denial of the right to vote based on race, color or previous condition of servitude.

16th Permits Congress to levy an income tax without apportioning it among the various states or basing it on the United States Census.

17th Establishes the direct election of United States senators by popular vote.

18th Prohibited the manufacturing or sale of alcohol within the United States.

19th Prohibits the denial of the right to vote based on sex.

20th Changes the date on which the terms of the president and vice president and of members of Congress end and begin (to January 20 and January 3 respectively). States that if the president-elect becomes vacant, the vice president-elect is inaugurated as president in their place.

21st Repeals the 18th Amendment and makes it a federal offense to transport or import intoxicating liquors into U.S. states and territories where such is prohibited by law.

22nd Limits the number of times a person can be elected President.

23rd Grants the District of Columbia electors in the Electoral College.

24th Prohibits the revocation of voting rights due to the non-payment of a poll tax or any other tax.

25th Addresses succession to the presidency and establishes procedures both for filling a vacancy in the office of the vice president and responding to presidential disabilities.

26th Prohibits the denial of the right of US citizens eighteen years of age or older to vote on account of age.

27th Delays laws affecting Congressional salary from taking effect until after the next election of representatives

When Bonaventura Enlisted in the U.S. Army. Back in 1890, 15% of the U.S. population was foreign born. (That's nearly twice the 8% it was in 1999, over a hundred years later.) Immigrants were a bigger numerical factor near the turn of the 19th century, and they formed the backbone of our labor force. There was plenty of land to be cleared, available for farming. While we didn't have any wars going on then, immigrants were quite welcome in the Army too.

The beginning of this Chapter presents the essentials of Bonaventura's enlistment in 1892 at Davids Island, just off New York City.

1892, really? Way over a century ago; how'd you get that? From the National Archives in Washington. They keep these records deep in the basement.

Actually, I assumed that when my dad first enlisted in the Army, he was put right to work building the Erie Canal, but later found out that excavation and construction of the canal had already been long completed.

The **Erie Canal** is a waterway in New York that runs about 363 miles from Albany, on the Hudson River north to Buffalo, at Lake Erie, completing a navigable water route from the Atlantic Ocean to the Great Lakes. First proposed in 1807, it was under construction from 1817 to 1825. Today, it's part of the New York State Canal System. The canal passes through the center of the appropriately named city of Lockport.

Eventually, my dad, Bonaventura, having been in the Army for all of six years, got himself promoted to Sergeant in the U.S. Army – on his way to becoming career military. When the Spanish-American war broke out in 1898, Teddy Roosevelt made going to war sound exciting and patriotic.

Bonaventura? As explained to someone else, it was his given name: translates roughly to "good luck." There was a Saint Bonaventura, a Franciscan theologian born 1221 in Tuscany, Italy.

I'm not sure how Bonaventura's medical history compares with other soldiers, but he reported ill in December 1896, this time with intermittent fever from malaria. Originally thought he had caught it much later in the Philippines, but from his records it looks like he picked it up in his first enlistment. Here are some of the gruesome details about three types of serious illnesses to which the troops were exposed at maneuvers and in bivouacs.

About Bonaventura. His name might have meant good luck, but not good behavior. His enlistment papers have unfavorable notations added after he was discharged in 1897. The enlistment papers, partly reproduced in the preceding Figure 28, mentions his Regiment (13th Infantry) and Company (H) along with the evaluation associated with his discharge.

Note that at discharge his five years of service were graded as "Good," while many other enlistees were listed as having had "Very Good" or "Excellent" service. Also he mustered out as a Private. The circumstances will become clear in the next Chapter.

But how did he get from there to the Philippines? Oh, when the Spanish-American war broke out, the Army called for volunteers. He rushed to join. But it's another story, another Chapter, because – although he served during the Spanish-American War – he didn't see any action. I'll have to bring you (and myself) up to date later on the Philippine Insurrection – and the Boxer Rebellion, for that matter – in Chapter III. First, let's introduce the 1898 Spanish-American War.

Malaria is a parasitic mosquito-borne infectious disease that involves high fevers, shaking chills, flu-like symptoms, and anemia.

It is widespread in tropical and subtropical regions, including parts of the Americas, Asia, and Africa. Each year, there are more than 250 million cases of malaria, killing between one and three million people, the majority of whom are young children in sub-Saharan Africa, where 90% of malaria-related deaths occur. Malaria is commonly associated with poverty, and can indeed contribute to poverty and be a major hindrance to economic development.

Malaria is caused by a parasite that is transmitted from one human to another by the bite of infected Anopheles mosquitoes. In humans, the parasites travel to the liver, where they mature and release harmful substances.

The majority of symptoms are caused by that release of parasite byproducts into the bloodstream, the anemia resulting from the destruction of the red blood cells, and the problems caused by large amounts of free hemoglobin that circulate after red blood cells rupture.

Malaria can be carried by mosquitoes in temperate climates like the United States, but the parasite disappears over the winter. Estimates are that there are 300-500 million cases of malaria each year, and more than 1 million people die. It presents a major disease hazard for travelers to warm climates.

In some areas of the world, mosquitoes that carry malaria have developed resistance to insecticides. In addition, the parasites have developed immunity to some antibiotics. This has led to difficulty in controlling both the rate of infection and spread of this disease.

Malaria is a medical emergency requiring hospitalization. Chloroquine is a frequently used in anti-malarial medication, but quinidine or quinine is also given.

American Military Forces During the Spanish-American War. The Spanish-American War was fought between May and August 1898. The four-month flare-up marked transformation of the United States from a developing nation into a global power. At its conclusion, the United States acquired the Philippines, Guam, and Puerto Rico. The war was also the first successful test of its new armored navy.

Almost 300,000 sailors, marines, and soldiers served in the American forces, and a little over 2,000 died from various causes. The number of participants was not large compared to the approximately three million men who served in the Civil War or the sixteen million men and women who served in World War II. The smaller numbers are in part due to the short length of the Spanish-American War – it ended before many soldiers had even been transported to the war zone. There was also no draft during this war, as there was for the Civil War and the two subsequent world wars.

At the time, African-Americans served in the U.S. Navy and Army, but not in the Marine Corps. Women served in the Army Nurse Corps. Native-Americans fought in the war, especially with the First Volunteer Cavalry (Rough Riders).

On board U.S. Navy ships, African-Americans were integrated with sailors of all nationalities. (Many aliens, including Japanese, Chinese, and Filipinos, served on U.S. Navy ships during that era. Some of them enlisted while the ships were in foreign ports.)

Over the ensuing years, a resurgence of racism led the Navy to relegate African-Americans to mess attendants, including some who had held much higher ratings during the Spanish-American War.

Shanghaiing (crimping) took place only at waterfront locations frequented by a tiny, boisterous segment of citizenry. Politicians and law officers could easily ignore the problem or benefit from it. The relevant laws served more to protect shipowners and captains from mutiny than to safeguard the rights of seamen. And most victims were not literate enough to record their plights and few non-seamen even cared about their fate.

The shipping master, charged with producing a crew, depended primarily on the boarding master, or boardinghouse keeper, for his supply of sailors. The boarding master provided food, shelter, liquor, and entertainment for men awaiting berths. In addition, the ship's captain had to pay the crimp a commission per man.

Like today's high-level drug traffickers, crimps defied law enforcement, bribing city officials and threatening captains, who accepted the system partly from fear. Exact numbers are of course impossible to pin down, but it is likely that crimps used various forms of shanghaiing to fill perhaps as much as 20 percent of merchant-ship berths. In 1890 The *New York Times* reported that shipping masters still had "a complete monopoly" on supplying sailors for outgoing ships.

Sailing masters clubbed and flogged men, sometimes to death, for misreading a compass, responding too slowly to an order, or simply getting sick. Shanghaied landlubbers, knowing nothing of halyards, jackstays, and jib booms, suffered most of all.

With no recourse and very little money, escape was difficult even when the ship was in port. Sailors knew they could be arrested as deserters even if their service had been involuntary. Considered riffraff, few people cared.

As the crimps' network expanded through the late 1800s, menacing neighborhoods grew even more perilous. In New York crimps mostly employed contact men called runners, whose strong arms and weak principles might find a likely candidate in any wanderer making his way through the swarms of streetwalkers, procurers, panhandlers, thieves, gang members, seamen, and drunks at the lower end of the Bowery. No fewer than two hundred boardinghouses were interspersed among the rough-and-tumble bars and brothels in lower Manhattan.

An article in the Coast Seamen's Journal in 1908 reported: "The more ignorant or complaisant man they found, the better the blood-money-hungry crimps liked him. All sorts and conditions of humanity were regularly shanghaied on board outward bound windjammers and turned over to the bucko mates to be 'combed out' and remodeled into a sailor. If his alternative was being bloodied by a belaying pin, he became a willing deck hand." The seaman writer had himself once been shanghaied in Norfolk, Virginia.

Women, too, took part in crimping. In San Francisco a Mother Bronson ran a boardinghouse and bar on Steuart Street, and a Miss Piggott is reported to have owned a similar establishment on Davis Street. Perhaps following the example of "Shanghai Kelly," their drugged victims were sent by trapdoor to waiting boats. Mother Bronson was capable, according to a reporter, of "lifting a customer from the floor to the top of the bar with one kick."

One boardinghouse keeper of low repute was convicted and sent to prison in 1894 for murdering a man while attempting to shanghai him.

Some successful crimps never resorted to force. The San Francisco boardinghouse keeper Mike Conner trained greenhorns briefly with a back-yard contrivance consisting of a ship's wheel, mast, jib, and rigging and then passed them off on captains as experienced hands.

Seasoned crimps did not always wait for victims to come ashore; they might send runners to meet vessels just entering the harbor. The runners gathered seamen with promises of good times and bribes of liquor, loaded them into boats, and delivered them to the docks. From there they could be carted to boardinghouses by draymen (drivers of a dray — a low, flat-bed wagon without sides, pulled generally by horses or mules, used for transport of all kinds of goods.

[This preceding "How-to" episode was adapted from a copyrighted on-line article SHANGHAIED! by David Neal Keller, a freelance writer and independent documentary film-maker, in the September 1995 issue of *American Heritage Magazine*.]

Judging by the scars on my father's head, I'd say he went the hard way.

Ending the Practice of Shanghaiing. In 1884 Congress passed a law banning all advance payments of sailor wages except when made voluntarily to dependent relatives. The Supreme Court had previously ruled that the 13th Amendment freeing slaves did not refer to seamen.

The American Seamen's Friend Society planned in 1904 to build "the world's largest and best equipped sailors' home" in New York. Two years later Congress made shanghaiing punishable by a fine or imprisonment. The Seamen's Act of 1915 abolished all wage prepayments to "original creditors," namely the crimps. It made crimping a federal crime, and finally put an end to it.

This legislation was successful primarily because of the widespread encroachment of steam-powered vessels in the world's merchant marine services. Without acres of canvas to be furled and unfurled, the demand for unskilled labor greatly diminished. Steamships gradually replaced sailing vessels on the open seas. While a landlubber could pull a rope, he would not be expected to tend an engine.

Even though the practice passed into history, many wealthy families were not eager to have the world discover that their ancestral fortune began with a blow to somebody's head.

Actually, I assumed that when my dad first enlisted in the Army (1892), he was put right to work building the Erie Canal, but later found out that excavation and construction of the canal had already been long completed.

1892, really? Way over a century ago; how'd you get that info? From the National Archives in Washington. They keep these records deep in the basement.

The **Erie Canal** is a waterway in New York that runs about 363 miles from Albany, on the Hudson River north to Buffalo, at Lake Erie, completing a navigable water route from the Atlantic Ocean to the Great Lakes. First proposed in 1807, it was under construction from 1817 to 1825. Today, it's part of the New York State Canal System. The canal passes through the center of the appropriately named city of Lockport.

Incidentally, one of the stories was that Bonaventua actually fought in the West during the Indian Wars, but there was no reason to give that any credence. It looks like he got sent there just a little bit too late for the fighting.

Eventually, my dad, Bonaventura, having been in the Army for all of six years, got himself promoted to Sergeant in the U.S. Army – on his way to becoming career military. When the Spanish-American war broke out in 1898, Teddy Roosevelt made going to war sound exciting and patriotic.

Bonaventura? As explained to someone else, it was his given name: translates roughly to "good luck." There was a Saint Bonaventura, a Franciscan theologian born 1221 in Tuscany, Italy.

His name might have meant good luck, but not good behavior. His enlistment papers (Figure 28) have unfavorable notations added after he was discharged in 1897. The enlistment papers mention his Regiment (13th Infantry) and Company (H) along with the evaluation associated with his discharge.

Notable in connection with modern-day illnesses are the lingering illnesses that followed Bonaventura throughout his life, including while serving with the Canadian Army in World War I.

Located in what was then part of the Cherokee Outlet, Camp Supply almost immediately had become the headquarters of Lieutenant Colonel George Armstrong Custer and the 7th Cavalry. It was from there that Custer led his Cavalry south to the banks of the Washita River to destroy the village of Cheyenne Indian chief Black Kettle. Custer later came to his Hollywood-dramatized end in the Battle of the Little Bighorn in eastern Montana.

Custer's Last Stand. The Battle of the Little Bighorn, also known as Custer's Last Stand, was known by the Native Americans involved as the Battle of the Greasy Grass. It was an armed engagement between the 7th Cavalry Regiment of the United States Army against the combined forces of Lakota, Northern Cheyenne and Arapaho indigenous people, occurring on June 25 and June 26, 1876, near the Little Bighorn River in eastern Montana Territory.

The battle, the most famous action of the Great Sioux War of 1876-77, was an overwhelming victory for the Indian tribes, who were led by several major leaders, including Crazy Horse and Gall, inspired by the visions of Sitting Bull.

The U.S. 7th Cavalry, including the Custer Battalion, a force of 700 men led by Lt. Col. George Armstrong Custer, suffered a severe defeat. Five companies were annihilated; Custer was killed, as were two of his brothers, a nephew, and a brother-in-law. Total U.S. deaths were 268, including scouts, and 55 were wounded.

Later, Camp Supply served to protect the Cheyenne and Arapaho reservations from incursions by "Whites." The Camp was renamed Fort Supply in 1878, several years after the Red River War of 1874-1875.

Fort Supply was primarily active in the first ten years of its existence. The post was also given responsibility to escort and protect cattle drives along the trails from Texas to Kansas. Its soldiers were called into action for three Indian uprisings, and the troops protected Cheyennes and Arapahoes from depredations by other Indian tribes, by White stock thieves, and by whisky traders from Kansas and New Mexico.

Fort Supply quickly became an Indian-Territory hub of transportation, with troops building roads and telegraph lines that linked the forts and reservations – protecting travelers along the many trails. In the 1880's, Ft. Supply troops provided protection for the emerging cattle industry of western Indian Territory.

By 1880, the Indian Wars on the Southern Plains were nearly over and the fort was in bad repair. Army officers in the Department of Missouri recommended its abandonment. But General of the Army Philip Sheridan objected and worked to establish the Fort Supply Military Reservation, thus giving permanence to the fort and an accompanying land reserve of 36 square miles.

General Sheridan said, "[Fort Supply] has been valuable heretofore strategically and as a supply camp, and is now valuable strategically for the protection of the Indian Territory, the Atlantic and Pacific Railroads and the cattle trail from Texas. I cannot give my approval for its abandonment."

As the frontier continued to diminish after 1890, Fort Supply served as headquarters for the opening of the Cherokee Outlet to settlement. Troops from Fort Supply helped clear 9,000 square miles in the Outlet of cattle and "Sooners." They provided support and supervision in the opening of the Cheyenne-Arapaho Reservation in April 1892.

"Sooners" was a name given to settlers who entered the Unassigned Lands in Oklahoma before President Grover Cleveland officially proclaimed them open to settlement on March 2, 1889. The name derived from the "sooner clause" of the Act, which stated that anyone who entered and occupied the land prior to the opening time would be denied the right to claim land.

The earliest Sooners were often deputy marshals, land surveyors, railroad employees, and others who were able to legally enter the territory early. Other Sooners crossed into the territory illegally at night, and were originally called "moonshiners" because they entered "by the light of the moon." These Sooners hid in ditches at night and suddenly appeared to stake their claim after the land run started, hours ahead of legal settlers.

Problems with Sooners continued with each successive land run; in 1895 as much as half of the available land was taken by Sooners. Litigation between legitimate land-run participants and Sooners continued well into the 20th century, and eventually the U.S. Department of the Interior was given ultimate authority to settle the disputes

As 115,000 homesteaders entered the Outlet at noon on 6 September 1893, troops from Ft. Supply guarded land offices and registration booths in the four military districts.

After the Cherokee Outlet was open to settlement, Fort Supply was officially closed in September 1894. One of the last missions that troops from Fort Supply performed was bringing to end violence against the railroads during the summer of 1894. Troops from Fort Reno had been unable to quell the wrecking of trains, destruction of tracks, and demolition of trestles by residents from nearby communities.

On February 26, 1895, operation of the old Fort Supply was turned over to the Department of the Interior. The garrison – the 3rd Calvary and the 13th Infantry – left the post.

In its quarter century of history, Fort Supply played a part in the lives of three important elements in Western Plains history: the red man, the cowboy, and the sodbuster. What was left to the Indian Nations in 1902 is shown in Figure 33.

The preserved historic Fort Supply post is located in Woodward County, in northwest Oklahoma, not far from the Texas Panhandle (around 125 miles northwest from Oklahoma City and 1400 mi. southwest of Lockport, New York.)

All this gets my attention, indeed, but what's it got to do with your father? Good question, and the answer in a nutshell is simply "quite a bit," it turns out.

As shown in Figure 28, Bonaventura's original hitch in the U.S. Army started at Davids Island, New York, a general recruiting depot for the U.S. Army, located in Long Island Sound, off the coast of New Rochelle. When he enlisted (as "Weiss, Bonaventura"), he gave his occupation as "sailor." That would be consistent with his likely fate if shanghaied as soon as he first arrived in the States.

Also, the enlistment papers say he was assigned to Company H of the 13th Infantry.

Actually, when writing just that sentence, I had a true eureka: It caused me to take a look at the history of Ft. Supply, and suddenly noticed that the 13th Infantry had been sent there, to Oklahoma! In fact, it came to me just as I typed the words: "The garrison – the 3rd Calvary and the 13th Infantry – left the post."

That settled it; my father must have indeed been stationed as a foot-soldier in the Oklahoma Indian Territory at the beginning of his enlistment.

Indeed, according to his military records, Bonaventura was billeted at "Ft. Supply" from January 1893 to 6 October 1894 – nearly two years.

Originally I was put off by its prosaic name: simply dismissed it as a supply facility in New York where Bonaventura would pick up his uniform and join his unit.

Having found that a real Ft. Supply was in Oklahoma, in Indian country, and would have been the origin of his sometimes-repeated tales about having served in the American West, I finally saw the connection.

In any event, after re-reading what I wrote up earlier in this Chapter about Ft. Supply and its role in U.S. history, I realized something: that – because of the opening of the Oklahoma Outlet, and the expected surge of settlers, including pressure from the "sooners" – the 13th Infantry was recruiting in New York City. My father just happened to be at the right place or the right time, or he heard from scuttlebutt about the opportunity to enlist.

So, his very first posting came about during what is now viewed as an exciting period in history. For Bonaventura, as a raw recruit, it might have been pretty heavy duty.

Fort Supply was closed officially in September 1894; so my dad might have been shipped back east anytime around then. What we know for sure is that he was at his Fort Niagara post in upstate New York by late 1894.

CHAPTER IV:
HERITAGE AND UPBRINGING

I've written and published a number of books, before and after retiring from my lifelong professional occupation (nuclear physics and engineering). Now my pensioned retirement is mostly fulfilled with the help of a comfortable rolling chair, computer screen and touch-type keyboard, and a supportive family. Such a semi-active combination requires or least nurtures patience and attentiveness — keeping me from simply watching endless TV.

My wife, Bobbi, is the family "technician" who keeps the computer system running, as she had to fix and reboot this morning, after my hour or so fright. Now we just leave the computer on 24/7. Having learned touch-typing back at SMA high school, that has served me well. And a optimized tilted keyboard from Goldtouch helps too.

Listed here, briefly without hype, are the titles of my monographs and coauthored technical books: *Proliferation, Plutonium, and Policy, Nuclear Shadowboxing* (2 coauthored volumes), *Nuclear Insights* (3 coauthored volumes), *Cold War Nuclear Challenges.* and lastly *Cold War Brinkmanship*. Most were written and published after retirement from full-time employment. A former W&L classmate, Gerry Lenfest, helped financially and motivatingly sponsor publication of the *Nuclear Insights* set.

THIS SAGA, AN EARLIER BOOK, AND NOW THIS BOOK

Some — or maybe a lot — of the underlying factual input so far in this saga about the Fox Millennium, is derived from an earlier book I wrote and had published: *Lover, Soldier, Reprobate* — a thoroughly researched and documented biography of my wayfaring father. Its subtitle, "International Odyssey of Love and War," reflects that book's topical scope, as well as my father's opportunistic travels, wives, and children around the world. He truly became a soldier of fortune (good or bad).

Although this book, *The Fox Millennium*, similarly contains enough story-line foundation for an engrossing movie or TV series, it would never be expected to be as popular or meaningful like Alex Haley's *Roots*. Yet, the narratives in this book could meld into a saga of popular interest.

As for now, this book's foundational story that covers a thousand years of history should suffice for you the reader, and for my extended family — an overdue historical narrative about resilience, survival, luck, often hard work and individual sacrifice. While not claiming you'll get worked up, it should be worthy of reading — especially during the protracted Covid-19 crisis.

As prefaced, this history begins with the ancient Volpi clan, traced back in Italy hundreds of years, with family ancestry records supplemented by additional vital records, assembled repositories, personal files — nowadays frequently available on-line.

Long ago, the civilized human role on earth often began as a matter of heritage or even valuable legacy in the form of wealth, land or simply title. For women it had been mostly a matter of marriageability; for men it was a matter of honor, inheritance, manhood, impoverishment, or survival. None of it was to be taken lightly.

In *Lover, Soldier, Reprobate* there's a complete story told of finding out about my mother's quest during the economic depression (of the 1930s) to obtain a share of Bonaventura's pension. In fact, that's how I got started in researching my family history, having requested and eventually received a (nearly 500-pp) surprising copy of Bonaventura's military records (first from the U.S. Army and eventually another unexpected batch of files from the Canadian Army).

My archival quest can be specifically traced back to a portion of a VA letter kept in my mother's safety-deposit box in Florida. Not until she passed away did I follow up on the identifying information found in that top portion, as reproduced in Figure 44.

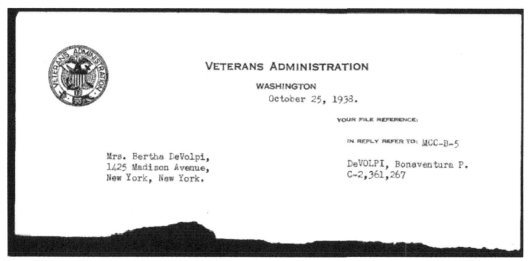

VETERANS ADMINISTRATION

WASHINGTON
October 25, 1938.

YOUR FILE REFERENCE:

IN REPLY REFER TO: MCC-D-5

Mrs. Bertha DeVolpi,
1425 Madison Avenue,
New York, New York.

DeVOLPI, Bonaventura P.
C-2,361,267

Figure 43. Top portion of VA letter to my mother, as kept in her safety-deposit box.

The full content of the letter was a eye-opener, as it turned out that there were three former wives of Bonaventura simultaneously trying, unbeknownst to each other, for years (during the economic depression of the 1930s) to get a share of his pension For whatever personal reason, my mother had torn off the bottom half that revealed the existence of the former Bonaventura's wives, but she kept this letterhead portion in her safety-deposit box. Since it contained the VA's file number on Bonaventura, it opened up years later my successful quest for more information about him. It was decades before I found a copy of the full original letter from the VA to my mother.

Because my book *Lover, Soldier, Reprobate* has the complete story of Bonaventura, I'll cop out here by providing only a few noteworthy highlights (or lowlights) of his career and meanderings.

As mentioned, we have a foundation of records from his military-service files, both American and Canadian. First, from historical records on line, here are some selected maps and then-contemporary illustrations.

In particular, Figure 44 is a map of the Philippine Islands, where Bonaventura spent a decade or so apparently in some kind of military role.

Figure 44. Map of Philippine Islands

Figure 45 is an old photographic rendition of a canon used by the U.S. Army at the time of the Spanish-American War and the Philippines Insurrection.

Though superficially resembling a Gatling gun its internals are very different, having only one firing pin rather than a firing mechanism for every barrel. It was a built-up, rifled, rapid-fire gun, designed to be light enough to travel with horse cavalry.

HOTCHKISS REVOLVING CANNON

Figure 45. Hotchkiss Revolving Cannon, Spanish-American War vintage.

Besides the field-gun version, several other variants of the 37mm Hotchkiss revolving cannon were in existence, notably for naval defense against torpedo boats as well as fortresses firing shrapnel or canister shells in defense of moats. The naval variant was adopted by Russia and the United States, amongst others. The field-cannon version was accompanied by a horse-drawn ammunition cart.

A Hotchkiss revolver 3-pounder cannon was also adopted by the US and Russian navies in the 1880s. This cannon had five rotating barrels.

Figures 46 and 47 hark back to the days when we depended on thick catalogs, especially from Sears-Roebuck, as a standard of what was available and at what price.

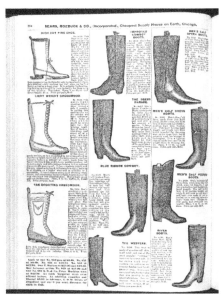

Figure 47. Boots advertised in an old Sears-Roebuck catalog.

Figure 46. Cover of Sears Roebuck catalog for 1897, about the time my father immigrated to the United States.

U.S. Army Camp Alger in Virginia.

Camp Alger, near Falls Church, Virginia, was established May 18, 1898, for the Spanish–American War effort. It was approved by Secretary of War Russell A. Alger for whom it was named. By August 1898, more than 35,000 troops were stationed at the camp.

Camp Alger was about 1½ miles from Dunn Loring, a train station on a branch of the Southern Railway, 7 miles from Washington, D.C., and about 5 miles from Fort Myer. The field surface was rolling, partly wooded, with cultivated clearings and with good drainage. The soil was of clay and sand and nearly impervious to water. Immediately after the selection of this camp preparations were made for the reception of troops by the erection of storehouses at Dunn Loring, where the Southern Railway had put in extra sidings to accommodate the increased traffic.

Figure 48. Old postcard, depicting rifle practice at Camp Alger, Va.

AUTHOR'S UPBRINGING, EARLY ON

Since you've delved into this books this far, you — the reader — are owed some relevant (but succinct) autographic background information.

Adjacent is an old grainy archival photo (Figure 49) of me as a baby in my mother's (Bertha's) arms, next to my father (Paul, as she called him), appropriately staged just before he left once again by ship to an overseas destination.

Figure 49. My father Bonaventura with my mother holding me just before my father was departing again by ship overseas.

My working mother (as a pedicurist in Greenwich Village) found it too difficult to care for me in Manhattan; so she arranged to board me out in the Bronx (Figure 50) with a French-Italian-American family, the De Leons. They had a dog named Spot that I walked around the block each day.

After a few grade-school years in the Bronx (that included recreational swimming in Pelham Bay, stepping on barbed horseshoe crabs), and religionizing (that didn't take hold) in a Catholic Church across the

Figure 50. Where I boarded in the Bronx. There was a nice backyard with some grape vines.

street, I was shipped off to military school when World War II broke out.

Maternal Heritage

When World War II broke out after the bombing of Pearl Harbor, it became a particularly difficult situation for my mother. She was then working, I think part-time, for a Japanese restaurant owner. The restaurant was on 8th street in New York Manhattan's downtown Greenwich Village. My mother was then going by her husband's name which was Italian, thus from a nation that had also declared war on the United States after the Japanese bombing of Pearl Harbor. Moreover, she was never really sure of her family heritage, sometimes explaining that they came from Austria (but the Gaber name sounded Germanic — somewhat awkward for a family name after the United States declared war on Germany).

Later I discovered, after extensive genealogical research, that the Gaber family emanated from a city called Cernovice or Chernivtsi located in what is now upper Ukraine; at the time of her family's emigration it was part of the Austrian-Hungarian Empire (which helps explain my mother's reference to Austria).

Moreover, decades later, microfilm records at the LDS genealogical library in Salt Lake City revealed that the Gaber family came across the Atlantic on two different ships, the first bearing the father — a garmentmaker — and the second the mother, along with the remainder of the immigrating Gaber family. My mother probably never knew of her actual genealogical origins.

I had always listed my mother and her family as Austrian, which is what I was told. But with some spare time during a business trip in Austria, I tried and never did find any record of her family. (Now it's clear why: The family actually had emanated from a remote and hapless part of central Europe, Chernevtsi (or Chernevisti), in Bukovina, now part of Ukraine. (It wasn't easy to trace, lots of microfilm to go through, and many false leads, but found her listed among siblings with her mother Minna Gaber arriving on the SS *Naderland* in 1909.)

Family Allegiances

After you absorb the last few paragraphs, you'll note that I had some sort of familial connection with each of our sworn deadly World War II enemies: Italy, Japan and Germany. The Italian part of the connection was difficult to avoid because of my last name. That linkage was awkward in grade school, especially during World War II, when kids could sometimes be especially mean.

Decades later, my background was routinely investigated for clearance to handle national-security classified-information. Originally the investigations were authorized by the Navy during the Korean War, but later by the FBI and civil service, for my employment at a national nuclear laboratory located in DuPage County suburbs outside of Chicago, Illinois. Argonne National Laboratory became my place of employment for 40 years.

Having had a mixed national-family origin was a matter specifically noted in the government investigation reports, but it was never a problem in granting the security clearances for working at Argonne. Usually, investigations for security clearance commence with your origins, family and friends, and work their way to school and eventually to employment, recreation and diversion associations. During wartime — that is, World War II — my family origins and linkages (with Austria, Italy, and Japan) were of course an initial matter of official concern, but I never had any problems being approved for the highest level of U.S. government national-security clearance.

That's not to say that my family origins didn't result in some awkward moments for me as a kid, especially in military school. Kids, not excluding me, could be mean to each other.

As a matter a fact, the family name Gaber also had Jewish undertones. I was never sure if any of my mother's relatives were practicing the Jewish faith. Even more complicating was the fact that they mostly lived on the upper East side of Manhattan, where a lot of Jewish families resided. And, especially in those days, anti-Semitism was widespread. Of course, that was not a problem for my federal security investigations, but it was a factor in my surrounding awareness during adolescence.

EDUCATION AND SUMMERS IN VIRGINIA

My education in Virginia started anomalously with my wartime midterm 5th-grade entry into the Staunton Military Academy (SMA) in southwestern Virginia, well inside the Shenandoah Valley of Virginia (Figure 51).

To get there, I was pinned with a destination tag when shipped off at the railway station in New York City, and met at the Staunton, Virginia, train station by the grade-school (underschool) headmaster. I had been carefully detrained by a caring conductor with my meager luggage, after a full day of lonely travel over the landscape of New Jersey and Pennsylvania into the delightful Shenandoah Valley in southwestern Virginia.

The Blue Ridge mountains are to the East, and the Washington National Park is to the West. The Blue Ridge Parkway runs from north to south. It is a National Parkway and All-American Roadway, noted for its scenic beauty. The Parkway, America's longest linear park, runs for 469 miles through 29 Virginia and North Carolina counties, linking Shenandoah National Park to Great Smoky Mountains National Park.

Figure 51. Map of the northern part of the Shenandoah Valley in southwestern Virginia ("breadbasket of the South during the Civil War"). Various counties, such as August, Rockingham, and Shenandoah, and a few cities are labeled on the map. The Shenandoah River runs north down through the middle of the valley, and underground there are numerous limestone caves and caverns. Callouts on the map locate some cities like Staunton.

The parkway has been the most visited unit of the National Park System most every year since 1946. The land is maintained by the National Park Service, and in many places parkway land is bordered by United States Forest Service property.

People love to hike the Appalachian Trail along the Blue Ridge Mountains. In the Eastern United States it is a marked hiking trail extending between Springer Mountain in Georgia and Mount Katahdin in Maine. As a kid, I often dreamt of making the trek, at least from Virginia to Georgia. There are designated camp sites and cabins along the trail. Usually first-come, first-serve.

As a cadet at SMA, I often hiked Shenandoah Valley roads and the trails, especially during warm-weather school vacations when I didn't have to return to New York. On some occasions I used to hitchhike, something my mother frowned on. Now that I recall, I even hitchhiked from college at W&L during spring vacation all the way down to southern Florida. Those were the days. I don't see hitchhikers on the road nowadays.

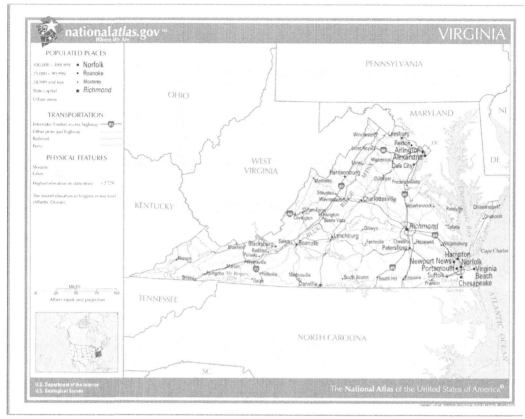

Figure 52. Map of Virginia with modern Interstate Highway 81 running down the Shenandoah Valley.

The City of Staunton (pronounced Stanton) — filled with churches, spires and institutions — is an independent city in Virginia. As of the 2010 census, the population was 23,000 (about double what it was when I went to school there) with its government offices now in Verona, contiguous to Staunton. Later, when I went on to college at nearby Washington and Lee University, I did some journalism-type research to report about the history of Staunton and its Augusta County institutions of the Shenandoah Valley.

Notably Staunton has been a city of churches, their spires prominent in the landscape from almost any angle. I seem to recall a hotel named after Confederate leader Robert E. Lee; instead, the web indicates that the city was once home to about ten hotels, only one of them still in operation — the Stonewall Jackson Hotel. General Jackson was another important Confederate leader, especially known for military battles in the Shenandoah Valley.

This Stonewall Jackson hotel was renovated in the early 2000s, and is now in operation as both a hotel and a conference center. The Ingleside Resort north of Staunton is no longer in operation. During World War II it was used by the federal Immigration and Naturalization Service as a detention center for enemy aliens held under U.S. government Executive Order. (As a cadet at SMA, I sometimes hiked by Ingleside, but don't recall being aware of its wartime use.)

The city of Staunton is also home to Stuart Hall, then a private girls' preparatory school, as well as the **Figure 53**. Staunton Military Academy location of the states' Virginia (SMA) logo. School for the Deaf and Blind. Staunton was the first city in the United States with a fully defined city-manager system.

As cadets at a mens' school, we were often angling to somehow get the attention of girls at Mary Baldwin or Stuart Hall.

Figure 54. Downtown Staunton (Virginia) at night. As cadets we weren't allowed downtown after dark, but often marched into town on Sunday mornings to attend church.

Staunton is the **birthplace of Woodrow Wilson**, the 28th U.S. president, and home of Mary Baldwin University, historically a women's college. Staunton Military Academy (SMA) was perched on a hilltop a few blocks above Wilson's birthplace home; so we cadets from SMA in uniform often walked individually or in formation past the historic-site manse on the way downtown.

The highly educated Wilson was the only U.S. president to earn a PhD (from Princeton University). He worked as college professor and university president before being going into politics and ultimately elected as the 28th U.S. president. Wilson served for two terms (1913-1921) as president of the United States, and he led the country through WWI. He fought for democracy, world peace, and progressive reform. Wilson is often lauded by historians for being one of our nation's strongest presidents. However, he was brought up and persisted as an latent apologist for slavery and its consequences in the United States.

Visitors to Staunton can tour the house and grounds at the Woodrow Wilson Birthplace and Presidential Library, as well as Mary Baldwin University and the former SMA site on the hilltop.

Having been a lowly **cadet at Staunton Military Academy**, I learned to march, grit my teeth and take orders from staff and ranking cadet officers. We marched in platoon unison, carrying rifles without firing pins. Most staff, I recall, were former military: It was wartime then — early 1940s. SMA provided high-quality grade- and high-school-level training and a full range of sports and extracurricular activities. My main competitive sport was swimming (breaststroke and butterfly), working my way up on the team with state/region competition and earning medals/trophies. For me academically, SMA emphasized writing, composition touch typing, and I worked on the school newspaper and yearbook, all of which steered me toward college as a journalism student.

I recall hiking sometimes from SMA to Verona north along Route 11 — in fact, to the south too, past the Virginia School for Deaf and Blind, and to and up Betsy Bell Mountain, both of which I could see at a distance from my quarters at SMA.

Staunton was the first city in the world to adopt a city manager form of government (in 1908) — an outgrowth of the Progressive movement (for which Woodrow Wilson is considered to have been one of its leaders). Staunton has become a featured location for period-type movie films.

Staunton is also home to the former Western State Asylum, a hospital for the mentally ill, which originally began operations in 1828. The hospital was renamed Western State Hospital in 1894. In its early days, the facility was a resort-style asylum, with terraced gardens where patients could plant flowers and take walks, with roof walkways to provide mountain views, and with many architectural details to create an atmosphere that would aid in the healing process. However, by the mid 19th century, this utopian model of care had vanished, replaced by overcrowding in the facility and the warehousing of patients. Ankle and wrist restraints, physical coercion, and straitjackets were apparently used. When I hiked by in the 50s, the inmates would scare me by standing on balconies and clanging utensils.

After the passage of the Eugenical Sterilization Act of 1924 in Virginia, patients were forcibly sterilized at Western State but not until the law authorizing the practice was repealed in the 1970s. Later, electroshock therapy and lobotomies were practiced at the facility. When Western State vacated the property and moved its adult patients to its present site, the facility was renamed the Staunton Correctional Center and turned into a medium-security men's penitentiary.

A separate complex, DeJarnette State Sanatorium, was constructed in 1932 and acted as a location for patients with the ability to pay for their treatment. I used hike by the sanatorium and was scared by the patients (who I thought were involuntary inmates that would clank utensils from their balconies).

Summer Camps in Virginia

While my grade and high school years were at SMA, the first summer camp I recall attending was in fact called Camp Virginia. Situated at the Maury River at Goshen in the midst of the Allegheny Mountains, it was founded back in 1928.

In the following years I spent summers at a camp in the Nimrod Hall Valley (the name of which I don't recall) near Clifton Forge, Virginia.

In folklore and in historical fact, the Nimrod Valley camp area along the Cowpasture River was once occupied by the Powatan Confederacy, a native American tribe that left a rich legacy of a habitat it occupied centuries ago along the river. (See Figure 56 for an early indication of where the First Americans had dominated in Virginia.)

Figure 55. Me in cadet uniform, with my mother at SMA graduation (1949).

Tribes from over the mountains to the west, in what is now West Virginia, were said to have been their warrior rivals.

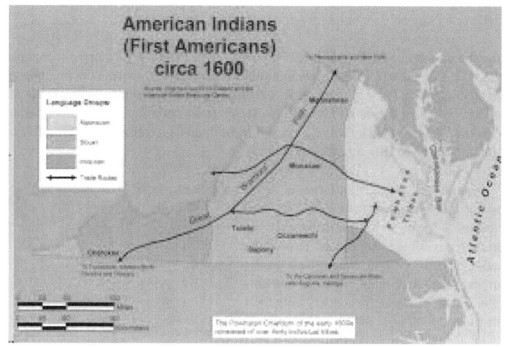

Figure 56. Map of land range for First Americans in Virginia (native Indians) circa 1600. The Powatan Confederacy inhabited the eastern-most, coastal zone.

Just across from the camp on the Calfpasture River (also to the south of the camp, along the river) were some farm fields that belonged to the Metheny family. It was short walk, crossing a rustic swinging bridge anchored to trees on each side of the river, to reach the home of the family that farmed that land.

While I got to know the Metheny family closely, old man Metheny was supposed to be half-breed offspring of a native American of the Powatan tribe. He certainly knew where to look for artifacts, especially in what appeared to have been a tribal campsite just above the Calfpasture River. I spent a lot of time on their porch, chatting with him and his family, which included a couple of girls more or less my age.

According to Wikipedia, prior to European settlement, all of the area that is now Virginia was inhabited by **Native-American tribes**. The pre-colonial population were Algonquian-speaking peoples, Nottoway and Meherrin in the coastal (or Tidewater) region... while the interior was inhabited by either Siouan or Iroquoian-speaking tribes.

Here in Figure 57 is a photograph of the Cowpasture River coursing through the Nimrod Hall Valley, taken from a bridge on Route 42.

Figure 57. Cowpasture River through the Nimrod Hall Valley in Virginia.

Revisiting Virginia Summer-Camp Grounds

Many years later, on a memorable vacation from work at Argonne, I drove in our station wagon there from Chicago with my kids. We toted a canoe that we could portage on a dirt road to the horseshoe bend, run the rapids, and fish downstream back to our campsite.

I think the Calfpasture River ran into the into the Maury River, which downstream flowed into the New River. As shown in a vintage photo, the rivers were (probably still are) pastoral, bucolic — with rapids that we could (and did) shoot on canoes.

In the Nimrod Hall Valley, the Calfpasture River had plenty of overhanging branches, trees and deep pools to cast bait or lures into. We fished often (particularly for bass and other small river fish, such as perch and catfish). I recall gingerly stepping bare foot through the rapids, picking hellgrammites from under rocks as great bait for fishing. Once in a while there were some turtles, sometimes the snapping variety (to be feared). Occasionally a few snakes, and watch out for the water moccasins!

Moccasins (not the snakes). I didn't know it at the time, but water-moccasin snake skin made for good footwear used by the Indians. Yeah, that's apparently where we got the term for what became popular as casual shoes.

Now, recalling the Calfpasture River, brings back especially fond memories, captured in black and white in some of my photos taken from the Virginia Route 42 highway bridge in the Nimrod Hall Valley. I had spent many summers in camp there, and decades later drove back as a tourist.

It was there at camp cabins in the Nimrod Hall valley area during World War II, that I met the Metheny family. They lived across the river on a farm and were very kind to me, especially old-man Metheny, and wife and their children, who were my cohorts in age. I still remember vividly one time when he had taken me on a hike up nearby Bear Mountain: I got bit by a bumble bee on the forehead; binged enough that he had to carry me on his shoulders most or all of the way back to his home.

Small fallfish in the rapids were fun to fish and hook. I don't recall much in the way of trout, but there might have been some. There were trout to be caught further downstream, maybe in the Cowpasture River or the Maury River. Mostly we hoped for bass, but sometimes caught small colorful perch. I think there had once been some fishing camps upstream that might have planted some bass or pan fish. We often used natural bait like hellgrammites and worms.

Figure 58. Another view of the Nimrod Hall Valley in Virginia, with the Calfpasture River running through it (down the middle of the photo).

During my early years visiting there, it was wartime, so everybody pitched in during harvest. My volunteered job was toting a bucket of water to thirsty workers across the field.

At one time when at SMA, I imagined canoeing from the Maury back upstream and portaging across the mountains to the New River in West Virginia, which I think flowed into the Kanawa River and eventually into the mighty Mississippi and thus ultimately to New Orleans. That would have been a magnificent (and lengthy and hardy) trip, a couple of thousand miles — just a adolescent daydream. But so did Mark Twain dream, and probably I read many of his works while in high school and college in Virginia.

Old man Metheny was half American-Indian heritage, I recall, and he introduced me to indigenous culture. On a cliff overlooking a bend in the Calfpasture River, there used to be an aboriginal Indian campsite. That was confirmed by the number of artifacts recoverable there, best soon after the land was plowed or after a good rainfall on furrowed land. I once had a collection of arrowheads, bird points, and spear points that I had gathered from walking the plowed land and other paths.

Both sides of Rt.42 north-south through the remote Nimrod Hall Valley are surrounded by forests of national parks. Along the highway itself are just a few homes and stores, even now. Douthat State Park with cabins and lake-country swimming/fishing could be reached from the Valley by a couple-hours hike through and over the mountains where you could look for deer, varmints and bugs. We kept an eye out for bear and a legendary wildcat who roamed at night.

The swinging bridge across the Calfpasture River, going from the Metheny's farm property, over to their land on the other side, was still there when I last visited in the 1990s. Their old family house looked unoccupied and dilapidated, as did their barn and outbuildings. The road through their farm fields was rutted and looked largely unused. A blacksnake and many bugs stood guard.

Hellgrammites are the larval stage of an aquatic river insect which lives two very distinct lives. Hatching from an egg case placed on a rock ledge or an overhanging branch, young hellgrammites fall into the water that will become their home for one to three years.

These amazing, rather ugly creatures are found in river bottoms. Growing to a length of two to three inches long the hellgrammite resembles a centipede with a powerful set of pinching mouthparts, but it possesses six legs. Hellgrammites live underneath rocks, submerged logs, and debris in swift river currents, hunting and feeding on other macro-invertebrates.

Hellgrammites are a useful in identifying the quality of their river habitats because they can survive only in relatively clean and well oxygenated water. Fisherfolk consider them to be one of the prime live baits for fishing. The creature will emerge from complete metamorphosis into a winged Dobson fly which has a short but intense winged life.

Washington and Lee University

Seven years later, I was enrolled under partial scholarship in a liberal-arts college — Washington Lee University — just about 40-miles further south in the

Shenandoah Valley at Lexington. In those four years, fraternity life became important, in my case pledging and joining in my sophomore year the Beta Theta Pi fraternity, which had a front-row house location facing the campus.

Somehow at W&L, I managed to keep a car, usually parked in front or in the university lot across the street. Cars were not officially allowed for freshmen, but pretty popular with my fraternity brothers, especially for occasional trips to the nearest college-girls schools, such Hollins, Sweetbriar or Mary Baldwin, each about an hour north or south.

Aged Kentucky bourbon was my alcoholic drink of choice — Old Forester, in particular. Not cheap, but we managed to buy it from the Virginia ABC alcohol-beverage control store not too far from our fraternity house. My "Beta" (ΒΘΠ) fraternity frat house was just downhill from the W&L campus. That's where I roomed after freshman year (just off campus) as did most students, in their respective fraternity houses, there being little other housing for upperclassmen (no women accepted and maybe one black student) during my years at W&L.

The street our fraternity house faced was the route VMI cadets would sometimes march in unison down from the "Hill" into town, a parade and singsong reminiscent of my days at SMA. *Ring-tum-Phi* was the University's academic honor society. I never made it, a particular disappointment to my mother.

Figure 59. My (BΘΠ) fraternity house at W&L I recall rooming on the upper floor for at least one year.

Lexington, by the way, also had a downtown movie theater, a few blocks from the campus. I don't recall how often they changed shows, but it wasn't every day, maybe twice a week. "Colored" could sit in the balcony. At the time (early 1950s), the [Robert E.] Lee highway, Rt. 11, passed right by our fraternity house. It was many years before a highway bypass was built around town.

The Lenfest Center for the Arts, now home of the W&L Department of Theater and Dance, Music and Art and is a multi-use facility designed and equipped to accommodate a broad spectrum in one complex of the performing arts, including dramatic and musical theater, opera, choral and band music, as well as dance and performance art. W&L alumnus Gerry Lenfest, who set up a fund for the Center, was a classmate (and

Figure 60. Postage stamp issued 1949 honoring bicentennial for Washington and Lee University in Virginia. That was the same year I enrolled as a freshman student.

decades later) a supporter of some of my patented nuclear-technology initiatives. Having been '49 classmates, we refreshed our college memories at periodic class reunions. (Both Gerry and I began active duty in the Navy sometime soon after graduation, he I think into minesweepers and me assigned to landing ships.)

I still recall some pleasant sociable picnics on the rock-filled Maury River running through north Lexington, its rapids visible from a bridge on Route 60. (That was the main highway through the Shenandoah Valley, which ran north and south). The Maury originated further west with the Calfpasture River near Millboro. In the Millboro Springs Valley there was a convenient U-shaped bend on the Calfpasture River, which we could portage across overland to launch a canoe in upstream rapids.

Summers in Chelsea, Coney Island, Long Island, and Jersey Shore. Because this book is somewhat autobiographical, I should acknowledge some of my hang outs, other than Greenwich Village, on school vacations.

My varsity sport at SMA was swimming, so in New York City I sought out public pools that could be used for practice. One was in Chelsea, a residential neighborhood on the West Side of Manhattan, reachable by subway. I had some friends that had summer homes on Long Island.

Coney Island was accessible by subway too, I think BMT. Nathan's hot dogs, topped with everything, were great.

My hangout for many college summers was the Jersey Shore, including Bradley Beach, Allenhurst, Deal and Belmar, usually lifeguarding daytime and drinking beer with friends in the evenings.

Because the Maury River was named after Confederate naval officer Matthew Fontaine Maury, it might be renamed at some time. It runs into the James River past Richmond, the capital city of Virginia. The name of the Maury river and some monuments at W&L University are now also up for reconsideration, as are some names tied to U.S. Navy ships.

CHAPTER V:
U.S. NAVY MILITARY SERVICE

The War in Korea (Early 1950s)
Much of text content and map for the following section are largely taken from my previous published book, *Cold War Nuclear Challenges,* also available on Amazon in print and downloadable versions.

When Japan was defeated in World War II, the Soviet Red Army entered northern Korea, and the United States took over the southern half.

Afraid that the US was interested in taking North Korea as a base for operations against Manchuria, the People's Republic of China secretly had sent an army across the Yalu River. One of the earliest and more significant consequences of U.S. global-containment strategy was outbreak of the 5-year Korean War involving a large number of nations.

The Korean War (1950-1953) began when the North Korean Communist army crossed the 38th Parallel and invaded non-Communist South Korea. Kim Il-sung's North Korean army, armed with Soviet tanks, quickly overran South Korea,

The invasion was largely contrived, prepared, and initiated by Stalin: He had ordered the creation of detailed war plans that were communicated to the North Koreans.

The UN Security Council backed South Korea's defense, which fell disproportionately on the United States. For more than three years, the bitter war dragged on, eventually stalemating in a reluctant armistice that remains today.

Figure 61 shows how the flood and ebb of military advances went back an forth, north and south, ending with an armistice that has prevailed to this day.

Stalin — after nearly 30 years of power — died before the armistice, having largely kept his nation out of the Korean War. When North Korea invaded South Korea, UN Commander General MacArthur organized the surprise Inchon amphibious landing in September 1950. A month later, China intervened.

The war in Korea (last from 1950-1953) was mostly between a UN force led by the United States fighting with the South, against China with assistance from the USSR fighting for the North. The Soviets had occupied Korea north of the 38th parallel after WWII, and American forces had occupied the south. By 1948, two separate governments had been set up, both claiming to be the legitimate government of Korea. Twenty-one member nations of the United Nations eventually contributed to the defense of South Korea, with the United States providing 88% of the military personnel.

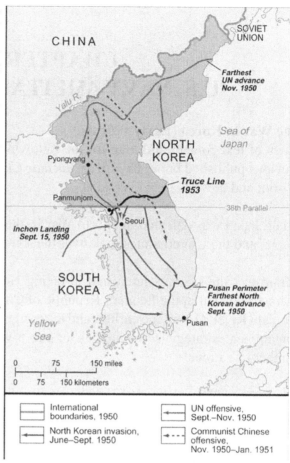

After the North Korea invasion, South Korean forces had been on the point of defeat in two months, forced all the way back to the Pusan Perimeter. Defeat looked imminent. But in September 1950, an amphibious UN counteroffensive was launched at Inchon, cutting off many of the North Korean attackers. Those that escaped envelopment and capture were rapidly forced back north gradually all the way to the border with China at the Yalu River, or into the mountainous interior.

Figure 61. Major military advances in the Korean War, which started in 1950 and ended in 1953.

However, in October 1950, Chinese forces crossed the Yalu and entered the war. That intervention triggered a retreat of UN forces which continued until mid-1951. The next two years of conflict became a war of attrition, with the front line being close to the 38th parallel. North Korea was subject to a massive bombing campaign. Jet aircraft engaged in air-to-air combat for the first time in history, and Soviet pilots covertly flew in defense of their Communist allies.

Fighting ended on 27 July 1953, when an armistice was signed. The agreement created a Korean Demilitarized Zone to separate North and South Korea, and allowed the return of prisoners. Some aroused but contained clashes have continued to the present.

Public opinion in heavily involved countries, such as the United States and Great Britain, was divided for and against the Korean war. Many feared an escalation into a general war with Communist China, and even nuclear war. The strong public opposition often strained Anglo-American relations.

With the breakout of the conflict in Korea, regional and localized hostilities spread worldwide. Many Cold War crises were ignited: Vietnam (1955–1975) and later Afghanistan, the latter a battleground that has lingered into the 21st Century.

Like the first two world wars, the Cold War's eventual demise in the early 1990s did not settle all issues, there being many leftovers: political, economic, ideological, military, ethnic, hegemonic, cultural, constitutional, and religious. Regarding nuclear brinkmanship and government spying, significant highlights — some personal — are described later in more detail.

Potential Nuclear Dimension of Korean War. John Foster Dulles, who had defined the policy of brinkmanship as "The ability to get to the verge without getting into the war is the necessary art," promoted the idea of using American nuclear superiority to make overt and direct threats in the Korean War. He was prepared, if necessary, to use atomic bombs and later thermonuclear weapons. If that happened, it would have broken down the psychological taboo that distinguished nuclear from other weapons. Dulles advised that we ought to treat them as any other weapon. When Eisenhower became president in January 1953, he subscribed to his new Secretary of State's strategy, despite some qualms.

Eisenhower made some fairly explicit public statements about the possibility of using nuclear weapons in Korea if a ceasefire were not arranged, and then even more explicit statements about the possibility of using them if the armistice should be violated. Because it was not violated, Eisenhower and Dulles believed that this no-nuclear-weapon strategy worked. But there's no independent evidence that the threat of using nuclear weapons had any impact on ending the Korean War. In any event, the Eisenhower administration started to cut back on national military-budget spending for conventional weapons, thus relying more heavily on the nuclear deterrent to protect American global interests.

Four months after Stalin's death on March 5, 1953, the Korean Armistice was settled. Despite what has turned out to be long-standing stalemate (still not finalized), the war had galvanized NATO into developing a viable military structure.

Even when the war was going badly for the South Koreans and the Americans, targets in North Korea were not considered useful enough for atomic bombs. As a result, the A-bomb already became viewed as a "wasting asset" rather than a "winning weapon."

China had entered the Korean war in November 1950. Of course, that was a major military setback to the allies. Later that month, President Truman caused a controversy when he stated at a news conference that the United States was considering using the atomic bomb in Korea in order to compensate for its losing conventional war.

World War II Atomic Destruction of Hiroshima and Nagaski. Because of the total (atomic) destruction of two cities in Japan that definitively quickened an end to World War II, it was not a hollow threat to consider using them in the Korean War.

On August 6, 1945, during the 2nd World War, over four square miles of central Hiroshima, including its factories, were destroyed by a single atomic bomb carried to the city by a B-29 bomber, creating the now-signature mushroom cloud indicative of its horrendous destructive power.

The United States detonated nuclear weapons over Hiroshima and Nagasaki on August 6 and 9, 1945, respectively, with the required consent of the United Kingdom. The two bombings killed between 129,000 and 226,000 people, mostly civilians, and remain the only uses of nuclear weapons in armed conflict.

In the final year of World War II, the Allies had prepared for a costly invasion of the Japanese mainland. The war in Europe had concluded three months earlier on 8 May. A conventional and a firebombing campaign had devastated 67 Japanese cities. The Allies called for the unconditional surrender of the Imperial Japanese armed forces in the Potsdam Declaration on July 26, 1945, the alternative being given as "prompt and utter destruction," but the Japanese government ignored the ultimatum and the war continued.

By August 1945, the Allies' secret Manhattan Project had produced two types of atomic bombs, and the US Army Air Forces (USAAF) was equipped with the specialized version of the Boeing B-29 Superfortress that could deliver the atomic bomb from a base on Tinian in the Mariana Islands. On July 25 the Allies issued orders to the USAAF for atomic bombs to be used on four Japanese cities On August 6, one of the modified B-29s dropped a uranium gun-type bomb ("Little Boy") on Hiroshima. Three days later another B-29 dropped a plutonium implosion bomb ("Fat Man") on Nagasaki.

The bombs immediately devastated their targets. Over the next two to four months, the acute effects of the atomic bombings killed between 90,000 and 146,000 people in Hiroshima and 39,000 and 80,000 people in Nagasaki; roughly half of the deaths in each city on the first day. Large numbers of people continued to die for months afterward from the effects of burns, radiation sickness, and other injuries, compounded by illness and malnutrition. In both cities, most of the dead were civilians, although Hiroshima had a sizable military garrison.

Japan surrendered to the Allies on August 15, six days after the Soviet Union's declaration of war and the bombing of Nagasaki. The Japanese government signed the instrument of surrender on September 2 in Tokyo Bay, effectively ending World War II. Scholars have extensively studied the effects of the bombings on the social and political character of subsequent world history and popular culture, and there is still much debate concerning the ethical and legal justification for the bombings and regarding alternative strategies.

Although commentators considered it doubtful that the threat to use the atomic bomb had elicited concessions from China or North Korea, President Eisenhower and his Secretary of State, John Foster Dulles, "claimed to believe it." The Korean War ended with an armistice on 27 July 1953, still enduring with no appearance of closure.

President Truman had created controversy when he stated at a news conference in 1950 that the United States was considering nuclear bombing in Korea in order to compensate for setbacks in the conventional war. In fact, his Commander in Chief, General MacArthur, wanted to use nuclear weapons, but Truman sacked him after he provoked a brutal retaliation from Chinese occupiers in Korea and began to publicly insult presidential policies. On his own, MacArthur had decided to go even further in antagonizing the Chinese. Without consulting Washington, he decided to send an ultimatum to the PRC, demanding that the Chinese withdraw their troops. If they didn't, MacArthur promised to force China to its knees. Truman was incensed at the rogue attempt to define and influence American policy. He decided MacArthur had to be fired.

Three years later, in 1953, Eisenhower as U.S. President threatened the use of nukes to end the war if the Chinese refused to negotiate. In any event, despite or unrelated to that threat, China and North Korea agreed to an armistice with the United Nations, signed July 27, 1953, formally ending the war. North and South Korea remained separate and occupied almost the same territory they had when the war began.

Although it is doubtful that the Truman threat to use the nuclear bomb elicited concessions, Eisenhower and his Secretary of State, John Foster Dulles, claimed to believe the threats were effective. Nevertheless, the A-bomb became viewed as a "wasting asset" rather than a "winning weapon." In effect, the bloody war set a lasting precedent: no nukes for regional conflicts. Nuclear weapons were never brought to bear in the Korean conflict.

Spring 1953 was also the time I graduated from W&L, with formal commissioning as an Ensign in the U.S. naval reserves, having drilled for several years of formal preparation. I was scheduled by the Navy to start my active duty at the end of the summer of 1953.

Military Service Obligation. Having spent my college years "drilling" with the NROTC and with two summers of formal training at naval stations in Rhode Island and California, I had fulfilled the requirement to be automatically commissioned upon graduation as an Ensign. This enabled me to be assigned for active duty to the amphibious fleet at the Navy Naval Operating Base, Norfolk, Virginia, beginning September 1953.

LSTs (Landing Ships). For nearly 2-1/2 years I served aboard LST landing ships — initially as supply officer, later as deck officer ("First Lieutenant"). First I was assigned to the LST 509 (see photo, Figure 66. Later, for me the most interesting cruise (called "Occupation Service" by the U.S. Navy Department) included a summer in the Med (Mediterranean) aboard another flat-bottomed LST, the1081 (USS Pima County).

In the Navy, I served aboard one of two amphibious seagoing ships (the LST 509 and the LST 1081— Figure 69) on many voyages at sea. During my period of naval service, these ships were assigned fleet duty in maneuvers and at ports along the Atlantic coast and throughout the Caribbean and its islands. Not the least memorable of the cruises took place off the coast of Cape Hatteras, where because of a hurricane our flat-bottomed ship rolled and pounded up and down at sea.

Rules of the (Nautical) Road. The International Regulations for Preventing Collisions at Sea set out, among other things, the "rules of the road" (navigation guidance) that are to be followed by ships and other vessels at sea to prevent collisions between two or more vessels. The Rules are derived from a multilateral international treaty.

Although rules for navigating vessels within U.S, inland rivers and lakes may differ, the international rules specify that they should be as closely in line with universal practice as possible. The rules for vessels navigating within the United States are published alongside the international rules.

Under normal sea conditions LSTs would be lucky to make 10 knots (about 11 mph) headway, but with our flat bottom it was somewhat less in choppy waters or when bucking the wind. Even the ship's skipper got seasick sometimes.

Having the watch at sea meant being on lookout "on the con" for other vessels or landfalls, and meant staying awake, essential to the safe operation of the vessel, and also allow the ship to respond to emergencies and other situations quickly. Keeping awake on one of he nighttime watches was easier said than done. There would usually also be a radar room or combat information center below deck.

On a typical seafaring vessel, be it naval or merchant, personnel "keep watch" in various locations and duties across the ship, such as the bridge and engine room. Typical bridge watchkeepers include a lookout and a deck officer who is responsible for the safe navigation of the ship; whereas in the engine room, an engine officer ensures that running machinery continues to operate within tolerances.

Having the "con" was always a challenge, especially if you had the dog watch — "first" dog watch from 1600 to 1800 (4 pm to 6 pm) and the "second" dog watch from 1800 to 2000 (6 pm to 8 pm).

I always found the middle watch midnight to 4 am. and the morning watch from 4 to 8am to be the most challenge to stay awake, especially when you had nothing but an empty ocean around you. Periodically you would do some star sighting for navigation when possible.

An officer of the deck (**OOD**) has a key watchstanding position in the U.S. Navy, tasked with duties and responsibilities for the ship, whether at sea or in port.

At sea, the OOD is stationed on the bridge and is in charge of navigation and safety of the ship, unless relieved by the captain or a qualified officer. The OOD is usually assisted in operation and navigation by a boatswain's mate, quartermaster, and signalman.

The OOD is supposed to keep continually informed concerning the ship's tactical situation and factors that may affect safe navigation of the ship, and take appropriate action to avoid grounding or collision according to the Rules of the (nautical) Road and orders of the commanding officer.

In port, the OOD is stationed on the quarterdeck, which is the entry point (gangplank) to the ship, where all personnel and visitors must cross to come aboard.

On smaller ships like an LST, a line officer takes turns as OOD. With maybe four line officers, at sea it means being on the bridge alternately around the clock.

My intended/enrolled/graduated journalism career after W&L was interrupted by a military obligation/stint: as an junior naval officer assigned to U..S. Navy amphibious-force LST landing ships operating out of home naval base (NOB) Norfolk, Virginia, just before the Korean War ended.

Partly in order to be able to graduate college without being pulled into full-time (Korean wartime) military service, I had enrolled in the NROTC (the Navy's version of recruiting officers from colleges). The unit "drilled" bi-weekly in nearby Fishersville, Virginia.

By graduation time from W&L, I did my usual summer semi-employed activity, mostly lifeguarding on the Jersey Shore (first Bradley Beach and later Bradley and Deal beaches). Otherwise during the of the summer break, I was chasing girls on the beaches and boardwalks.

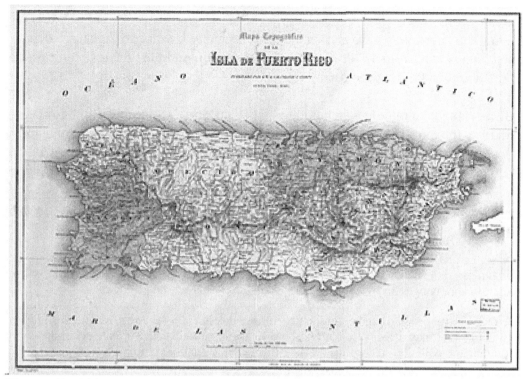

Figure 62. Old map of Puerto Rico, showing Vieques Island, to far right on the map, opposite what became Roosevelt Roads naval station on the mainland. The city of Ponce is to the south-east of the Island (bottom of the map) in what presents as well-formed horseshoe bay.

Entering the ancient harbors of such Carribean cities as San Juan, Puerto Rico and Havana, Cuba, brought about visions of ancient sailing-seafaring times when masted schooners plied the deep-harbor ocean ports of the Caribbean Sea.

Of course, most of my military service was and would be considered humdrum. (Nor did I ever become a professional journalist.). Nevertheless, a number of incidents are worth recalling.

I'll never forget our ship bombarding Vieques Island, opposite the U.S. Naval Base Roosevelt Island off eastern Puerto Rico. I was gunnery officer on our LST, in charge of the ship's meager cannon that our crew fired in live-ammunition practice. After all, it was wartime, although the fighting ravaged halfway across the world in Korea. We pounded the Vieques beaches, mostly imaginary targets, sometimes a few unlucky wild goats. Our five-inch gun or guns, I don't remember exactly, roared. Occasionally our machine gun or some rifles added to the excitement and noise of the live-fire exercise.

Figure 63. Recent map of Puerto Rico (slightly blurred in this version) showing major cities, with Vieques Island to the East. Ponce is midway along the South coast. The north-south girth of the island is roughly 40 miles, and east-west it is about 100 miles.

Sometimes, while at sea we were in formation with other ships of the line in a squadron. Maybe even a Commander or Admiral aboard a lead ship would direct the operation. Ours might take a turn as lead ship, when our squadron was on a joint exercise, which was not often. Most of the time, we sailed solo. We usually had a specific job to perform, standing orders to carry out, that is to transfer supplies from one place to another. Those orders came from Washington, DC, from the chief of naval operations.

When not loaded for resupply services, we carried out beaching exercises with sometimes with other LST's, often on Vieques.

LSTs were capable of hauling smaller landing craft too, as at WWII landings on beaches of Normandy and at Korean War assaults on Inchon.

Figure 64. Korean War naval landing ship (LST 509) underway at sea. World-War-II-vintage LSTs were reassigned to duty during the Korean War, particularly for the Allied landing at Inchon.

When you multiply our practice-shooting exercises with that of the U.S. naval fleet in the Caribbean, lot of rounds were expended. I don't recall if the rest of the amphibious fleet or the entire fleet practiced or only bombarded there, but sometimes they aimed at targets other than those being towed.

Figure 65. Harbor entrance San Juan, Puerto Rico, through choppy waters.

Ponce, on the south side of Puerto Rico, was several times our port-of-call, bringing provisions to what must then have been some remote, nearly-forgotten U.S. military installation or government office. We were always happy to visit strange places. Sometimes the crew was particularly pleased with the female reception, which depended in part on frequency of naval visits and the fact that crew members were paid in U.S. dollars.

Puerto Rico, officially the Commonwealth of Puerto Rico is a U.S. territory located in the northeast Caribbean Sea, approximately 1,000 miles southeast of Miami, Florida.

Puerto Rico is an archipelago located between the Dominican Republic and the U.S. Virgin Islands and includes the main island and several smaller ones, such as Mona, Culebra, and Vieques. The capital and most populous city is San Juan. The territory's total population is approximately 3.2 million, more than 20 U.S. states. Spanish and English are the official languages of the executive branch of government.

Originally populated by the indigenous Taíno people, Puerto Rico was colonized by Spain following the arrival of Christopher Columbus in 1493. It was contested by various other European powers, but remained a Spanish possession for the next four centuries. The island's cultural and demographic landscapes were shaped by the displacement and assimilation of the native population, the forced migration of African slaves, and Spanish settlement primarily from the Canary Islands and Andalusia. In the Spanish Empire, Puerto Rico played a secondary but strategic role compared to wealthier colonies like Peru and New Spain. By the late 19th century, a distinct Puerto Rican identity began to emerge, based on a unique creole Hispanic culture and language that combined indigenous, African, and European elements. In 1898, following the Spanish–American War, the United States acquired Puerto Rico, which remains an unincorporated territorial possession, making it the world's oldest colony.

Puerto Ricans have been citizens of the United States since 1917, and can move freely between the island and the mainland. Because it is not a state, Puerto Rico does not have a vote in the U.S. Congress, which governs the territory with full jurisdiction. Puerto Rico's sole congressional representation is through one non-voting member of the House called a Resident Commissioner. As residents of a U.S. territory, American citizens in Puerto Rico are disenfranchised at the national level, do not vote for the president or vice president of the U.S., and in most cases do not pay federal income tax. Congress approved a local constitution in 1952, allowing U.S. citizens of the territory to elect a governor. Puerto Rico's future political status has consistently been a matter of significant debate.

By Latin American standards, Puerto Rico has the highest GDP per capita and the most developed and competitive economy; however, its poverty rate is higher than the poorest U.S. state, and the territory struggles with chronically large debt, considerable unemployment, and a high rate of emigration. The 21st century has seen several major challenges, including a government-debt crisis and devastation by Hurricane Maria.

Figure 66. View of modern San Juan frontage. Of course, it was nothing like this modern when our naval ship ported there back in the 50s. The more quaint prevailed then.

132

1954 Hurricanes Devastate East Coast. On August 31 Hurricane Carol made landfall on New York's Long Island and produced wind gusts of 120 mph. The hurricane's storm-surge effectively isolated eastern Long Island for a period of time.

On September 10 Hurricane Edna tracked to the east of Long Island, producing 9 inches of rain. New York City had to order an emergency standby for the majority of its hospitals, and subways.

Oct 5 – Oct 18: Hurricane Hazel was the deadliest, costliest, and most intense hurricane of the 1954 Atlantic hurricane season. The storm killed at least 469 people in Haiti before striking the United States near the border between North and South Carolina as a Category 4 hurricane. Hurricane Hazel's wind gust of 113 mph at Battery Park has been the highest ever recorded in New York City.

Figure 67. LST 1081 (USS Pima County) underway (assigned to "occupation service in Europe" from 7 June to 20 September 1955).

During one of these hurricanes, I think we sailed our flat-bottomed LST from Atlantic City to Norfolk. It was an up and down roller-coaster ride, with a constant electronic bearing to Cape Hatteras on our starboard (to the right).

I think we withstood the other hurricane of the season while secuured in port at Norfolk Amphibious Base, along with everyone else.

We rarely beached our ship on a beachhead in peacetime during practice landing operations because that would entail considerable scraping and repainting of the ship's bottom. That's quite an refurbishment operation, both in outage time and in Navy-approved nautical paint.

Staten Island and Brooklyn Naval Shipyards. Our LST landing ship was overhauled in New York City, on Staten Island. On at least one occasion I had to drive over to the Brooklyn Naval Yard (since decommissioned) to pick up some parts. I recall having my car then, but whatever vehicle I used to get the parts ran into a (still-memorable) parking problem at the congested Brooklyn Naval Yard.

The second (and last ship) I served on was the LST 1081 (Figure 70), the USS Pima County, which during World War II had operated in the Asiatic-Pacific Theater. It had been commissioned on 30 June 1945 and was assigned to the Asiatic-Pacific Theater. Decommissioned in 1946, it was recommissioned in 1951 and lasted in service until late 1955, not long after I left active duty.

Naval Cruise in the Med. The final major naval deployment with the LST 1081 was for the summer of 1955, resupplying U.S. bases or American "interests" at coastal Mediterranean portst. We had crossed the Atlantic (back and forth) to get to the Med (which took about a week, only making 10 knots headway, or so). Of course a "cruise" on a U.S. Navy ship is not the same as on a commercial passenger ship.

In North Africa and the Med coastal cities, we pulled into ports where U.S. military and diplomatic stations needed resupply, including Port Leyote, Morocco; Casablanca, Morocco; Tripoli, Libya; Gibraltar; Taranto and Naples, Italy; Nice, France; the independent kingdom of Monaco; and Majorca of the Spanish Balearic Islands. I also memorably recall pulling into Palermo, Sicily, on a very hot Scirocco summer day.

Scirocco is an Italian word for a wind that comes across the Mediterranean from the Sahara desert, sometimes reaching hurricane speeds in North Africa and Southern Europe, especially during the summer season. In California, Santa Ana winds are the equivalent.

Memorably, we sailed into Tripoli, Libya, then under U.S. control. The Navy Exchange at the American naval base in Tripoli at the time was well stocked, and I recall buying a Leica camera there with some nice lens accessories and leather case at dirt-cheap prices for service members. We could also stock up on cartons of American cigarettes, which were fantastic commodities for exchange. (I don't recall just how many cartons or American dollars it cost me, but it was a bargain when I bought a Vespa motor scooter in Italy.

For that tour of duty in the Med, I was then "First Lieutenant," that is, officer in charge of the deck crew. That made me responsible mostly for the external decks and hull of the ship. For example, under my purview came responsibility for maintenance and painting of the ship's hull and topside; also, being officer responsible for the deck cranes, lifeboats and ship's anchor. It's a good thing we had experienced CWOs.

CWOs (U.S. Navy Chief Warrant Officers — grades WO 1-5) are a breed all their own. Chiefs are the ones aboard ships who make sure that orders from commissioned officers are carried out. In the United States Armed Forces, the ranks of warrant officer (grades W1 to W5) are rated above all non-commissioned officers, candidates, cadets, and midshipmen, but subordinate to the lowest commissioned officer (ensign in the Navy). We depended heavily on the "Chief" for directing the ship's crew to carry out assigned duties, at sea or in port. Warrant Officers usually had the most nautical experience and had separate quarters, aboard ship and at home port.

Shipboard Damage Control. In order to be as self-sufficient as possible when far from shore support, each ship of the line is equipped and the crew organized so as to deal with emergencies, which includes teams trained to deal with seamanship, combat systems, engineering, casualties, damage control, and medical problems. Even if your ship was in maneuvers at sea with a squadron or fleet, you have to be rather self-sufficient far out in the ocean.

134

Aft steering is a compartment at the back of a ship, with full steering controls and communication with engineering, combat-information center, and the bridge. It also has an engine-order telegraph for communicating speed and shaft revolution orders to the engine room. Normally it is manned only during General Quarters, or in case of casualty to the bridge helm. If the bridge sustains significant battle damage, the ship can still be maneuvered from aft steering, even though that space is below deck and has no view. A qualified Officer of the Deck with an outside view communicates rudder and engine speed orders to aft steering in that case.

Figure 68. A photo taken in Venice. Note gondola and gondolier rowing to the left in this canal.

Scylla and Charybdis. At one point in our Med cruise, our ship passed through the Strait of Messina, between the island of Sicily and the Italian mainland. *Scylla* and *Charybdis* are mythical sea monsters noted by Homer in Greek mythology. As our ship navigated through, it was difficult to ignore the idiom, which has been associated with the proverbial advice "to choose the lesser of two evils." Several other idioms, such as "on the horns of a dilemma," "between the devil and the deep blue sea," and "between a rock and a hard place" express similar meanings. The mythical situation has developed a proverbial use in which seeking to choose between equally dangerous extremes is seen as potentially leading to disaster.

The movie *Casablanca* with Humphrey Bogart is probably the most famous Hollywood production of all time, for good reason. And of course once when our ship docked in Casablanca, I made a point of find the bar where Bogart famously sang "Here's looking at you, kid" in the Marseillaise scene of the movie.

Here are some factoids about the American-made movie: Besides Bogart, it starred Ingrid Bergman, Paul Henreid, Claude Rains, Sydney Greenstreet, and Peter Lorre. Music was by Max Steiner; cinematography by Arthur Edeson; produced by Warner Bros – First National Pictures; distributed by Warner Bros. Pictures; released 1942 (Hollywood Theatre) and 1943 (United States). The 1942 romantic-drama film was directed by Michael Curtiz.

Set during World War II, it focuses on an American expatriate who must choose between his love for a woman and helping her and her husband, a Czech resistance leader, escape from the Vichy-French controlled city of Casablanca to continue his fight against the Germans.

Although *Casablanca* was an A-list film with established stars and first-rate writers, no one involved with its production expected it to be anything other than one of the hundreds of ordinary pictures produced by Hollywood that year. *Casablanca* was rushed into release to take advantage of the publicity from the Allied invasion of North Africa a few weeks earlier. It had its world premiere on November 26, 1942, in New York City and was released nationally in the United States on January 23, 1943. The film was a solid if unspectacular success in its initial run.

Exceeding expectations, *Casablanca* went on to win the Academy Award for Best Picture, Best Director and Best Adapted Screenplay. Its reputation gradually improved, to the point that its lead characters, memorable lines, and pervasive theme song have all become iconic. It still consistently ranks near the top of lists for the greatest movie films in history.

After the Korean War ended, wartime LSTs were kept by the Navy in peacetime service largely to be nimble and capacious supply ships. While amphibious training was still carried out with marines and their vehicles, the bread-and-butter role of LSTs was as provisioning ships that could go into almost any port. Even though World War II had ended a decade earlier, the United States still had many military bases around the Med.

Having been a swimmer at SMA, I had learned to enjoy spearfishing off beaches and jetties along the Jersey shore. That hobby and experience ended up serving me well during my years on active duty in the Navy, especially when we sailed and ported in the Caribbean and Mediterranean. Most of the time, the waters were so clear you could see many meters under water, either from the ships' rail or when snorkling.

A Vespa (Italian for "wasp") Moto (scooter). Being in charge of the LST's deck crew and ship's cranes as First Lieutenant came in particularly handy in Taranto Bay (Italy) when I purchased a Vespa motor scooter from a store at the harbor's town. In order to get the scooter transported to my ship anchored in the bay, I hired a smallboat and oarsman who rowed me and the Vespa across from the harbor landing to our ship. Upon arrival I could order the deck crew to lower a crane hook and cable, and all went nervously well in hoisting my new vehicle aboard.

In fact, I learned to drive the Vespa on board the ship, mostly topside but sometimes on the cargo deck, largely by help from our bosun's mate. (In the U.S. Navy the ship's boatswain assists the first lieutenant in the execution of major seamanship functions and the maintenance of topside gear. The boson's mate supervised cargo handling and inspected and maintained rigging and deck gear.) He was usually the senior non-commissioned officer aboard.

Neither our upper deck nor tank deck had a lot of open space. I had never owned or rode a bicycle (either in Virginia or New York); so it was a double learning experience, both for being on a two-wheeled vehicle and on a motorized one at that. By the time we arrived at the *mole* (harbor dock) in Palermo, Sicily, I had mastered enough of the two-wheeled scooter to entice a girl to ride with me around the pier.

The Vespa *moto* turned out to be pretty handy whenever we pulled into a foreign port. In fact, that's the main reason I bought it, to be able to get around in Mediterranean cities where we pulled in. We needed a way to get some supplies.

The scooter served me well in later tours of naval duty, sometimes better able than our ship's jeep to help pick up crew mail from our naval stations or consulates in strange ports when and where we docked, both in the Med and the Caribbean. Being able to send postal mail off to the States, and pick up it up in distant foreign ports forwarded from the States, was never a simple logistical proposition when coping with it overseas. Often when we came across another U.S. naval ship, we would exchange old movies (then kept in canisters), as well as needed supplies.

After graduation from Virginia Tech and when leaving Blacksburg, I sold the Vespa (probably for $200) to my former thesis advisor, Dr. Andy Robeson. That might have been more than I paid for it in Taranto, Italy, having bartered it in exchange for cartons of cigarettes. While our ship was sailing around the Med in the mid-1950s, we could buy at discount from ship's store, and for a nonsmoker like me, they were valuable commodities. So were dollars, then the most sought-after medium of currency at the time.

Errol Flynn. Worthy of being recalled is a particularly unusual experience during my Med cruise. It took place in Majorca, of the Balearic Islands, where the expatriate film star Errol Flynn lived aboard his infamous yacht *Zaca* in the Bay of Palma with his wife, Patricia Wymore.

One night, while our ship was anchored nearby for a week or two, a small boat pulled aside, and we heard the boaters speaking English. Imagine our surprise when Flynn and his wife requested permission to come aboard, asking for fuel for their yacht lanterns and bringing some reels of his movies. Our crew got to watch the first movie with Flynn on the ship's deck while he mocked himself. Days later, I had opportunities to visit on his yacht and join him spearfishing in the Bay. Being officer in charge of our ship's deck crew had its perks!

Ship's Lanterns. Older seagoing yachts were outfitted mostly with lanterns fueled from animal fats, especially fish and whale oil. While-oil lamps were an ancient form of ship's lighting, the lighting was gradually replaced by kerosene-fueled lanterns beginning around 1850.

Kerosene — in the form of paraffin, lamp oil or coal oil — is a combustible hydrocarbon liquid derived from petroleum. It has been (and still) is widely used as a fuel in aviation, as well as homes.

Looking back now, Errol Flynn was quite a character. Besides being an actor of cinema, theater, radio and TV, he lived his life as an adventurous go-getter. He also became known as a trickster, movie hero, gallant character, womanizer, drinker (indeed), eccentric, navigator, researcher, writer. and journalist. I would add snorkeler, both of us having done some underwater diving together with snorkeling mask and spearguns in the Bay of Palma.

Malta, Naples, Monte Carlo. There three ports were among the many we pulled into in the Med. Occasionally we spent enough time docked so as to get some nighttime "shore leave" in the harbor district or inner city. In those days the casino in Monte Carlo was fun for a while (and affordable), but the city-nation back then was nowhere as busy as other ports in the Med, yet just as expensive. I mostly shot craps when visiting casinos in the Med in those days, playing table odds closely. I toyed with a little casino poker, primarily draw and stud.

Gibraltar is a British Overseas Territory located at the southern tip of the Iberian Peninsula. It has a land area of about 2½ sq mi and is bordered to the north by Spain. The landscape is dominated by the Rock of Gibraltar at the foot of which is the densely populated town area, now home to over 32,000 people.

On Gibraltar, I drove our jeep around on the other ("wrong") side of the road, evading Gibraltar's barbary macaque apes and all, in conformance with the British Colony rules and local traffic. As usual, the jeep was useful in getting us fresh supplies and picking up or dropping off mail.

In 1704, Anglo-Dutch forces captured Gibraltar from Spain during the War of the Spanish Succession on behalf of the Habsburg claim to the Spanish throne. The territory was ceded to Great Britain in perpetuity under the Treaty of Utrecht in 1713. During World War II it was an important base for the Royal Navy as it controlled the entrance and exit to the Mediterranean Sea, the Strait of Gibraltar (which is only 9 mi wide at this naval choke point), making it difficult even for Axis submarines to traverse. It remains strategically important, with half the world's seaborne trade passing through the strait. Today Gibraltar's economy is based largely on tourism, online gambling, financial services and cargo-ship refueling.

The sovereignty of Gibraltar remains a point of contention in Anglo-Spanish relations because Spain still asserts a claim to the territory. In a 1967 referendum the citizens of Gibralter rejected proposals for Spanish sovereignty, and, in a 2002 referendum the idea of shared sovereignty was also rejected.

Being ship's First Lieutenant had its perks. But duty aboard an LST was never easy, and whenever reaching port we had to share our job assignments and shore-patrol obligations (among four line officers). On shore patrol, I had to pack my 0.45-caliber sidearm. (While appearing tough, armed and in uniform, it was mostly a charade.)

Naval Exercises around the Caribbean (Early 1950s).

During some of my LST Caribbean cruises, we pulled into (usually docked) at any one of several naval bases and sites in Puerto Rico, including Ponce on the south coast. That was a welcoming port for shore liberty (free time for crew and officers).

Our ship sometimes carried and supplied provisions to the U.S. naval base on eastern Cuba at Guantanamo Bay and also up the river at nearby Santiago, Cuba. (This was long before it GTMO was used as a prison camp). We had a rather large reefer (refrigerator) aboard; when ship's supply officer, I remember having to crawl into the reefer in order to inventory our frozen meat supply. I don't recall anything specific about our visit to GTMO back in the early 50s.

Whenever possible, especially when anchored in clear water, we were able to do some snorkeling. Once, while near an island in the Caribbean, I speared a *langusta* (warm-water lobster) big enough to make the main course for a meal in the officer's mess (our designated dining area aboard ship). Incidentally I seem to recall that in those days, most of the attendants in the officer's mess were Filipino stewards.

The US Navy enrolled **Filipinos** to serve only as cooks, waiters and cabin boys aboard ships. As was the case for the LST on which I was assigned in the 50s, stewards recruited in the Philippines under an unusual treaty were apportioned aboard almost every large ship of the fleet, serving meals in the officers' mess and cleaning the officers' staterooms.

In 1992 the US Navy terminated a nearly century-old program of recruiting **Filipino males** to serve aboard ships as stewards. Tens of thousands of Filipinos had served in the Navy since the end of the Spanish-American War, when the Philippines became a US colony. Filipinos were the only foreign nationals allowed to enlist in the US armed forces without first immigrating to this country. And the Navy was the only military branch they could join.

Competition for the 400 slots was fierce. Carson said the Navy received as many as 100,000 applicants – 250 applicants per slot – each year. After weeding out those viewed as unqualified to enlist, the Navy tested about a quarter of the applicants and picked the top 400.

In addition to the economic rewards, the enlistment slots were also coveted because they represented the first step toward eventual US citizenship. Immigration laws allowed Filipinos and other foreign-born US residents serving on active duty in the military during a declared conflict to apply for naturalization.

Guantanamo Bay Naval Base, also called GTMO, is a US military base and now a detention camp in Cuba, which the U.S. had leased as a coaling station and naval base in 1903. The United States assumed territorial control over the southern portion of Guantánamo Bay under the 1903 Lease agreement after the Spanish-American War, well more than a century ago.

Guantánamo Bay is located in Guantánamo Province at the southeastern end of Cuba. The Bay provides the largest harbor on the south side of the island. and it is surrounded by steep hills which create an enclave cut off from its immediate hinterland.It is at the southeastern end of Cuba and is the oldest overseas U.S. Naval Base.

The lease was $2000/yr in gold until 1934, when the payment was set to match the value in gold in dollars. In 1974, the yearly lease was set to just over $4000.

This was the time when Castro was just beginning to mount a revolution in the mountains. On our LST, we brought supplies to GITMO (Guantanamo Bay military installation, which the United States has hung on to since the Spanish-American War). While U.S. possession of that base became an irritant to the Castro government, it was and probably still is a welcome source of employment and American dollars for Cuban workers and vendors.

Since the Cuban Revolution of 1959, the Cuban government has consistently protested against the U.S. military-base presence on Cuban soil and called it illegal under international law, alleging that the base was imposed on Cuba by force.

Since 2002, the naval base has contained a military prison (the Guantanamo Bay detention camp) holding alleged unlawful combatants captured in Afghanistan, Iraq, and other places during the U.S. War on Terror. Complaints of torture and denial of protection under the Geneva Conventions have been condemned internationally.

The United States still exercises jurisdiction and control over this territory, while recognizing that Cuba retains ultimate sovereignty. Some legal scholars argue that the lease may be voidable.

Guantánamo Bay is now home for a U.S. Naval Base and the Guantánamo Bay detention camp, both governed by the United States. Since the 1959 revolution, Cuba has only cashed a single lease payment from the United States government, as doing so would tend to legitimize American jurisdiction over the base. In January 2018, President Donald Trump signed an executive order to keep the detention camp open indefinitely. In May 2018, the first prisoner was transferred during Trump's term, reducing the number of forgotten inmates to 40.

The **Geneva Conventions** are rules that apply only in times of armed conflict and seek to protect people who are not or are no longer taking part in hostilities. The first Geneva convention dealt with the treatment of wounded and sick armed forces in the field. The second convention dealt with sick, wounded, and shipwrecked members of armed forces at sea. The third convention dealt with treatment of prisoners of war during times of conflict. The fourth convention dealt with treatment of civilians and their protection during wartime.

Controversy has arisen over the US designation of irregular opponents as "unlawful enemy combatants," especially in U.S. Supreme Court judgments regarding the Guantanamo Bay brig facility. Attorneys-General have claimed that any person, including American citizens, suspected of being a member, agent, or associate of Al Qaeda, the Taliban, or possibly any other terrorist organization, is an "enemy combatant" who can be detained in U.S. military custody until hostilities end.

The **Cuban Revolution** began with an armed revolt conducted by Fidel Castro's revolutionary 26th of July Movement and its allies against the military dictatorship of President Fulgencio Batista. The revolution continued sporadically until the rebels finally ousted Batista on 31 December 1958, replacing his government with a socialist state. (The *Dia de la Revolución*, 26 July 1953, is celebrated in Cuba). The 26th of July Movement later formed itself along communist lines, becoming the Communist Party in October 1965.

The Cuban Revolution had powerful domestic and international repercussions. In particular, it transformed Cuba's relationship with the United States, although efforts to improve diplomatic relations have gained momentum in recent years. In the immediate aftermath of the revolution, Castro's government began a program of nationalization, centralization of the press and political consolidation that transformed Cuba's economy and civil society. The revolution also heralded an era of Cuban intervention in foreign military conflicts in Africa, Latin America, Southeast Asia and the Middle East.

Among the impoverished peasantry, several rebellions occurred in the six years following 1959, mainly in the Escambray mountains, which were repressed by the Revolutionary government. More recently, many self-exiled Cubans made the 100-mile sea-crossing to Florida, which has a large population of ex-patriots.

Final Navy Cruise. My last tour of duty ended auspiciously. When sharpening a screwdriver for whatever reason in the LST machine shop, I managed to grind off part of my left thumb and nail. It was a bloody mess, ending my active-duty career. I had to be transferred to a naval hospital ship in the Caribbean. The ship's surgeon re-attached what he could of my thumb, which eventually regrew the nail. Meanwhile, my arm was put in a sling, and they dropped me off at Norfolk at first opportunity, whereupon I was summarily discharged a little before the intended discharge date.

Awaiting me was my wife and newborn baby. Just before embarking on the Med cruise I had married Helen Genopolis, who was pregnant with what turned out to be our first child, which we named Paul. She was from a Norfolk family. Helen bore three other children of our marriage, one other while we were in Virginia.

After Discharge from the Navy.

Upon military discharge, enabled by the GI veterans bill, and spurred on by an encouraging physics (or nuclear-engineering) department head at Virginia Tech in Blacksburg, I converted academically to a flexible technical curriculum. Thus I ended up eventually with a PhD in nuclear physics, having progressed though advanced mathematics via correspondence courses in the Navy and later advanced-placement technical classes at Virginia Tech. There in Blacksburg, my wife Helen with me, she

4

soon had the first of our four children. (I had to finish my language and dissertation requirements in Illiniois.)

Another thing I picked up at Virginia Tech was gardening. Originally VPI was a land-grant school, and one of the curricula it prided itself on was agriculture. Thus it had a horticulture department which among other things had veterans grow a victory-type garden requiring something like 25 different vegetables. When I enrolled, the previous class had graduated and left their gardens behind giving an opportunity for veterans like me to cultivate and reap the harvest. Ever since, I have had a veggie garden in my backyard, usually with several varieties of tomatoes.

POST-GRAD YEARS: BLACKSBURG, VIRGINIA

Virginia Polytechnic Institute is located in the mountains of the Virginia's southwest (see Figure 56). VPI is the largest land-grant university in the Commonwealth of Virginia.

Residing there in Blacksburg with my nascent family, I spent two straight years, starting as a graduate student still satisfying some undergrad course requirements while taking graduate-level courses (mostly in mathematics).

One thing for sure: I was never cut out to be a chemist, having nearly flunked freshman-college chemistry at VPI.

The GI Bill was my main source of support, for living and tuition, with some supplemental income from "drilling" with the military reserves (I think at the Fishersville Naval Reserve post near Waynesboro). That involvement meant I would still have to spend two weeks (paid) summer training/research, alternating each year at NRL in DC and NRDL in San Francisco. That part is rather fuzzy in memory to me because at Virginia Tech I was immersed in my academic work.

I was fortunate at VPI to be under the close tutelage of Dr. Marshall Hahn, who was then head of the nascent but expanding Physics Department, and Dr. Andy Robeson, who became my thesis advisor. Dr. Hahn eventually became president of VPI.

While living and studying in Blacksburg, my MS-degree research requirement was centered on a graphite-moderated sub-critical reactor then under construction. This program allowed me to finish in two years the requisite undergraduate and graduate courses. VPI was one of the first universities to get involved in nuclear-reactor research and development, then a matter of major national interest. It turned out to be a good and timely career choice for me.

CHAPTER VI: ARGONNE

EISENHOWER ATOMS FOR PEACE PROGRAM

The major determinant for me and my family in deciding to go to the Chicago area upon graduation was a 2-year fellowship at Argonne National Laboratory, located in the southwestern suburbs (see Figures 7o and 71).

As a nascent nuclear engineer, there were a number of commercial- and research-oriented employment opportunities. However, accepting the financially supported fellowship at Argonne in Illinois turned out to be a career-long decisive choice. Under a new program promoted by President Eisenhower, applicants were accepted from all over the world, and from many academic or administrative levels, to study nuclear science and engineering at a special purposed school attached to and using Argonne personnel as educators.

Figure 69. Logo of President Eisenhower's international Atoms for Peace program which kickstarted the development of peaceful nuclear power around the world.

The specific nuclear-science and engineering program INSE to which I was admitted, compensated for me and my family to travel to Argonne, housed us in temporary quarters near the lab, and paid a salary. The first year consisted of formal professional classroom nuclear education, and the second year was an assignment of mutual agreement in a working program or facility at Argonne. I chose the sub-critical/critical reactor-experimental facilities on the site's Building 315/316 laboratory complex because of my prior experience at VPI. That choice turned out to dominate my subsequent professional career.

As for other graduates of the INSE program — from Japan, South Africa and elsewhere — they went back to their countries of origin and operated or built nuclear reactors or even national programs for nuclear energy research and development. The Eisenhower Atoms for Peace program for developing constructive nuclear energy in nations around the world was successful in meeting its goals.

ARGONNE NATIONAL LABORATORY

Argonne is a science and engineering research national laboratory operated by the University of Chicago under contract to the U.S. Department of Energy. The lab is located in DuPage county near Lemont, Illinois, outside Chicago (see Figure 70 area map).

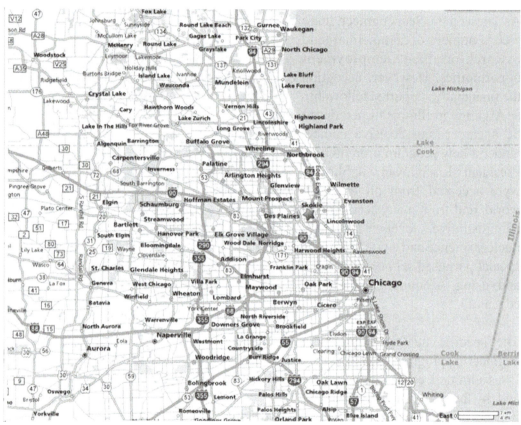

Figure 70. Map of Chicago area. Argonne National Laboratory is located westward near Interstate 355, between the towns of Bollingbrook, Lemont, and Romeoville.

Argonne was initially formed to carry out Enrico Fermi's work on nuclear reactors as part of the World War II Manhattan Project. After the war, it was designated as the first national laboratory in the United States. Originally, the lab focused primarily on non-weapon-related nuclear physics, designing and building the first power-producing nuclear reactors, helping design the reactors used by the USA's nuclear navy, and a wide variety of similar projects. In 1994, the lab's nuclear mission ended, and today it has been assigned a broad portfolio in basic science research, energy storage, renewable energy, environmental sustainability, supercomputing, and national security.

After the close of World War II, the Manhattan Project was disestablished by Congress and a new federal department for nuclear energy was organized by the Atomic Energy Commission. The laboratories that helped develop the atomic bomb were given new missions, with the DOE labs at Los Alamos, Livermore and Sandia receiving most of the weapons-related assignments and with Argonne and Brookhaven becoming fully peace-oriented nuclear-development national labs.

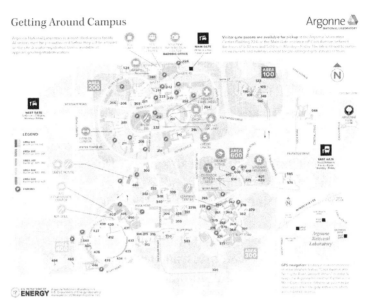

Figure 71. Map of Argonne National Laboratory and surrounding area.

Originally, during and just after World War II, Argonne National Laboratory evolved separately in a distant forest area southwest of Chicago. Within that fenced-in area simply called Argonne is where I became a member of the nuclear-reactor research staff upon completion of my fellowship in the Eisenhower program; it's also where I eventually finished the thesis requirements for masters and PhD degrees in nuclear engineering and physics.

Argonne is currently a part of the expanding Illinois Technology and Research Corridor. The lab formerly ran a smaller facility called simply Argonne-West in Idaho next to what is now the Idaho National Engineering and Environmental Laboratory. In 2005, the two Idaho-based laboratories merged to become the Idaho National Laboratory.

To the extent I recall, Argonne then had programs in nuclear-related areas of engineering, chemistry, chemical engineering, biology, experimental physics, accelerators and the environment. The national weapons laboratories out West — mainly Los Alamos, Livermore and Sandia — carried out most of the weapons-oriented R&D. Oak Ridge in Tennessee was the site for production of enriched uranium. At one time or another, I visited all of the DOE facilities on official business.

Maria Goeppert-Mayer. Aside from some visiting scholars and local or state politicians, we had a number of visits and lectures at Argonne from notable scientists and engineers. One was Goeppert-Mayer. She was a noted theoretical physicist who had discovered underlying features of the atomic nucleus, and those discoveries led to her sharing the Nobel Prize in 1965, the first woman in the United States to do so (and the last one for another half-century). During World War II, Goeppert-Mayer worked for the U.S. Manhattan Project — first, on isotope separation at Columbia University and, later, with Edward Teller at Los Alamos Laboratory.

After the Mayers moved to Chicago in 1946, she had received a faculty appointment, splitting her time between the University of Chicago's Institute for Nuclear Studies and the newly opened Argonne National Laboratory as a Senior Physicist in the Theoretical Physics Division.

As part of my job at one time, I got to see so many nuclear weapons at such facilities as Pantex that it became psychologically sickening. Image: Just one of even the smallest nuclear warhead detonations could kill almost everyone in a small city.

Argonne R&D was limited strictly to non-military applications of nuclear energy, mostly in the development of research, test and power reactors. Once in a while a few Nobel-prize winners involved in (non-military) nuclear research came to our site to give a lecture or carry out some specialized work. One of Argonne's novel accelerators has drawn people from all over the world to do experiments, now including research on the SARS Covid-2 coronavirus.

Marie Curie. Marie Skłodowska Curie (1867 – 1934), was a Polish and naturalized-French physicist and chemist who conducted pioneering research on radioactivity. She was the first woman to win a Nobel Prize, the first person and the only woman to win the Nobel Prize twice, and the only person to win the Nobel Prize in two different scientific fields. She was part of the Curie family legacy of five Nobel Prizes. She was also the first woman to become a professor at the University of Paris, and in 1995 the first woman to be entombed on her own merits in the Panthéon in Paris.

Marie Curie was born in Warsaw, in what was then the Kingdom of Poland, part of the Russian Empire. She studied at Warsaw's clandestine Flying University and began her practical scientific training in Warsaw. In 1891, aged 24, she followed her older sister to study in Paris, where she earned her higher degrees and conducted her subsequent scientific work. She shared the 1903 Nobel Prize in Physics with her husband Pierre Curie and physicist Henri Becquerel. She won the 1911 Nobel Prize in Chemistry.

Her achievements include the development of the theory of "radioactivity" (a term she coined), techniques for isolating radioactive isotopes, and the discovery of two elements, polonium and radium. Under her direction, the world's first studies were conducted into the treatment of neoplasms using radioactive isotopes. She founded the Curie Institutes in Paris and in Warsaw, which remain major centers of medical research today. During World War I she developed mobile radiography units to provide X-ray services to field hospitals.

While she became a French citizen, Marie Curi never lost her sense of Polish identity. She taught her daughters the Polish language and took them on visits to Poland. She named the first chemical element she discovered (polonium) after her native country.

Ironically, Marie Curie died of anaemia from exposure to radiation in the course of her scientific research and radiological work at field hospitals during World War I. Awareness of radiation hazards had not yet become widespread knowledge.

Invention of Hodoscope. Presumably, my main claim to an enduring professional reputation will be invention of the fast-neutron/gamma hodoscope, a multichannel/multidetector system used primarily at the TREAT reactor in Idaho. Patent records also substantiate my subsequent development of several variants of the hodoscope that could be used for detection of banned or clandestine substances or objects.

In order to avoid having to present here an overly complex description, suffice it to say that the hodoscope technical scheme involves a multitude (hundreds) of radiation detectors assembled in an array so as to be able to record and reproduce an image of the object of interest. It is basically a nuclear-imaging scheme. For its initial incarnation, the hodoscope was developed and implemented at the test reactor TREAT in Idaho. A couple of smaller hodoscope systems have since been installed and evaluated for use at other reactors. Overall, maybe a thousand detectors were involved in the most advanced system.

The hodoscope is a fast-neutron/gamma-ray nuclear-detection system devised for application and specifically installed at TREAT. In fact, it became a major achievement in my technical career, resulting at one time in my having management responsibility for a fully-committed team of designers, engineers, operators, and analysts at Argonne. Quality control was an integral and formal factor.

The hodoscope operated for many successful years operation at the TREAT testing reactor (ultimately involved in some 200 nuclear tests). I also pitched it for use in nuclear-arms-control treaty verification, for which neither the hodoscope nor any other technical method was ever implemented. As I understand it, the TREAT testing program, including the hodoscope, has been restarted with new nuclear-reactor safety goals.

Ad-hoc specialized mobile hodoscope-style systems could conceivably be applied for the purpose of scanning road vehicles or rail-train cargo. (No nuclear reactor would be needed, but an radiation source or radiation accelerator is required for most applications.) For some time after my retirement, there was considerable federal funding available for development of technical means of detecting hidden accumulations of nuclear and other clandestine materials, particularly if concealed in trucks or railcars or aircraft.

Besides the unique combination of hardware involved in the hodoscope at TREAT, we had developed at Argonne various state-of-technology methods of promptly and reliably transferring huge amounts of digital data across the country in rapid sequence, much more quickly that previously achievable. Those were heady days at the office when we could demonstrate with novel visual reconstruction the outcome of experiments with short turnaround.

Report-generation at Argonne. Perhaps one of my most enduring professional contributions is probably in technical-report generation, which fittingly combined my early journalism college training with my later professional activities at Argonne.

If I can claim to be sort of a pioneer in something besides the hodoscope, it would be the means we developed for the hodoscope project at Argonne to process large quantities of data and subsequently consolidate and report the data and results for technical reports generated at a rapid pace. That preceding sentence implies a number of challenges that we solved with a unique and original combination of hardware and software.

FORTRAN is a general-purpose programming language especially suited to numeric computation and scientific computing.

Originally developed by IBM in the 1950s for scientific and engineering applications, FORTRAN came to dominate this area of programming early on and has been in continuous use for over six decades in computationally intensive areas such as numerical weather prediction, finite element analysis, computational fluid dynamics, geophysics, computational physics, crystallography and computational chemistry. It is a popular language for high-performance computing and is used for programs that benchmark and rank the world's fastest supercomputers.

Successive versions have added support for structured programming and processing of character-based data, array programming, modular programming and generic programming, high performance, object-oriented programming, concurrent programming, and native parallel computing capabilities.

Fortran's design was the basis for many other programming languages. Amongst the better-known is BASIC, which has a number of syntax cleanups, notably better logical structures, and other changes to work more easily in an interactive environment.

Fortran programs were originally written in a fixed-column format, reflecting punched card (Figure 72) input practice, with the first 72 columns read into twelve 36-bit words. A letter "C" in column 1 caused the entire card to be treated as a comment and ignored by the compiler. Otherwise, the columns of the card were divided into four fields: the label field: a sequence of digits for use in control statement; a continuation field which served as the statement field; and Columns 73 to 80 used for card-identification information, such as punching a sequence number or text, to re-order cards.

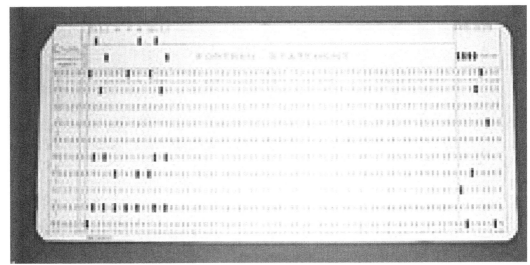

Figure 72. A punched IBM card — used for early digital-computer programming. In fact, that's how in college at VPI, I was introduced to data processing and computer programming. The actual card is about the width of this book.

Text Processing for Technical Reports: Direct Computer Assisted Origination, Editing, and Output of Text. (By A. De Volpi, M.R. Fenrick, G.S. Stanford, C.L. Fink, and E.A. Rhodes, Argonne National Laboratory) Oct 1, 1980. (55 pages). Report number: ANL-80-52. (This report generated nearly a thousand requests for reprints.)

Abstract: Documentation often is a primary residual of research and development. Because of this important role and because of the large amount of time consumed in generating technical reports, particularly those containing formulas and graphics, an existing data-processing computer system has been adapted so as to provide text-processing of technical documents. Emphasis has been on accuracy, turnaround time, and time savings for staff and secretaries, for the types of reports normally produced in the reactor development program. The computer-assisted text-processing system, called TXT, has been implemented to benefit primarily the originator of technical reports. The system is of particular value to professional staff, such as scientists and engineers, who have responsibility for generating much correspondence or lengthy, complex reports or manuscripts - especially if prompt turnaround and high accuracy are required. It can produce text that contains special Greek or mathematical symbols. Written in FORTRAN and MACRO, the program TXT operates on a PDP-11 minicomputer under the RSX-11M multitask multiuser monitor. Peripheral hardware includes videoterminals, electrostatic printers, and magnetic disks. Either data- or word-processing tasks may be performed at the terminals. The repertoire of operations has been restricted so as to minimize user training and memory burden. Secretarial staff may be readily trained to make corrections from annotated copy. Some examples of camera-ready copy are provided.

Hodoscope Data. The hodoscope generated reams of data, and we had to have a "system" with reliable procedures to handle and process the data. In fact, we ended up with a full team of operators, analysts and support staff, forming altogether

150

formally a "Hodoscope Section" administratively within the controlling reactor Division at Argonne.

Eventually, as this task grew, we had our own offices, staff and support personnel at Argonne, as well as designated and technical support at TREAT.

There were several stages involved in preparing and executing an experiment (which was expensive). First, the responsible "experimenter," a staff member at Argonne-East drew up and prepared the experiment in accordance with current requirements as conveyed by Divisional management. Since this was part of a broader DOE or NRC program, the Division management coordinated with the experiment sponsors. The experimenter then informed our Diagnostics team of any tests that needed the hodoscope to be operated. In fact, over the course of time, some 200 of the experiments involved the hodoscope, and as I recall in all but two of the experiments the hodoscope system produced useful data to complement the other results (such as temperature and coolant flow meters associated with the experiment).

Each experiment was expensive to perform, particularly when the experiment was meant to represent conditions in a nuclear-power reactor as faithfully as possible under the conditions that could be simulated in the experiment. At first only a single fuel pin in a cannister could be tested in TREAT. Eventually the test configuration grew to be 7 pins fully contained in a single cannister with hot liquid sodium being pumped through the closed-loop cannister during the experiment. All that took a lot of (expensive and time-consuming) preparation and performance, with coordination between Argonne East and Argonne West, and between the chief experimenter and the various support personnel.

At first, the hodoscope operated with a few hundred channels of detector instruments, each of which produced many thousands or millions of pieces of data over the course of some seconds or tens of seconds associated with a single experiment. Eventually the hodoscope was expanded to have many hundreds of one type of detector in parallel with additional arrays of another type of detector. Since the experiment might only last a second or so, the time resolution of the hodoscope system sometimes had to be in milliseconds, and usually many thousands of intervals of data had to be recorded fo many seconds.

Originally, at the very beginning of the program, the experiments had been carried out without any means of direct visualization. Soon after, the first efforts at visualization led to the use of high-speed framing cameras that recorded data on reels of cinephotographic film which had to be developed. The results of several hundred data channels could thus be visualized. However, most of the experiments produced a cloud of smoke that visually obscured the reactor fuel being tested. It was this visualization limitation that led to requirement that led to the hodoscope electronic system of nuclear detection and data recording.

Because of the immense amount of data produced, this also turned out to be spawn my pioneering and enduring contribution to writing technical reports. And since then, it has also ended up aiding me in writing and publishing my many articles and books, including this one.

Computer-compatible word-processing programs have been in the course of time commercially developed and sold to on-line users. I now use what is called WordPerfect X7. The corporation that supports WordPerfect is now based in Canada, and it has evolved, as have such user programs as Microsoft Word and LibreOffice, from the earlier text-processing systems for which I had a hand in developing out of necessity.

WordPerfect has been gradually expanded to enable creation and processing of all kinds of documents, letters, brochures, resumes, and more. It was adapted early on to have compatibility for other file-formats, including Microsoft. In my mind, WordPerfect's most powerful feature is its constantly-available "Reveal Codes" window, which greatly simplifies document editing. I usually keep three or four text lines revealed (visible on the screen) at the bottom of the WordPerfect window. PDF versions can be directly created for any WordPerfect file. As seen in this book, multi-color illustrations can be readily included and indexed.

IBM 5150, in 1981 the first PC, accomplished something very new and different. IBM had begun to produce in volume that highly competitive, desktop computer of top quality, intended for both consumers and businesses — at a price tag of less than $1,600. Now, four decades later, it's advent is underappreciated, but then it was eagerly adopted.

The PDP-11 (as in Figure 73) was a series of 16-bit minicomputers sold by Digital Equipment Corporation (DEC) from 1970 into the 1990s, one of a set of products in the Programmed Data Processor (PDP) series. In total, around 600,000 PDP-11s of all models were sold, making it one of DEC's most successful product lines. The PDP-11 is considered by some experts to have been the most popular minicomputer ever.

Figure 73. PDP-11/40 computer, 1970s vintage — used for early digital-data processing. The processor is at the bottom. A dual magnetic-tape drive is installed above the processor.

The PDP-11 included a number of innovative features in its instruction set and additional general-purpose registers that made it much easier to program than earlier models in the PDP series. Additionally, the innovative Unibus system allowed external devices to be easily interfaced to the system using direct memory access, opening the system to a wide variety of peripherals. (I recall going to California to learn how to program and operate it.)

The PDP-11 replaced the PDP-8 in many real-time applications, although both product lines lived in parallel for more than 10 years. The ease of programming of the PDP-11 made it very popular for general-purpose computing uses as well.

In other words, besides expediting the process of receiving and storing the data from the hodoscope at TREAT, we used the computer to process the mountains of digital information. Doing so, resulted in a short, timely turnaround in the experimental process.

In **current-day Sweden**, a country rich with technological advancement, thousands of people have recently had microchips inserted into their hands. The chips are designed to speed up the users' daily routines and make their lives more convenient — accessing their homes, offices and gyms is as easy as swiping their hands against digital readers.

They also can be used to store emergency- contact, medical details, social media profiles. or e-tickets for events and rail journeys. Proponents of the tiny chips say they're safe and largely protected from hacking, but one scientist is raising privacy concerns around the kind of personal health data that might be stored on the devices.

Around the size of a grain of rice, the chips typically are inserted into the skin just above each user's thumb, using a syringe similar to that used for giving vaccinations. The procedure costs about $180. So many Swedes are lining up to get the microchips that the country's main chipping company says it can't keep up with the number of requests.

An effort to expand the PDP-11 from 16 to 32-bit addressing led to the VAX-11 design, which took part of its name from the PDP-11.

The design of the PDP-11 inspired the design of late-1970s microprocessors including the Intel x86 and the Motorola 68000. Design features of PDP-11 operating systems, as well as other operating systems from Digital Equipment, influenced the design of other operating systems such as CP/M and hence also MS-DOS. The first officially named version of Unix ran on the PDP-11/20 in 1970. It is commonly stated that the C programming language took advantage of several low-level PDP-11–dependent programming features albeit not originally by intent.

WORLDWIDE GROWTH OF NUCLEAR ENERGY

Nuclear Power Reactors

From the World Nuclear Association, here are some statistics about nuclear power in the world today, with the first commercial nuclear-power stations having started operation in the 1950s:

▸ Nuclear energy now provides about 10% of the world's electricity from about 440 power reactors.

▸ Nuclear is the world's second largest source of available low-carbon power.

▸ Over 50 countries utilize nuclear energy in about 220 research reactors.

Civil nuclear power can now boast more than 17,000 reactor years of experience, and nuclear power plants are operational in 30 countries worldwide. (In addition to research, these reactors are used for the production of medical and industrial isotopes, as well as for training of reactor operators.)

Twelve countries in 2018 produced at least one-quarter of their electricity from nuclear power, according to the World Nuclear Association. Figure 74 shows the breakdown in relation to various alternative sources of total energy produced now (2020) in the world.

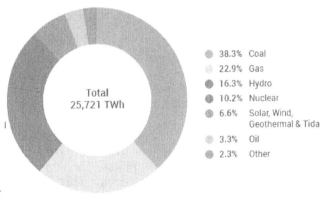

Source: IEA Electricity Information 2019

Figure 74. World energy production total in terrawatts — thousands of gigawatts — from by various sources throughout the world at this time, according to the International Energy Agency.

France gets around three-quarters of its electricity from nuclear energy, while Hungary, Slovakia and Ukraine obtain more than half from nuclear. Meanwhile Belgium, Sweden, Slovenia, Bulgaria, Switzerland, Finland and Czech Republic get one-third or more. South Korea normally gets more than 30% of its electricity from nuclear. The United States, United Kingdom, Spain, Romania and Russia obtain about one-fifth of electricity from nuclear. Japan has relied on nuclear power for more than one-quarter of its electricity despite the meltdowns at Fukushima.

Despite the serious Chernobyl accident, Ukraine and Russia have persisted — even expanded — the generation of electricity from nuclear power.

Through regional electrical-transmission grids, many more countries depend in part on nuclear-generated power; for example, Italy and Denmark which have no longer have nuclear plants within their borders, get nearly 10% of their electricity derived from imported nuclear power.

About 50 more reactors are under construction, equivalent to approximately 15% of existing capacity. In 2018 nuclear plants supplied 2563 TWh of electricity, up from 2503 TWh in 2017 (a TW [terawatt] being a 1000 megawatts). This was the sixth consecutive year that global nuclear-energy generation has risen, with output 217 TWh higher than in 2012.

Medical-Radiation Reactors. It has been found that radioisotopes are useful in improving or even curing some medical conditions that could not be resolved by other means. Some radioisotopes are readily produced in training and power reactors, but other radioactive curatives are better derived from specialized reactors.

There's now widespread use of radiation and radioisotopes in medicine, particularly for diagnosis (identification) and therapy (treatment) of various health conditions. In developed countries (a quarter of the world population), about one person in fifty benefits from diagnostic nuclear medicine each year, and therapy with radioisotopes is about one-tenth of this.

Nuclear medicine was developed in the 1950s for endocrine treatment, using iodine-131 to diagnose and then treat thyroid disease. In recent years specialists have also come from radiology, as dual PET/CT (positron emission tomography with computerized tomography) procedures have become established.

Nuclear medicine can use radiation to provide information about the functioning of a person's specific organs, or to treat disease. In most cases, the information is used to make a quick diagnosis of the patient's illness. The thyroid, bones, heart, liver, and many other organs can be easily imaged with x-ray or other radiation, and disorders in organ function revealed.

In some cases, radiation can treat diseased organs, or tumors. Five Nobel Laureates have been closely involved with the use of radioactive tracers in medicine. Over 10,000 hospitals worldwide use radioisotopes in medicine, with about 90% of the procedures for diagnosis.

The most common radioisotope used in diagnosis is technetium-99 (Tc-99), with some 40 million procedures per year, accounting for about 80% of all nuclear medicine procedures and 85% of diagnostic scans worldwide. In developed countries (26% of world population) the frequency of diagnostic nuclear medicine is about 2% per year, and the frequency of therapy with radioisotopes is about one-tenth of this. In the USA Eeach year there are over 20 million nuclear medicine procedures in the U.S. and about 10 million in Euroe.

Radiopharmaceuticals in diagnosis is now growing at over 10% per year. The global radioisotope market was valued at nearly $10 billion in 2016, with medical radioisotopes accounting for about 80% of this, and poised to reach about $17 billion by 2021. North America is the dominant market for diagnostic radioisotopes with close to half of the market share, while Europe accounts for about 20%.

Argonne also had its own medical-source facilities, accelerators and reactors, as well a dedicated program for making use of radioactivity in medical programs.

Nuclear Research and Test Reactors. Having spent a considerable amount of my professional time at Argonne initiating and managing a program in nuclear-reactor safety, I can't help but mention the TREAT reactor in Idaho and the hodoscope installed at the reactor. That versatile reactor has been and continues to be a major test platform for nuclear fuel intended for power reactors. In fact, I understand the reactor and the hodoscope were modernized a number of years ago.

Besides TREAT and its reactor-safety role, another Argonne program called the RERTR, sponsored by DOE gained international support leading to the safe dismantlement of obsolete research and training reactors.

Advanced Nuclear Research and Engineering

Much of the research and development funded at Argonne, as at other U.S. nuclear "peace" labs resulted in generational improvements for nuclear-power reactors. Nuclear-power reactors these days supply electricity with high reliability and produce economically competitive power for many decades — in some cases now going on 80 years. After carrying out R&D for about half (the first-half) of my professional career, I shifted more towards what would be called advanced nuclear technology research and engineering centered around a test reactor sited in Idaho.

The TREAT Nuclear Test Reactor. As part of a congressionally-designated national program for U.S. military and civilian nuclear development, a remote nuclear test site had been set up in Idaho. Designated "Argonne-West," it was near Idaho Falls, in potato and jackrabbit country, not all that far from Craters of the Moon. Argonne's TREAT (Transient Reactor Test Facility) achieved first criticality in 1959 at the Idaho site, and was being (and is still) used to study the effects of simulated reactor accidents on nuclear fuel and components.

TREAT was to be (and has been) used in realistically testing advanced nuclear-fuel designs. It has had an important role in design and engineering of new and redeveloped reactors intended for an expanding and improved nuclear-reactor program. Nuclear-power development, particularly as visioned under the Eisenhower worldwide Atoms for Peace program, was then and ever since has been part of national and international fission-power and radioisotope-supply strategy.

Capsules (test sections) containing nuclear fuel pins to be tested where inserted in the center of the reactor (see Figure 77). When all was ready, the reactor would be first be run at a low power and a traditional radiographic image would be obtained. Also, the hodoscope would be calibrated and aligned so as to have the test fuel within the design field of view. The "slotted elements" allowed radiation, particularly fast neutrons, to reach the hodoscope without attenuation, and the hodoscope instruments detected the radiation. As described below with a little more detail, after an experiment the hodoscope data would be analyzed and compared with the other instrument data. Teams of analysts worked on and interpreted all forms of the data collected from the experiment, the reactor, and the hodoscope.

Hodoscope. Overhead and cross-section renditions of the hodoscope instrument system at TREAT are depicted below in Figure 75. The hodoscope turned out to be my signature career achievement at Argonne. Basically, it was a (complex) instrument designed to monitor the behavior of nuclear fuel in the "Test Section" which is positioned at the center of the test reactor TREAT.

TREAT stands for "transient test reactor." It was (and is) capable of testing newly designed nuclear fuel pins that were being evaluated for their functional capability under relatively realistic conditions. It would be one thing to design a fuel pin (mostly for reactors then being considered), but another matter to find out if they could perform well under fairly realistic conditions.

TREAT did not provide a test of long-term durability or "burnup." That would have to determined in some other type of reactor with a high radiation flux and an extended period of operation. No, TREAT was an interim platform to find out if the fuel for an advanced nuclear reactor had at least some of the design features that could withstand operation in a power reactor, but without having to wait for many years of full-scale operation. Although thermal-flux reactors were already in full-power operation around the world, fast-flux reactors were being designed and tested by examining the potential performance in a reactor such as TREAT.

An "experimenter" or team of experimenters at Argonne would construct a fuel element or bundle of elements (limited to 7 fuel-pin elements), and that would be tested at TREAT after undergoing whatever possible pre-operational tests could be made without the radiation produced by TREAT. Although this testing procedure was not the same as full-scale operation, it was a lot quicker in identifying design limitations. Depending on whether intended for water- or liquid-sodium-cooled reactors, the fuel pins might have some internal liquid coolant (water or sodium) within a steel or zirconium metallic cladding. By irradiating such test pins in TREAT under rather severe but short conditions, it was possible to gain a foothold on their viability for the power reactor that they were designed for. After all, it didn't make sense (and would have cost too much money and time) to build a full-scale prototype reactor and find that it would be suitable. So reactor designers at Argonne would develop prototype fuel pins that could be tested at TREAT.

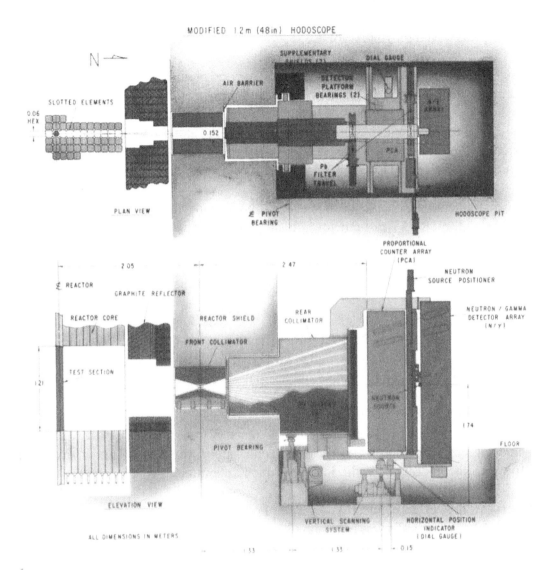

Figure 75. Hodoscope nuclear instrument system at TREAT for detection of radiation deliberately induced in the "TEST SECTION" which is at the center of the TREAT reactor core. The image on the top is the overhead view, and the image on the bottom is the side view. This figure is relatively large in order for the call-outs to be readable.

Origin of Hodoscope Program. As mentioned previously, I had been regularly fulfilling my annual military-reserve obligations (a 2-week tour of duty) by spending constructive time on alternating years at the Naval Research Laboratory in Washington, DC, and at the Naval Radiological Defense Laboratory in San Francisco.

Being then a research associate at Argonne, I happened to be shown an experiment at NRL conducted on behalf of Argonne and soon realized that the manner in which the experiment was being attempted would be better implemented by a different means I was developing at Argonne.

Long-story-short, we changed the exploratory experiment from one involving gamma-ray monitoring at NRL to one involving fast-neutron monitoring at TREAT. The fast-neutron experiment worked out well, and the single-channel apparatus grew into a large multichannel system installed at TREAT, along with its data-collection system, which initially was based on recording light-emitting diodes which were recorded on fast-framing camera film.

The instrument, which we designated the hodoscope nuclear-diagnostic system installed at the TREAT test reactor in Idaho, but devised and built at Argonne East, became for me a career-changing concept ultimately engaged in nuclear diagnostics for more than a decade. It also later provided an important foundation for accumulated expertise in sensing nuclear materials, a technology central to detection of nuclear weapons.

It gradually evolved through several modifications into a massive instrument with something like a 1000 detectors, and it worked nearly flawlessly in conjunction with the very detailed and complex experiments that were being conducted at TREAT for a couple of decades.

The hodoscope and TREAT reactor was recently revitalized (as of 2017) and upgraded for a new Energy Department reactor-safety program still underway at the sprawling site, redesignated the Idaho National Laboratory.

Overseas Travel. In connection with the hodoscope program and the subsequent arms-control program, it was occasionally necessary or professionally useful to travel to other laboratories, not just in the United States, but also nuclear facilities in Canada, Europe, and Japan.

Examples are the Canadian facilities, the IAEA laboratories and facilities in Vienna and Siebersdorf, as well as the Lake Como region. Also, that professional collaboration also meant visiting facilities of the Italian Nuclear Energy Agency in northern and southern Italy.

Maritime Nuclear Reactors. Nuclear reactors have earned a significant role in maritime applications. Because ship refueling is a major consideration, seagoing nuclear power has proven worthwhile for surface and subsurface vessels. Renewed attention is also driven by greenhouse gas emissions from fossil fuels on land and sea. Right now, merchant ship nuclear propulsion accounts for about one-third of the world's nuclear-plant capacity (which consists of about 450 electric-power producing reactors worldwide — 11% of the world's total electricity).

Maritime reactors have little or no pollutant discharges or carbon emissions while also providing shipboard electricity, desalinated fresh water, heated water — all with economic stability, high peak-demand capacity, and reliability, especially under highly variable seagoing conditions. Nuclear has been particularly suitable for ships, especially submarines, which need to be at sea for long periods without refueling. Worldwide, more than 140 ocean vessels are now powered by 180 small nuclear reactors. While most nuclear-powered marine vessels are subs, the rest range from icebreakers to aircraft carriers.

Although special procedures and crew are required for shipboard maintenance of a nuclear-reactor, that has not proven to be too difficult. The United States had built 219 nuclear-powered vessels to mid-2010 and has the most nuclear-powered aircraft carriers. All the American aircraft carriers and submarines are nuclear powered. Nowadays, it would hardly make sense to launch a military submarine that wasn't nuclear-powered. All it takes now is one nuclear-armed, nuclear-powered submarine to provide nearly everlasting national security, as well as the extended international security afforded by the standoff that nullifies any supposed quantitative or qualitative advantage a bigger nation might think it would have. Indeed, military nuclear reactors might be considered peacemakers more than warmakers.

Worldwide by now, several hundred naval reactors have been built, as well as over 400 land-based atomic-power reactors, 770 research and test reactors and 34 orbiting reactors — a grand total close to 2000 nuclear reactors of all types, government and commercial built and operated. We've come a long way in utilizing nuclear energy.

Experiments Using Nuclear Reactors. While at Argonne I made extensive use of their wide array of reactors in order to carry out various nuclear experiments. Initially some of the experiments required short-lived radiation sources such as Mn-56, and others made use of fission products or artificially produced spontaneous fission isotopes such as Cf-252. Even until late in my professional career, I was making use of radioactive sources and carrying out experiments at Argonne reactors (and accelerators).

In fact, the primary objective of my PhD thesis, which was integral to my job assignment at Argonne, was a more precise measurement of the number of neutrons per fission in Cf-252. (As best I can tell from current data, we published a result that has turned out to be about 1% below that which is presently considered the most accurate value.)

CP5, ZPRs, TREAT.... Argonne was populated with an alphabet soup of nuclear reactors and facilities that deliberately produced radiation, mostly gamma and neutron beams that could be applied in experiments. They were not "power" producing reactors, rather "testing" reactors. CP5 on site was a source of radiation for experiments.

In addition, access could be arranged to other reactors at Argonne West or within the national laboratory complex. Occasionally it was necessary to travel domestically and overseas to different facility locations and other national laboratories in order to carry out experiments.

At Argonne's Building 315/316 complex where I was first assigned, there were several sub-critical assemblies (ZPRs), test reactors, and radiation accelerators. It was an ideal location (heavily fenced and guarded) where one could also learn firsthand just about all you needed or could learn regarding nuclear reactors and radiation, with much hands-on experience.

Many advanced reactors were located in Idaho at the National Reactor Testing Site, near Idaho Falls and Pocotello. Throughout its history, the U.S. nuclear laboratory in Idaho (presently known as the Idaho National Laboratory or "INL") has been home to 52 nuclear reactors, the largest concentration of nuclear reactors in the world.

Two of the first self-sustaining "breeder" reactors were constructed on the Idaho site, including EBR-II, pictured in Figure 76.

Argonne West was where the TREAT nuclear-fuel-testing reactor was located (the one that I ended up working at the most, spending considerable time in setting up an experimental apparatus called the hodoscope.

Figure 76. EBR project in Idaho for development of the IFR. The containment dome on the reactor is visible. Nuclear fuel reprocessing is carried out on the site.

As a result of my two-week annual tours of military duty committed in the naval reserves, I had conceived of an experimental concept which was shepherded into operation at the TREAT test reactor. That (fast-neutron/gamma) hodoscope became a career maker, at its peak resulting in my being put in charge of a team consisting of a dozen or so Argonne employees and leading to some significant (and programmatically expensive) technological contributions to the development of nuclear fuel for commercial power reactors. Of course, this book is not the medium for technical specifics, but there is an ample documentary record in my specialized publications.

While working at the 315/316 reactor-development complex, I became acquainted with Chuck Till, who became my close friend and duplicate-bridge partner. Off and on, we'd have a drink together socially. Chuck became a leader in Argonne's and DOE's national program for fast-reactor development.

The IFR was an advanced-reactor system developed at Argonne National Laboratory in the decade 1984 to 1994. The design is that of a "fast" reactor — its chain reaction maintained by "fast" neutrons with high energy — which sustains itself in a closed fuel-cycle system. Electrical power is generated, new fissile fuel is produced to replace the fuel burned, and its used fuel is recycled by molten-fuel processing.

A fast-neutron reactor is a type of nuclear reactor in which the fission chain reaction is sustained by neutrons with energies above 0.5 MeV or greater, on average, as opposed to thermal-neutron reactors. A fast reactor needs no neutron moderator, but requires fuel that is relatively rich in fissile material when compared to that required for a thermal-neutron reactor.

Story of the Integral Fast Reactor. A 2011 book titled *Plentiful Energy: The Story of the Integral Fast Reactor*: describes the complex history of a the IFR technology, with emphasis on its scientific foundation. It was authored by Charles E. Till and Yoon Il Chang, both formerly at Argonne.

The IFR project developed the technology for a complete system. The reactor concept had important features and characteristics that were completely new. This was a advanced development using high-temperature chemistry — putting its nuclear waste into final form for disposal: all to be done on one self-sufficient site.

Charles Till was longtime Associate Laboratory Director for Engineering Research at Argonne, in charge of civilian nuclear-reactor development. This program at the Laboratory was the largest by far in the United States in the last decades of the century. It was devoted entirely to research and development of reactors for electrical power generation. Dr. Till was personally involved in promoting fast-neutron self-sustaining breeder reactors.

Nuclear Power at Sea. Over 140 sea-going ships worldwide are powered by more than 180 small nuclear reactors, which altogether have accumulated more than 12,000 reactor years of marine operation.

At the present time, many important vessels in the United States Navy are powered by nuclear reactors. All submarines and aircraft carriers are nuclear-driven. Several cruisers were nuclear-powered, but all have since been retired. Most active nuclear-powered naval vessels are submarines, while the remainder range from icebreakers to aircraft carriers.

The U.S. Navy has accumulated over 5,400 reactor-years of accident-free experience, and operates more than 80 nuclear-powered ships.

Between 1950 and 2003 Russia built 248 nuclear submarines and 5 naval surface vessels (plus 9 icebreakers) powered by 468 reactors, and was operating about 60 nuclear naval vessels altogether. For Russian operational vessels in 1997, Bellona listed 109 submarines (plus 4 naval surface ships), 108 attack submarines (SSN) and 25 ballistic missile subs.

At the end of the Cold War, in 1989, there were over 400 nuclear-powered submarines operational or being built. At least 300 of these submarines have since been scrapped and some on order cancelled. Russia and the US thus had over 100 each left in service, with UK and France less than 20 each, and China six. The total today is understood to be about 120. Most or all naval reactors are fueled by high-enriched uranium (HEU).

India launched its first nuclear submarine in 2009 with a single 85 MW PWR fueled by HEU driving a steam turbine. It is reported to have cost US$ 2.9 billion.

Mostly after retirement from Argonne, I became an advocate promoting molten-salt reactors because of their inherently safe configurations and their profuse production of radioisotopes useful in medical applications. In fact, with the help of John Ross, I filed several patent applications.

Molten-Salt Reactors. A molten-salt reactor (MSR) is a class of nuclear-fission reactor in which the primary nuclear reactor coolant and/or the fuel is a molten-salt mixture. MSRs offer multiple advantages over conventional nuclear power plants, although for historical reasons they have not been deployed.

The concept was first established in the 1950s. The early Aircraft Reactor Experiment was primarily motivated by the small size that the technique offered, while the Molten-Salt Reactor Experiment was a prototype for a thorium fuel cycle breeder nuclear-power plant. Increased research into Generation IV reactor designs has renewed interest in the technology.

CHAPTER VII:
CHICAGO-AREA PUBLIC ACTIVISM

On 1 November 1945, the loosely organized Federation of Atomic Scientists in Chicago had become the Federation of American Scientists. That same year, the *Bulletin of the Atomic Scientists* was established by scientists, engineers and other professionals of the Manhattan Project who feared the horrible effects of these new nuclear weapons and devoted themselves to warning the public about the consequences. Those early activists, many who had transferred to Argonne, also worried about military secrecy, dreading that leaders without the full and knowledgeable consent of their citizens might draw their countries into increasingly dangerous confrontations.

The Ongoing, Endless Wars in Indochina. The Vietnam War was a conflict that involved the Indochina peninsula of Vietnam, Laos and Cambodia from November 1955 to the fall of Saigon at the end of April 1975. Perhaps 1.5 million Vietnamese and some 58,000 Americans were killed in the war, and maybe that many French soldiers.

Public opposition to United States involvement in the Vietnam War began to manifest itself with peacenik demonstrations in 1964 against the escalating role of the United States and grew into a broad social movement over several ensuing years. This movement informed and helped shape the vigorous and polarizing debate, primarily in the United States, during the second half of the 1960s and early 1970s, on how to end the war.

Many in the peace movement within the United States were students, mothers, or anti-establishment hippies. Opposition expanded among African-American civil rights, women's liberation, and Chicano movements, and sectors of organized labor. Additional protest in the United State increasingly came from many other groups, including educators, clergy, academics, journalists, lawyers, scientists, physicians — notably Benjamin Spock — and Vietnam military veterans.

Their protest actions consisted mainly of peaceful, nonviolent events; few were deliberately provocative or violent. On the other hand, police sometimes used violent tactics against peaceful demonstrators. By 1967, according to Gallup polls, an increasing majority of Americans considered military involvement in Vietnam to be a mistake, not echoed until decades later by the former American head of Vietnam war planning, Secretary of Defense Robert McNamara.

The CAS. In 1969, with the war in Vietnam lingering on, a second employee organization — Concerned Argonne Scientists (CAS) — was formed at Argonne, and I became its perennial co-chair. It was a time when many national professional and scientific associations ultimately became outspoken about the risks of nuclear war and about the seemingly endless procession of new means of mutual devastation.

Nationally, the American Physical Society, particularly its subgroup Forum on Physics and Society, increasingly took public positions in opposition to expansion of the nuclear-arms race. (In fact, I was later elected as a "Fellow" of the APS because of public activities on behalf of nuclear-arms control.) Nevertheless, such affiliation could not have been professionally particularly helpful at Argonne, where management labeled me as an "activist." Some Argonne and CAS colleagues, particularly George Stanford, Carolyn Hertzenberg and Gerry Marsh, were frequently involved in our joint activities, both locally and nationally.

It was with CAS urging that I was designated as a voluntary technical voice within a couple of community organizations in the city of Chicago, where public opposition was being formed against the federal government's ABM system. A group of Argonne physicists had already been publically expressing their unease about siting anti-ballistic-missile installations in the suburbs around the city. There were still remnants of an anti-aircraft system in the suburbs to defend against imagined Soviet nuclear-armed bombers, but ballistic missiles were so fast and evasive that a stationary defense made no sense and it placed those who lived nearby at even greater risk. Having been a former military officer, now with a nuclear technical background, I was well qualified to provide perspective to worried Chicago citizens.

At about the same time, a number of civil-rights outrages were taking place. In 1968, as elsewhere in the nation, there were riots in the West Side of Chicago after Martin Luther King's assassination. A year later the Black Panther Party combined forces with Latino and white Chicagoans to form the radical "Rainbow Coalition," which targeted the city's structural inequalities.

In the Fall of 1968 the Black Panther Party of Chicago was established, drawing power from a radical and militant perspective. Near the end of the following year, on 4 December 1969, a fatal and counterproductive police raid was carried out by city and county authorities against the Chicago Black Panthers.

The **Black Panther Party** was a revolutionary-minded socialist political organization founded by Marxist college students Bobby Seale (Chairman) and Huey Newton (Minister of Defense) in October 1966 in Oakland, California. The party was active in the United States from 1966 until 1982, with chapters in numerous major cities, and international chapters in the United Kingdom in the early 1970s, and in Algeria from 1969 to 1972. At its inception in October 1966, the Black Panther Party's core practice was its open-carry armed citizens' patrols ("copwatching") to monitor the behavior of the Oakland Police Department and challenge police brutality in the city.

In 1969, a variety of community social programs became a core activity. The Party instituted the Free Breakfast for Children Programs to address food injustice, and community health clinics for education and treatment of diseases including sickle cell anemia, tuberculosis, and later HIV/AIDS.

Black Panther Party members were subsequently involved in many fatal firefights with police.

Civil-Rights Movement in Chicago. Although the struggle for civil rights of black citizens had been going on for centuries, it began to gain the high ground with the leadership of Martin Luther King, Jr., who was assassinated in 1968. In the wake of his death, a wave of riots swept major cities across the country, while President Johnson declared a national day of mourning. Looting and riots had followed, putting even more pressure on the Johnson administration to push through additional civil rights laws. By December 1971, Jesse Jackson had organized Operation PUSH in Chicago.

In 1972, New York's **Shirley Chisholm** became the first major-party African-American candidate for President of the United States and the first woman to run for the Democratic presidential nomination. Four years later, Alex Haley published his novel *Roots: The Saga of an American Family*, which became a bestseller and generated great levels of interest in African-American genealogy and history. It became adapted as a TV series that attracted a huge audience across the country.

One thing in Chicago led to another. In December of 1989, two leaders of the Black Panthers were assassinated by city and county police. As a result, the local ABM-opposition group had to shift priorities into becoming a social-justice organization, the Chicago Alliance to End Repression. That brought me along too. We had been dealing with some relatively minor civil-rights problems in DuPage county outside Chicago. On one occasion, I had to join the mayor of our small town of Lisle in a 2-person sit-in at a local barbershop until the barber would cut the hair of a black man (who was emloyed at the nearby Bell Labs). In another case, one of my sons and I tried (unsuccessfully) to convince the pastor of a Lutheran church in our neighborhood to accept black parishioners.

Bell Labs: Currently designated Nokia Bell Labs, formerly Bell Labs Innovations (1996–2007), AT&T Bell Laboratories (1984–1996), and Bell Telephone Laboratories (1925–1984), it is an American industrial research and scientific development company now owned by Finnish company Nokia. With headquarters located in Murray Hill, New Jersey, the company operates several laboratories in the United States and around the world. Bell Labs has its origins in the complex past of the Bell System.

In the late 19th century, the laboratory began as the Western Electric Engineering Department and was located in New York City. In 1925, after years of conducting research and development under Western Electric, the Engineering Department was reformed into Bell Telephone Laboratories and under the shared ownership of American Telephone & Telegraph Company and Western Electric.

Researchers working at Bell Labs are credited with the development of radio astronomy, the transistor, the laser, the photovoltaic cell, the charge-coupled device (CCD), information theory, the Unix operating system, and the programming languages B, C, C++, and S.

Nine Nobel Prizes have been awarded for technical developments completed at Bell Laboratories.

Here are a few other notable **civil-rights highlights and highlighters in the Chicago area**: 1983, Harold Washington became the first African-American mayor of Chicago; mid 1990s, Operation PUSH merged with the national Rainbow coalition; 1992, Carol Moseley Braun, Chicago born, became the first African-American woman elected to the U.S. Senate; and 2008, Illinois Senator Barack Obama was elected the 44th President of the United States, the first African-American to hold that office. Unavoidably, many other noteworthy contributors to civil rights in the Chicago area are not now mentioned in this book.

CHICAGO ALLIANCE TO END REPRESSION

While so much was evolving nationwide in the 60s about civil rights, other public protest activities were brewing because of objectionable government Cold War policies, including resistance against installing nuclear-tipped anti-ballistic missiles (ABMs) in the Chicago area. That proposed nuclear-armed ABM system eventually became one of the first major Cold War U.S. military programs to suffer reversal because of public protest. The organized community opposition, especially in the Chicago area, stands as a model of successful resistance to a governmental steamroller.

After the 1957 launch of *Sputnik*, ABM defense (or BMD) became a prominent American military and political objective because of domestic U.S. national-security concerns that had been aroused. Senator Barry Goldwater, the Republican candidate for President in 1964, made the lack of U.S. ballistic-missile defense progress a political football. However, widespread public opposition had been aroused by open-ended U.S. emphasis on military spending, especially during a time of competing domestic priorities. And now the government wanted to make us targets for nuclear ballistic-missile attack.

On the Beach is a 1959 American post-apocalyptic science-fiction film that starred Gregory Peck, Ava Gardner, Fred Astaire, and Anthony Perkins. This black-and-white film was based on a 1957 novel of the same name depicting the aftermath of a nuclear war. Unlike in the novel, no one is assigned blame for starting the war; the film hints that global annihilation may have arisen from an accident or misjudgment.

In early 1964, in the months following World War III, the conflict has devastated the entirety of the Northern Hemisphere, killing all of its humans after polluting the atmosphere with nuclear fallout. Air currents are slowly carrying the fallout south; the only areas still habitable being in the far reaches of the Southern Hemisphere.

Survivors in Australia detect an incomprehensible Morse code signal coming from the presumed devastated West Coast of the United States. The American nuclear submarine, USS Sawfish, now under Royal Australian Navy command, is ordered to sail north and make contact with the sender of the signal.

Chicagoans Against the ABM. Protests in opposition to locally siting anti-ballistic-missile-defense site propagated from the suburbs to city centers. Part of the concern had to do with the perception that the ABM sites would themselves become attractive targets for the Soviets to eliminate pre-emptively, and the aspect of concern was realization that the U.S. government had a huge military-defense budget.

In Chicago, a 1969 rally of the ad-hoc organization Chicagoans Against the ABM drew 1200 people to nearly fill Orchestra Hall. Nationally and locally prominent speakers included Tennessee Senator Albert Gore, Nobelist George Wald, and Chicago Congressman Sidney Yates. Organizers were Rev. C.T. Vivian. Robert Johnson, and Dr. Herbert N. Hazelkorn (Chairman). There were 34 cosponsoring local organizations — religious, labor, student, political, scientists. The ABM system soon grew into the object of nationwide grassroots opposition.

Other contemporary national-security issues emerged. As pointed out, first we had the bomber gap, later a missile gap, and then a national-security credibility gap: Now, there was a credulity gap, which grew out of government efforts to push forward with the improbable — in the form of ABM technology, capability, threat and spending. But not in our backyard!

President Nixon contended (1) that the Safeguard (modified Sentinel) ABM system would not provoke an escalating arms-race response from the Russians and (2) that if the United States did not immediately start with ABM development, American diplomacy would not be credible.

He was wrong on both counts: Soviet military planners let it be known that they would consider ABM an escalation in threat and a move toward a first-strike long-range, nuclear-tipped missile capability; and it was our huge nuclear deterrent that, in fact and appearance, had kept the United States in a formidable diplomatic power-policy position.

Government ABM Reversal. In February 1969, Secretary of Defense Melvin Laird, recognizing a national groundswell of opposition, ordered a halt to further investigation of ABM sites around the cities. However, this didn't end major federal missile-defense programs and spending. As mentioned, the Nixon administration proposed the more advanced Safeguard ABM program; all such BMD systems focused and was configured around hardware designed to protect missile installations, not the cities.

Even though ABM facilities in the Chicago area at Belmont Harbor and Argonne forest had long been deactivated, a group of American Indians in June 1971 with great fanfare temporarily occupied the former ABM missile sites. A contingent set up tepees and other living arrangements on the onetime missile-defense site just across the road from Argonne National Laboratory. That fenced area in the forest once hosted Nike-Hercules nuclear-tipped rockets that would detonate nuclear warheads above Chicago in order to intercept incoming ballistic missiles. How ironic!

Except for the brief and expensive (about $5.5 billion) deployment in 1974 of a single Safeguard installation at a North Dakota ICBM site, the ABM system never materialized. Research and development on ABM continued, however, until the next (also futile) phase in the history of ballistic-missile defense: reincarnation as SDI during President Reagan's administration.

Those of us active with the CAS had reason to temporarily celebrate (although we didn't) the demise of such futile, provocative, and expensive ABM government overtures.

1960's FEDERAL GOVERNMENT PRIORITIES

The U.S. military-industrial complex had came under widespread public attack during the late 1960s. Critics around the country raised questions about the amount spent on defense compared to education and other nonmilitary activities. The question of priorities for the federal budget, at a time when the expensive war in Vietnam was still going on, with no end in sight — either in terms of human or financial cost.

ORIGIN OF CHICAGO'S ALLIANCE TO END REPRESSION

The slaying in December 1969 of two members of Black Panther Party in Chicago startled and shocked many individuals who were previously uninvolved in civil-rights issues, or thought those were problems were primarily in other cities. As one result, the Alliance to End Repression (AER) was organized early in 1970 as a Chicago-area citizens' organization to coordinate human-rights advocacy groups.

Many individuals and organizations who previously had been involved in other public issues — civil rights, labor unions, immigration, ABM, defense spending, government priorities — joined in the new Alliance. The initial executive coordinator was John Hill, a priest who had organized the first union of priests in Chicago; here's his recollection:

> The slaying of the two Black Panther leaders was like the ultimate in repression. This really got a lot of people off the fence. Even the Chicago Bar Association, which was as much a part of the establishment as you can find, called for an investigation. And we did. We went out and got about seventy groups, block clubs and all kinds of organizations, to write a petition. That's when the Alliance to End Repression got started.

> We moved into our downtown Chicago office on April 1, 1970, having decided we were going to attack repression wherever it was. There were so many wrongs that needed to be righted. We had a lot of people with religious background. There were Catholics. There were Protestant housewives who had been visiting inmates in prisons for fifteen years. There were tiny organizations that had popped up all over, either having to do with prisons or with bail reform or with the rights of welfare mothers. And we became the place where they could gravitate....

The organization Chicagoans Against the ABM morphed in, along with its chairperson, Dr. Herb Hazelkorn who was given the same role in the new organization. The newly created Alliance opened an office with two staff members and the support of close to seventy participating organizations. According to records preserved at the Chicago Historical Society, approximately fifty of these organizations became Alliance affiliates.

Chicago Alliance to End Repression. Horrified by the brutal slayings of the Black Panthers in Chicago, a newly created Alliance to End Repression opened a downtown office in April 1970 by some appalled do-gooders. It started with two staff members and grew with the support of close to 70 participating local activist organizations. Approximately 50 of these organizations became Alliance affiliates. Activists and their leadership previously had focused on a variety of local, civil and political issues, but became galvanized because of the assassinations conducted by law-enforcement officers in our city.

The Alliance ultimately engaged in a wide range of public-interest issues, including the trial of the Chicago Seven, defense of Angela Davis, repeal of Emergency Detention Laws, defense of the right to bail, and opposition to police repression.

Local and state law-enforcement perceived the Alliance to be such a serious threat — to law and order and prevention of subversive takeover — that government agencies engaged in illegal spying and other unlawful acts against the Alliance. Eventually the

Alliance sued in federal court and successfully gained a court order prohibiting government spying. Because of infiltration and interference by local and federal agencies, it took several decades for the Red Squad spying suit to be settled in federal courts.

The organizations participating in creation of the Alliance ranged from the Amalgamated Meat Cutters union to the Black P. Stone Nation. Other supporting organizations were churches and synagogues, trade unions, human relations and community groups "working together to change government practices that threaten civil liberties."

In ideology and in programs, the Alliance was a microcosm of the 1970s social activism: politically liberal or leftist and broadly participatory; opportunistic in choosing issues to investigate; and decentralized, as it created and spun-off new organizations focused on particular issues. Affiliate organizations took part only in initiatives that they chose to support.

The Alliance attempted to create an inclusive mass movement. Representatives of affiliated and cooperating organizations selectively became members of task forces. A wide range of pressing issues became included: the Chicago 15 (of the 1968 Chicago Democratic Convention riots), defense of Angela Davis, repeal of emergency-detention laws, defense of the right to bail, and opposition to police repression.

A central concern of the Alliance throughout its existence was the Chicago criminal-court system. Four related issues prominent in the early life of the Alliance were: political influence on the Cook County Coroner's office, bias by the Chicago Police Board, discriminatory patterns in the granting of bail, and the Chicago Police Red Squad's surveillance of social and political activists.

As mentioned, and as documented, the Alliance openly conducted constitutionally lawful activities. However, that didn't prevent state and city officials from organizing (unlawful) operations at public expense from spying on and disrupting community organizations such as the Alliance. A special and secret "Red Squad" of the Chicago city police was formed, and they engaged in systematic spying of the Alliance and other citizen organizations.

Vindication. From its beginning, Alliance founders had considered suing the Chicago Police Department to stop the politically motivated surveillance. By April 1972 such a lawsuit was under active discussion. In November 1974, a lawsuit, *Alliance to End Repression, et al. versus James M. Rochford, et al.*, was filed in U.S. District Court. The discovery process in the case included files of the Chicago Police and the FBI's Chicago field office.

During an investigation by the Afro-American Police League, evidence of extensive illegal surveillance by the Chicago Police Department had already been found. After noticing the mysterious pay code 099 in the department's Intelligence Division, the Alliance's lawyers suspected that some community and civil rights activists were actually police officers or paid informants.

The lawsuit eventually resulted in a 1981 court order that barred police surveillance outside of specific criminal investigations. The Alliance had succeeded in its central project: elimination of political surveillance by the Chicago police. Eventually, as a consequence of victory in the "Red Squad" lawsuit, a collection of documents, known as the "Chicago Police Department Red Squad and related records," was deposited at the Chicago History Museum, in accordance with a court order issued by a Judge of the U.S. District Court.

Civil-liberty concerns were high on the agenda in the 1970s for activists in the Chicago area, partly because of local issues and police overreach, and partly because of federal (and local and city) police and agents. The ACLU was a major civil-rights support organization that could be relied upon for legal intervention.

The American Civil Liberties Union (**ACLU**) is a nonprofit organization founded in 1920 "to defend and preserve the individual rights and liberties guaranteed to every person in this country by the Constitution and laws of the United States." Steadfastly nonpartisan, the organization has been supported and criticized by liberal and conservative organizations alike. The ACLU works through litigation and lobbying. Local affiliates of the ACLU are active in all 50 states, the District of Columbia, and Puerto Rico. The ACLU provides legal assistance in cases when it considers civil liberties to be at risk. Legal support from the ACLU can take the form of direct legal representation or preparation of *amicus curiae* briefs when another law firm is already providing representation.

In addition to representing persons and organizations in lawsuits, the ACLU lobbies for policy positions that have been established by its board of directors. Current positions of the ACLU include: opposing the death penalty; supporting same-sex marriage and the right of LGBT people to adopt; supporting birth control and abortion rights; eliminating discrimination against women, minorities, and LGBT people; decarceration in the United States; supporting the rights of prisoners and opposing torture; and opposing government preference for religion over non-religion, or for particular faiths over others.

CHICAGO'S AMERICAN CIVIL LIBERTIES UNION

I don't recall precisely my first meeting with Ruth Adams as head of the Chicago branch of the ACLU, but at the time she had an ACLU office at the southside University of Chicago. She also had or organized a chapter in the suburbs and I was attending some of their meetings. She also took over editorship of the *Bulletin of the Atomic Scientists,* to which I contributed some articles.

172

Many years later, when she and her husband Bob Adams had settled in San Diego, I recall meeting them at their home near the university. We had a lot in common to share in terms of Cold War and civil-liberties interests.

Bulletin of the Atomic Scientists. Dedicated topical magazines such as the *Bulletin of the Atomic Scientists*, frequently carried and published in-depth studies and opinions about the arms race. The *Bulletin* was originally headquartered at the University of Chicago campus. It had its beginnings in December 1945, a few months after World War II ended, when the Atomic Scientists of Chicago (with Eugene Rabinowitch as editor) began publishing the *Bulletin of the Atomic Scientists of Chicago*.

After its long-time editor Ruth Adams passed away, the *Bulletin* drifted for a while into becoming an anti-nuclear-power mouthpiece. Recently the *Bulletin* seems to have corrected its course, focusing on nuclear-arms risk, climate change, and disruptive technologies. Now with its iconic Doomsday Clock set at 100 seconds to midnight, here's the 2020 *Bulletin* pronouncement:

Washington, D.C.. January 23, 2020. Humanity continues to face **two simultaneous existential dangers** — nuclear war and climate change — that are compounded by a threat multiplier, cyber-enabled information warfare, that undercuts society's ability to respond. The international security situation is dire, not just because these threats exist, but because world leaders have allowed an international political infrastructure erode....

CHAPTER VIII: WARS AND PEACE

In parallel with local and regional public engagement regarding government Cold War policy drift toward ever more horrific nuclear strategies, quite a few national and international organizations started to develop campaigns against the growing threat of atomic war. Here's a few of them:

CDI. As a private, non-governmental research organization, the Center for Defense Information was (and still is) an independent monitor of military spending. It has held that strong social, economic, political, and military components and a healthy environment have contributed equally to the nation's security. CDI has sought realistic and cost-effective military spending without excess expenditures for weapons and policies that increase the danger of war and without wasteful spending or compromising our national security. When visiting Washington, the author often met Admirals LaRoque and Carol, the founders.

The organization has continued its fundamental work opposing excesses of the MILC. Even now, CDI keeps track of defense spending, as part of the Project on Government Oversight, and continues to publish *The Defense Monitor*.

The **Center for Defense Information** (CDI) is a nonprofit, nonpartisan organization based in Washington, D.C. It has specialized in analyzing and advising on military matters.

CDI was founded in 1971 by an independent group of retired military officers, notably including Adm. Gene La Rocque and Adm. Eugene Carroll. In 2005, CDI expanded by creating the Straus Military Reform Project for the purpose of promoting military reform in the Pentagon and Congress. In 2012 CDI joined the Project on Government Oversight (POGO) which continued publication of *The Defense Monitor*..

After the 2008 U.S. elections, CDI released *America's Defense Meltdown: Pentagon Reform* for President Obama and the New Congress, a collection of briefing papers by a dozen defense intellectuals and retired military officers. In 2010, CDI released a second anthology, *The Pentagon Labyrinth: 10 Short Essays to Help You through It.* Since the mid-2000s, CDI has focused on the Lockheed Martin F-35 Lightning II as the embodiment of the Pentagon's acquisition problems — being both unaffordable and a huge disappointment in performance.

ACA. The venerable Arms Control Association, founded in 1971, is another of the many organizations that reacted to the threatening state of international affairs in the early 1970s. I was one of the original members, as well as many, in or out of government, who were active in national-security problems.

Under the dependable leadership of Executive Director Daryl G. Kimball, ACA has continued to be a national nonpartisan membership organization dedicated to promoting public understanding and support of effective arms-control policies.

Through its public education and media programs and its magazine, *Arms Control Today*, ACA provides policymakers, the press, and the interested public with authoritative information, analysis and commentary on arms proposals, negotiations and agreements, and related national-security issues.

NOMOR. Using the acronym nuclear overkill moratorium, NOMOR was organized in 1976 by Chicago-area citizens pressing for a unilateral U.S. pause in the production and testing of nuclear weapons.

During the height of the nuclear freeze debate, NOMOR prepared and distributed a "Primer" on "You, the Nuclear Arms Race, and Survival: Nine Questions and Answers." The contemporary "problem" was described as "nuclear roulette" — a nuclear arms-race game being played by governments with human survival as the stakes. NOMOR challenged the basic assumptions of the Pentagon's defense program, which were (1) that producing evermore nuclear weapons enhances "national security," and (2) that the nuclear race or a nuclear war could be "won."

Mobe. Mobilization for Survival was a mixed-issue "environmentalist" group. It held that "nuclear energy and nuclear weapons are merely different sides of the same coin." Concurrent with demonstrations as part of "International Action Week" against the neutron bomb and "teach-ins" at universities and colleges in August 1978, Mobe arranged more than 100 marches, demonstrations and sit-ins, mostly at military bases and nuclear-power stations in 36 states. In 1979 Mobe held a protest with other "affinity groups" and war-resisters at DOE headquarters in Washington.

Nuclear Freeze Campaign. Although a primary NGO goal was halting and reversing the arms race, the concept of simply freezing (suspending) the arms competition at the then-current levels in the late 1970s seemed politically more palatable.

Major religious, civic, and political organizations became early endorsers of the Freeze, including the YWCA, the National Conference of Black Mayors; the national-board and social-issues offices of the National Council of Churches, the United Presbyterian Church, the Unitarian Universalists Association; as well as the bishops and diocesan conventions within the Episcopal and Roman Catholic Churches.

Designating "Disarmament Week" for late October 1981, the Nuclear Weapons Freeze Campaign called on local organizations to create exhibits, show films, and hold lectures, press conferences, religious services, and teach-ins about the danger of nuclear war. The campaign also held a national "Call-In" on 26 October 1981, encouraging Americans to telephone the White House and urge President Reagan to propose a mutual freeze to Premier Brezhnev of the Soviet Union. In the spring of 1982, the Freeze Campaign reported that 20,000 volunteers were working in 140 offices throughout 47 states.

It is estimated that by 1985 the total number of local and national peace *groups* had increased to about 8000. Besides those connected with the Freeze campaign, other Cold War opposition groups grew, such as Physicians for Social Responsibility, the Council for a Livable World, and SANE — the latter's membership growing from

4000 in 1977 to 150,000 in 1986. President Reagan's policies had instilled so much fear that it catalyzed widespread public protest. (Although Republicans still idolize Reagan as a peacemaker, his bellicosity brought the world closer than any other presidency to nuclear Armageddon.)

Committee of Soviet Scientists. The Committee of Soviet Scientists for Peace and Against the Nuclear Threat (shortened to CSS), a non-governmental group of senior Soviet scientists, was established in 1983 "for the purpose of studying the technical feasibility of disarmament agreements and discussing these questions with Western groups." The CSS became a key intermediary for the Soviet side in dialogs with Westerners.

Academicians Yevgeni Velikhov and Roald Sagdeev were the primary organizers of the CSS. The Committee, formed during the early stages of Gorbachev's premiership, presented the boldest of unofficial Soviet efforts to bring in more moderate arms-control policies. Hewing closely enough to the Party line, the activists were officially tolerated in carrying out approved activities with Western NGOs.

Velikhov and Sagdeev, through the CSS, accelerated the East-West side-channel dialog after Reagan's "Star Wars" speech in March 1983. Based on their own analysis, which indicated that the American SDI could be neutralized by much-lower-cost countermeasures, the Committee was successful in persuading Gorbachev not to launch a Soviet "Star Wars" program.

By having access to the respective government leaders, Velikhov and Sagdeev were able to get Chairman Andropov to agree to a moratorium on testing Soviet ASAT. The Academicians also influenced Gorbachev's decision to begin a unilateral halt of Soviet nuclear tests, an initiative brushed off by the Reagan administration, which argued that the Soviet Union would test clandestinely. Velikhov then suggested that a non-governmental group set up seismometers in Kazakhstan, and that led to an extraordinary NGO experiment carried out under the auspices of the CSS and the NRDC (Natural Resources Defense Council, headquartered in Washington, DC).

The Chicago Connection. A regional public-interest group, the Chicago Committee on National Priorities, had been organizing public hearings in the late 1960s. According to the Committee's findings, two-thirds of the federal budget was being spent on the ongoing Vietnam war, the defense establishment and accrued interest from past wars. After taking into account government operating cost, only 15 percent of the federal budget was left for public health, education and welfare.

This was at a time when the Defense Department was allocating billions of dollars for the multiple-warhead MIRV weapon system. If the United States deployed MIRV, the Soviets would also have to do so — as indeed they later did. Because so much of the federal R&D budget was for military rather than peaceful research, scientists had additional reason to join the national-priorities realignment movement.

NOMOR jointly challenged the military view that "continued high-level spending on nuclear weapons and delivery systems would contribute to national security." It was unlikely that Soviet leaders would be "so myopic as to think they could win a meaningful victory in a nuclear war."

But newspapers like the *Chicago Tribune* were opposed to a military moratorium in Vietnam and badmouthed the anti-war public demonstrations. They editorialized against "well-meaning and sincere opponents of war" who might be "sucked in on such revolutionary designs" and are "contributing to the breakdown of all order in this country." According to the *Tribune*, "virtually every seditious group in the nation was represented" in planning a forthcoming November 1969 university-oriented moratorium demonstration. The newspaper derided the "dogma of the far left," warning that "[it might not be] far from the time when there will be barricades in the streets." (It was so easy to through around words like seditious and treason, and it took a decade or so before the newspapers came around to change their editorial stance.)

National priorities and defense spending began to trigger significant public dissent because broader and festering societal issues were opened up: civil rights, human rights, police repression, women's indignities, etc. Misplaced government military spending stood in stark contrast to underfunded human priorities.

Taking explicit aim at arms-control policies promoted by President Trump, the *Bulletin* has recently added the following urgent editorial protestation regarding strategic nuclear arms control:

> It would be a crippling blow to the world if New START is not extended beyond 2021, when it is set to expire. This would not only eliminate remaining constraints on deployed nuclear arsenals, but also remove the monitoring and inspection capabilities which have provided both sides with increased transparency regarding nuclear capability.

THE WARS IN VIETNAM

First Indochina War (50s-60s). The ideological spasm that surfaced as the first Indochina War was mostly fought between North Vietnam (supported by the USSR and China) against South Vietnam (sustained by the United States and allies). As in the case of Korea, the Vietnam wars arose because the nation had been divided North and South after WWII, as well as because of global tensions that developed immediately afterwards. There were other similarities between the Indochina conflicts and the 1950-53 Korean War.

The Vietcong (a South Vietnamese communist common front aided by the North) fought a guerrilla war, while the North Vietnamese Army engaged in a more conventional war. Laos and Cambodia were also engulfed in the fighting.

As the war continued, the Vietcong role in the fighting decreased as the strength of the North Vietnam Army grew. Meanwhile, American and South Vietnamese forces relied on air superiority and overwhelming firepower in search and destroy operations, involving ground forces, artillery, and airstrikes. In the course of the war, the United States conducted a large-scale strategic bombing campaign against North Vietnam.

American involvement took several indirect forms: Naval and aircraft assistance, CIA covert bombing operations, and transport of civilians to South Vietnam. Napalm, exploited extensively by the United States in incendiary attacks in World War II, was also used during the Vietnam War. Ultimately, all this was ineffectual.

Napalm. Named from combining the words "naphthene" and "palmitate," napalm is a highly incendiary weaponized liquid. Americans developed and began to render it by air during World War II. From 1950, thanks to supplies from the United States, the French Air Force began using napalm in Indochina against the armed forces of the Democratic Republic of Vietnam, although civilians were often victims of its use. Not only does napalm burn its targets, but it also deoxygenates the area within its zone, often causing death to humans and animals by asphyxiation.

Vietnamese sources revealed that napalm provided a horrifying experience. During the battle of Dien Bien Phu, the French used American-supplied "Flying Boxcar" C-119s to drop more than six tons of napalm on enemy communication lines and targets.

Second Indochina War (60s-70s). While Ho Chi Minh was determined to reunite Vietnam, President Johnson was determined to prevent it. Although South Vietnam was on the verge of collapse, the stage was set for massive escalation of the undeclared war. Within two years of taking office, the Johnson Administration dispatched 1.5 million Americans to Vietnam to fight a war they found deadly, baffling, tedious, exciting, and (ultimately) unforgettable.

Domino Theory. The Western domino theory arose from fears that the fall of post-WWII independent Vietnam and Laos would trigger the toppling of other nations into the communist sphere of influence. Based on that unproven notion, President Kennedy increased the number of American military personnel in South Vietnam, although he resisted Pentagon proposals for major escalation. When LBJ came into office, he committed a large force of American combat troops in reaction to a (questionable) triggering event in the Gulf of Tonkin.

Four American Presidents Directly Involved in Vietnam Wars. In 1955, Vietnam became a Republic with Ngo Dinh Diem as its first leader. Eisenhower attempted to stop communist influence in Southeast East Asia. When President Kennedy pledged extra aid to the Diem regime in 1961, more advisers and machinery (but not troops) were sent to South Vietnam. However, two years later, just three weeks before being assassinated, Kennedy had tacitly approved a coup to overthrow Diem.

In 1964, the Gulf of Tonkin incident occurred and a Congressional resolution gave President Lyndon Johnson more powers to wage the war in Vietnam. He ordered a bombing campaign and sent the first combat troops to South Vietnam in March 1965. Soon after that, an involuntary civilian draft in the United States was instituted, causing many anti-war protests nationwide especially inside campuses.

The next president, Richard Nixon, started a so-called "Vietnamization" policy in 1969. During his years in office, Nixon escalated the war into Laos and Cambodia in an attempt to destroy Communist supplies of food, weapons, and manpower through the Ho Chi Minh Trail to South Vietnam. Nixon ordered a "Christmas Bombing" in 1972 to keep North Vietnam at the negotiating table as well as to convince South Vietnam to agree to a peace treaty. In January 1973, the Paris Peace Accords were signed ending the American direct involvement in Vietnam, which subsequently ended the war.

Opposition to American involvement in the war gradually swelled into outright civil disobedience throughout the nation. The opposition manifested itself in the United States in the form of peaceful protest through the formation of many anti-war organizations.

Figure 77. Young Vietnamese child, Kim Phúc, center left, running down a road naked near Trng Bàng, after a South Vietnam Air Force napalm attack (credit: Nick Ut/ The Associated Press, June 8, 1972).

Trying to help bridge such mixed cultural and technological issues, I was one of the founders of an informal organization at Argonne called the Concerned Argonne Scientists. We separated ourselves from the Federation of Atomic Scientists in order to take a proactive view in opposing the war in Vietnam. The CAS grew into an organization free to discuss, evaluate, and take positions on many quasi-technical issues that bordered between technology and politics.

During the Vietnam War, Greenwich Village (the downtown Manhattan part of New York City where I had once lived) was home to many "safe houses" used by the radical anti-war movement. Even now, the Village is known as a center for off-beat causes that implicitly or explicitly challenge traditional American culture.

Yet to be fully acknowledged are the contestable government tactics used to root out overseas communism, which was attempting a foothold despite America's Cold War anti-communism effort. American "truth commissions" were once proposed to look into specific situations like the massacre at My Lai, the use of napalm and defoliants in Vietnam and Cambodia, the mining of harbors in Nicaragua, support for the repressive regime in Chile, the CIA role in installing a dictator in Iran, and clandestine activities in Guatemala.

In South Africa and Argentina, retrospective inquiries to promote accountability and catharsis were established.

Johnson's successor, Richard Nixon, tried to make the Vietnam War his presidential hallmark, but he ended up extending the war until forced out of office in 1974. His successor, Gerald Ford, terminated the Indochina conflict before the end of his term in 1977.

This book on *The Fox Millennium* offers my personal — and sometimes involved — survey of those events regarding the wars in Vietnam, particularly from the viewpoint of anti-war activists.

CHAPTER IX: INTERNATIONAL POLITICS

BILATERAL AND INTERNATIONAL ARMS CONTROL

During much of the Cold War, nations East and West were held in a phase of political and military stagnation. The Soviet Union maintained a tight leash on its domains inside the Iron Curtain, thus keeping the superpowers militarily and rhetorically separated. Although there were several overtures on the table for discussion to alleviate this situation, the ongoing verbal dialog was obstructed by Cold War ideology and semantics.

Even so, a number of nuclear-related inter-governmental events were taking place on the international stage, in particular national and international pressure and debates about technical verification of nuclear arms control and of nuclear treaties between East and West.

One overture was arranged by the respective Academies of Science through the Nova Scotia Pugwash movement. Another approach (in 1981) was organized by the Natural Resources Defense Council (NRDC — a U.S. non-government organization — NGO), working with the Federation of American Scientists — FAS. The NRDC had previously been involved largely in environmental issues, of which the danger of nuclear warfare became recognized as the largest peril.

Because of my long-term membership in the FAS, coupled with my specialized technical knowledge about nuclear-fission materials, I too was invited on behalf of the FAS to participate in the 1981 first NGO meeting at Key West, Florida. One thing led to another, and not too much later progress began through unofficial NGO face-to-face E-W conversations. About a third of a century of Cold War had inhibited official communication, leaving only a few unauthorized overtures. The unofficial NRDC NGO, especially represented by Tom Cochran, working with the FAS led by Princeton professor Frank von Hippel, had remarkably overcome a long-standing bureaucratic impasse between adversarial Cold War governments.

Pugwash Conferences on Science and World Affairs are arranged by an international organization that brings together scholars and public figures to work toward reducing the danger of armed conflict and to seek solutions to global security threats. The conferences were founded in 1957 by Joseph Rotblat and Bertrand Russell in Pugwash, Nova Scotia, Canada, following the release of the Russell–Einstein Manifesto in 1955.

Rotblat and the Pugwash Conference jointly won the Nobel Peace Prize in 1995 for their efforts on nuclear disarmament. International Student/Young Pugwash groups have continued despite their founder Cyrus Eaton's death in 1979. In addition, an offshoot program has been carried on since 1966 by ISODARCO, the International School on Disarmament and Research on Conflicts, an Italian Pugwash derivative group.

ISODARCO stands for International School on Disarmament and Arms Control. Organized and conducted by the Italian branch of Pugwash, it has provided a 2-week-long biannual *corso* in Italy, often in Trento, sometimes in Venezia, and once in a while in China.

Since 1966 the Italian Pugwash Group (E-mail: isodarco@gmail) has been sponsoring the arms control and disarmament courses, which continue into the present. One of the organizers is Mirco Elena, from Trento. He graciously helped me with my personal search for relatives in Trento and my professional associations with ISODARCO. Over the years, I attended several of their "courses" which were more like mini-symposia. These courses were one of the first and only opportunities during early stages of the Cold War for scientists East and West to come together in an informal, non-polemic, long-lasting setting.

These overtures were taking place at a time when the hodoscope was becoming very successful in my professional role at Argonne National Laboratory. Accordingly, I was able to have some suggestions put on the negotiation table with respect to non-intrusive verification of the number of warheads on missiles, an issue that had become prominent and even the subject of some of my quasi-technical publications

A hodoscope-like system was candidate as a tool for unintrusive verification of warheads, that is, treaty verification without revealing militarily-sensitive nuclear-design features. So-called nonintrusiveness was sought for arms-control verification, that is, counting the number of treaty-limited military items without revealing design or operation secrets.

The Cold War was then near its peak (not subsiding until the collapse of the Soviet Union in late 1991), but national resources were still being diverted from pressing domestic needs. That diversion challenged the best interests of any nation, often preserving and expanding the power of dictators, ideological extremists, and other vested interests. Of course, autocratic governments with mostly nationalistic goals had been ignoring those lessons as long as they could.

Among the issues that influenced U.S. national policy were the very strategy (or philosophy — or thoughtless dependence) on Cold War brinkmanship. Our government, acting through the President and Congress, increasingly brought upon itself public protest and resistance to warlike policies, especially those which might get our nation and the world involved in a nuclear conflict. Factors that most strongly affected domestic policies and politics are included in my earlier book, *Cold War Nuclear Challenges*. Its first Chapter, Cold War Convulsions, describes East-West disputes that placed international security into a tenuous and dangerous stage during the Cold War. The accompanying turmoil on the domestic stage is detailed in the second Chapter of the book.

In fact, public involvement and protest during the Cold War was a major — perhaps the most important factor — in keeping the worldwide ideological conflict from becoming an extremely deadly, suicidal nuclear exchange. Our CAS group shared and tried to mitigate this danger, our members often giving public talks, our invitations to speakers joining us or giving talks at lunch time in the Argonne cafeteria, and as much activism as we could muster without abridging our tenuous status.

From that monograph book of mine, *Cold War Nuclear Challenges*, published long after retirement from Argonne, is this summary-type paragraph:

History still conveys lessons for any nation that contemplates an atomic arsenal: Potential adversaries will react, sometimes preemptively; and nuclear arms races are deceptively expensive. The new millennium's legacy has been interpreted by some not sufficiently qualified or experienced authors. That's one reason I've attempted to update and clarify where we stand, a quarter of a century afterwards. Having once been a naval officer — and later a nuclear physicist with access at one time to our innermost national secrets — has given me a unique vantage in narrating Cold War history, without having to disclose any still-classified information.

ARMS-CONTROL TREATY VERIFICATION

Verification of arms-control treaty obligations has turned out to be a important as wearing socks in shoes. You could — but rarely — went without socks or stockings. Yet, in an adversarial world, as existed during the Cold War, not much could be taken for granted. Treaty adherence needed to be verified by all signatories. This also became politically important at the time because rightwingers in the United States tried to undermine E-W treaty negotiations by (falsely) asserting that the treaties could not be verified and that the Soviets couldn't be trusted. In fact, "trust, but verify" became a politically boosted phrase, especially in right-wing conservative politics.

Those of us with a technical bent realized that technology could assist in treaty verification, especially if you wanted the treaty to work.. Those in favor of the treaty insisted that it be verifiable, especially by available and sometimes multiple national technical means. Those who opposed the treaty often argued against the potential for verification, contending that the other side would use any possible means to cheat.

Trust, but verify (Russian: Доверяй, но проверяй, a rhyming Russian proverb) was a phrase often bandied about during the Cold War. The catchword phrase became internationally known in its English form when used by President Ronald Reagan on several occasions in the context of nuclear disarmament discussions with the Soviet Union. The proverb was adopted as a signature phrase by Reagan, who used it frequently when discussing U.S. relations with the Soviet Union and may have helped relations between the two nations.

Reagan used the phrase to emphasize the extensive verification procedures that would enable both sides to monitor compliance at the signing of the INF Treaty, on 8 December 1987.

Originally, early in the Cold War, high-flying aircraft were used for overhead surveillance. That was before satellites were placed in space orbiting with impunity around the earch, overflying borders that included those isolating the Iron Curtain from the rest of the world. Even with overhead satellites, there some weapon systems, such a nuclear armaments, that were too small for reliable verification. A standard conventionally-armed missile warhead was no larger than a nuclear warhead. So size of a warhead was not something that could be a matter of control in an nuclear-arms-control agreement. Instead, both sides would have to agree to close-in, on-site inspection that could differentiate whether a warhead was nuclear or conventional. Proving that such differentiation was practical without revealing any technical details of the weapon became a major undertaking at the U.S. national labs.

Those of us at Argonne who were arguing in favor of arms control (mostly CAS members) also had to put meat on the bone, so to speak, to show how the particular treaty could be verified (without disclosing national secrets). For example, if the proposed agreement called for a limit on the number of nuclear warheads carried by a missile, we would need some way to tell if a particular type of missile had one or more nuclear warheads.

Reactors: Engineering, Physics, Technology. In the course of time at Argonne National Laboratory, I was assigned to various technical Divisions and nuclear programs, mostly those that had the term "reactor" in its name, which reflected its mission. Our assigned goal was to help the designated national government agency — DOE or NRDC or whatever it went by at the time — to develop and ensure the safety of nuclear reactors for civilian power and other nonmilitary purposes.

Technical Means of Treaty Verification. If a treaty were to call for differentiation between nuclear and conventional explosives, it would require special technical methods that could distinguish nuclear from conventional warheads. That would be particularly essential for any treaty dealing with cruise-missile warheads, because just looking at them from the outside you couldn't tell the difference between those armed with conventional or nuclear warheads.

As a matter of historical fact, cruise-missile warhead differentiation by detecting their radiation emanation became established in the NGO "Black Sea Experiment." (I was supposed to participate as an expert on behalf of the NRDC in that experiment, but for reasons never explained was denied government permission — see details in my earlier books). So, the technical means of verification for cruise-missile warheads has been long validated.

In any event, during the latter portion of my career at Argonne, much of my professional time was devoted to the development of technical means of verification of potential arms-control treaties. Of course, the means and goals of verification depended much on the items and their design sensitivity. If it was a nuclear weapon, little about it could be allowed to be disclosed in the verification process. If it was a non-nuclear weapon, part of the problem was that there were a great number of them (think armored tanks, for example).

Verifiability was a major stumbling block, a negotiation obstacle often raised by those who actually were opposed to the treaty — or any treaty — with the Soviet Union, that is, with those Communists.

Theoretically, the biggest military consequence would occur if warhead was a nuclear — not conventional — weapon; so major efforts East and West went into devising means for detecting nuclear armaments, either with or without a treaty. It was a challenging task for which our program at Argonne was well suited. Moreover, you couldn't get too fancy, that is, reveal anything about the object being inspected other than whether it was a nuclear or conventionally armed warhead, if it was under limitation by a treaty. That technical challenge was one that we at Argonne were well qualified because we had much experience in monitoring small and large reactors and subcritical assemblies for reactive nuclear behavior.

In fact, the hodoscope at TREAT was designed specifically to monitor nuclear materials placed at the center of that test reactor. With the aid of radiation deliberately delivered from within the reactor, we readily distinguished between the types and amounts of nuclear materials ranging from zero to high levels of fissile content purposely positioned in the middle of the reactor.

Because nuclear weapons emitted their own telltale radiation. that experience at TREAT gave us a leg up on devising technical means for detection of nuclear materials enclosed within various types of containers, even if no reactor could be used in the actual weapon verification process out in the field.

At the time the various strategic-arms treaties were under consideration or negotiation, Argonne along with the other DOE national laboratories promoted various technical means for consideration in verification of the proposed treaties. Depending on what would be the TLI (treaty-limited-item), each lab would check to see what it had that might be applicable. Of course, both the weapons and the non-weapons nuclear laboratories had experience relevant to verification of nuclear devices; in fact, it was a strong point for the Argonne program because we did not need to control or reveal any national-security-classified information, a limitation that hobbled the weapons labs.

The weapons labs of course had substantial experience in monitoring nuclear explosions underground as well as above ground. That, however, was nowhere near the same as verifying the existence or absence of a nuclear-weapon package; so their proposals never did get accepted for treaty verification.

Tagging Treaty-Limited Items (TLI's). When arms-control negotiations during the Cold War began in earnest, whether bilateral or multilateral, one of the foremost stumbling blocks was whether a potential treaty could be verified with sufficient confidence. War-hawks who were opposed to any treaty whatsoever often plmied their overt objections on verifiability. Those who favored the treaty argued that the agreement was to be and could reliably be verified by each side.

In the course of time, I had been put in charge of Argonne's program for treaty verification. At first, it was just a programmatically growing additive to our Reactor Physics Division program in nuclear diagnostics, the bulk of which dealt with the fast-neutron and gamma hodoscope. Because we were routinely engaged in detecting nuclear materials, our team was the logical Argonne National Laboratory grouping for delving into an further application of our equipment and experience. I thereupon became at first the *de-facto* and later the lab-wide head of a nascent Argonne program on arms-control verification, and was appointed to represent Argonne at what became a DOE designated multi-lab coordination for treaty-verification technology.

Aside from the logical role of hodoscope-type systems in treaty verification, Argonne had been conducting some relevant technical work using high-resolution electronic microscopes. One staffer of our Division, Bob Palm, proposed a method of accounting for TLIs by "fingerprinting" them. The process would be rather simple: a plastic-casting fingerprint would be made.

Simply soaking a plastic film attached to the surface of a TLI would result in a three-dimensional image of that area. Our proposal was to choose a convenient spot on the surface of the TLI, attach a thin plastic film, drench it with acetone, and store it after removal from the TLI surface. It would be similar to ordinary fingerprinting in criminal investigations, except that the fingerprint would preserve the three-dimensional aspects of the surface region being tagged. Because surfaces of weapons were likely to be made of some hard metal like steel, putting a little acetone on it would have no military aftermath. Bob would use the electronic

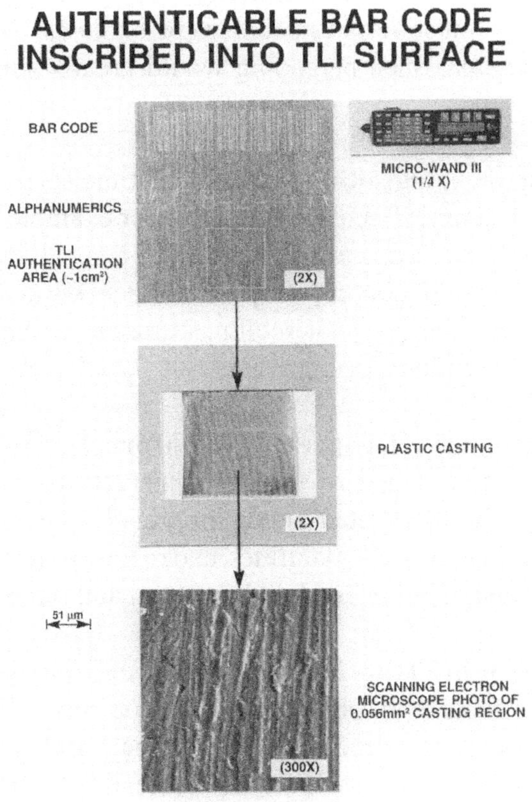

AUTHENTICABLE BAR CODE INSCRIBED INTO TLI SURFACE

BAR CODE

ALPHANUMERICS

TLI AUTHENTICATION AREA (~1cm²)

(2X)

MICRO-WAND III (1/4 X)

PLASTIC CASTING

(2X)

51 μm

SCANNING ELECTRON MICROSCOPE PHOTO OF 0.056mm² CASTING REGION

(300X)

Figure 78. Illustration of surface-casting method of "fingerprinting" an external surface of a TLI (treaty-limited item) weapon or military vehicle.

microscope to verify the fingerprint images by comparing the surface casting with the stored-data.

Figure 78 illustrates an alternative method where the bar code is inscribed into the TLI surface and/or a nearby area on the surface is used as the TLI identifier. In this case, as illustrated, a faithful plastic casting can be made of the TLI identification area and later checked against the data base.

In the course of time, I would illustrate the simplicity of the process by traveling to federal-agency meetings with a small kit that consisted simply of some plastic film and a vial of acetone. That was all that was needed to readily demonstrate the simple, low-cost method by taking a fingerprint of a penny or something.

In order to protect the area that was tagged and reidentify it for monitoring purposes, the tagged area was to be covered with a steel barcode. It was rather straightforward to have protective plates that were barcoded adhesive sheets made to cover the targeted area. Such barcoding would greatly simplify keeping an inventory of the TLIs.

An important logistical factor was that the surface of the TLI need not be modified or permanently affected in any way. For example, a nuclear weapon could be tagged by simply making a plastic casting of a specified area on its outer surface. Such a process would not impair performance of the weapon, nor leave any kind of permanent marking, nor require intrusion within the weapon — thus importantly preserving military secrecy.

Extensive Travel, Especially in Europe. Because of the wide scope of international arms control, I had to travel extensively on official business domestically and overseas. In the United States my travel brought me to essentially all the national laboratories and major facilities, and in Europe to corresponding national laboratories. In England, that included Aldermaston and other UK nuclear facilities.

DOE Role in Treaty Negotiations. In negotiations with foreign powers, each nation has its official representatives and support staff. The U.S. government operates mostly by a committee process, wherein the various cabinet-level offices support the Department of State which has the lead role in treaties with foreign nations. The Department of Energy would provide expert advice on matters dealing with nuclear matters and weaponry. For that purpose, technical experts from the national laboratories were seconded to the negotiating team. Such experts came from all the laboratories, sometimes including a couple of selected Argonne staff members.

DNA Role in Treaty Verification. The Defense Nuclear Agency normally receives and manages nuclear weapons after they are turned over from the weapons labs (that is from DOE to DOD). While at Argonne I was responsible for a program that supported the development of verification technology, and thus interacted directly with SAIC and with other beltway bandits that provided technical and analytical support to DNA.

In the course of time I gave a number of unclassified and some classified seminars at DNA, including some of keen interest after the NGO Slava cruise-missile verification. In addition, unofficially on behalf of DNA I was funded to travel around the world to learn what I could learn about pending arms control and verification interests, especially those that might lead to a treaty and to its verification.

In fact, with my assistance and making use of overseas contacts I had developed, DNA organized some verification-technology conferences both before and after the Soviet Union fell apart. The connections I had established enabled me to arrange through Argonne the invitations and travel of many of the participants, especially those that came from what (a couple of weeks later) became the former Soviet Union.

The 1992 DNA U.S.-Russian Conference (hosted in Williamsburg) brings to mind an anecdote: As the technical coordinator, it was my responsibility to arrange for the travel, care, and feeding of the Russians — just recently our sworn enemies, now in transition as colleagues. On the weekend day off, I took about a half-dozen of them on a van trip over to Hampton Roads. Crossing the bay bridge, we stopped at for an all-you-can eat buffet on a island across from the U.S. Naval Operating Base at Norfolk, Virginia. We had a delightful and sumptuous buffet, but somehow the question came up whether we could visit the naval base. (Remember, the East-West Cold War had just come to an end.)

Because I had served in the Navy at nearby Little Creek, Norfolk, it seemed like an easy trip extension; so we drove across the bay bridge, and as we got close to the main naval-operating base, I gave some thought to seeing if my Navy (reserve) officer's ID card would be enough to bring the former Soviets on to the base and escort them around. Much to my surprise, my ID was accepted, and we drove along the main harbor base, where many U.S. Navy warships were docked — even aircraft carriers, like ships of the line. Our guests, sworn enemies just two years earlier, took plenty of photos to amaze their families, friends and colleagues at home.

Needless to say, access to the base since then became much more restricted. I was given a friendly token of appreciation in the form of a collectively signed paper napkin, as shown in Figure 79.

In the Figure, recognizable signatures (*inter-alia*) are those from Bill Sutcliffe of Livermore National Lab, Tom Cochran of NRDC, Chris Paine of NRDC, Harold Agnew of Los Alamos National Lab, as well as Dave Hafemeister and Tom Neff, along with a number of important Russian/Soviet guests. As mentioned in its caption, the Soviet Union disassembled just a week later. I wonder if any of the well-connected Soviet scientists or administrators had an inkling of what was just about to happen back home?

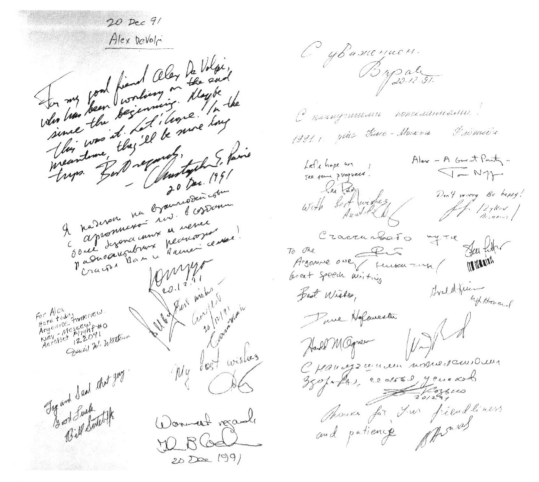

Figure 79. Signatures in remembrance of joint US-Soviet meeting that I organized in Williamsburg, Virginia, on behalf of DNA just a week before the USSR collapsed.

DOE LAG (Laboratory Advisory Group). At one time, I was the representative designated by Argonne to participate in a DOE laboratory advisory group about technical means that could be used for treaty verification. Each of the DOE labs usually had someone nominated and appointed to represent them at the treaty-specific LAG.

While any of the DOE labs could contribute ideas and technology to the verification process, Argonne technology was often well-suited for that purpose, particularly because very little of our work was national-security classified. Thus, technological details promoted by Argonne could be divulged in discussions with the Soviets, whereas some concepts considered by the DOE weapons labs were avoided because they might reveal classified national-security information.

In particular, one of the concepts that I put forth was the use of hodoscope-type multi-channel detection of gamma and neutron radiation. Technical information about the hodoscope has been published in the open literature. A hodoscope-type instrument would have been particularly applicable to the purpose of recognizing and counting nuclear warheads without revealing technical details about the warheads. Using "non-intrusive" means of verification was a major constraint for any proposed nuclear-arms-control treaty: You had to verify compliance without learning any more internal details about the weapon being verified.

The existing body of published work regarding the hodoscope and its capabilities provided a solid foundation for verification of some types of treaties being considered.

COOPERATIVE THREAT REDUCTION

As the collapse of the Soviet Union appeared imminent in 1991, the United States and their NATO allies grew concerned of the risk of nuclear weapons held in the Soviet republics falling into enemy or terrorist hands. The Cooperative Threat Reduction (CTR) Program, better known as the Nunn–Lugar Act based on the Soviet Nuclear Threat Reduction Act of 1991, was cosponsored by Sens. Sam Nunn (D-GA) and Richard Lugar (R-IN). This Act, created in 1986 in a congressional meeting, had the purpose "to secure and dismantle weapons of mass destruction and their associated infrastructure in former Soviet Union states."

The program provided funding and expertise for states in the former Soviet Union (including Russia, Ukraine, Georgia, Azerbaijan, Belarus, Uzbekistan, and Kazakhstan) to decommission nuclear, biological, and chemical weapon stockpiles, as agreed by the Soviet Union under disarmament treaties. After the nuclear warheads were removed from their delivery vehicles by the post-Soviet successor militaries, Nunn-Lugar assistance provided equipment and supplies to destroy the missiles on which the warheads had been mounted, as well as the silos which had contained the missiles. The warheads themselves were then shipped to and destroyed in Russia, with the highly-enriched uranium contained within was made into commercial nuclear-reactor fuel; which was purchased by the United States under a separate program.

After the collapse of the Soviet Union, I recall making a number of visits to various laboratories and agencies in Russia in connection with a DOE program for all U.S. national laboratories to assist the former weapons-labs in converting their activities toward peaceful R&D, including border security.

Agreed Bilateral Arms-Control Verification. Although many strategic-arms limitations were topics of intense bilateral negotiations (some that resulted in strategic-arms treaties such as SALT and START), few of them actually ended up with detailed on-site inspection procedures, despite years of R&D directed for that specific purpose.

Once the politics of strategic weaponry no longer became a right-wing obsession (particularly in the United States during the Reagan years), it turned out to be a relatively straightforward process for government negotiators to agree to arms-control measures that no longer needed any form of on-site verification. In particular, that verification process emerged from what had become the very successful INF Treaty.

The Intermediate-Range Nuclear Forces (INF) Treaty was an arms-control agreement reached during the Cold War between the United States and the Soviet Union. President Ronald Reagan and General Secretary Mikhail Gorbachev signed it on 8 December 1987. The US Senate approved the treaty the next year, and it came in effect on 1 June 1988.

The INF Treaty banned all US and Soviet land-based ballistic missiles, cruise missiles, and missile launchers with ranges of 500–5,500 km (310–3,420 mi). The treaty did not apply to their respective air- or sea-launched missiles, nor to shorter- or longer-range missiles. Under the treaty, by May 1991, the two nations had together eliminated 2,692 missiles, followed by the agreed 10 years of on-site verification inspections.

According to terms of the original treaty, each party has had the right to withdraw with six months' notice "if it decides that extraordinary events related to the subject matter of this Treaty have jeopardized its supreme interests." President Donald Trump announced on 20 October 2018 that he was withdrawing the US from the treaty due to supposed Russian non-compliance. The US thereupon formally suspended its INF compliance on 1 February 2019, and Russia did so on the following day.

However, for practical purposes, the INF Treaty had by 1991 fully accomplished its stated objectives. After all, we had permanently withdrawn our intermediate-range missiles from Europe, yet we could still attack Russia with a great many nuclear warheads that were delivered from strategic submarines or aircraft.

Since then, growth of China's strategic-missile forces has also been put forth by President Trump as an (irrelevant) reason for US withdrawal from the INF Treaty.

Negotiations for an Open Skies Treaty. While I don't recall the specific arguments, any agreement to allow aircraft reconnaissance flights over nuclear facilities (particularly nuclear-weapons development laboratories in the Soviet Union and the United States) was anathema to weaponeers. Thus, an Open Skies treaty would have been widely opposed. However, very little of military interest could be ascertained by overflying any nuclear lab (or armed-force installation). I don't recall that our DOE interlab treaty-verification working committee came up with any substantive objection to an Open Skies treaty.

In November 1992, President Bush assigned responsibility for overall training, management, leadership, coordination and support for U.S. Open Skies observation missions to the On-Site Inspection Agency (now a part of the Defense Threat Reduction Agency). Until entry into force in January 2002, DTRA support for the treaty involved U.S. participation in training and in joint trial flights.

Since 1992, the U.S. has conducted over 70 JTFs. The United States successfully flew its first Open Skies mission over Russia in December 2002. By March 2003, DTRA had certified 16 camera configurations on observation aircraft. DTRA also had contributed to certification of Bulgarian, Hungarian, Romanian, Russian, and Ukrainian equipment for observation flights under the treaty.

With entry into force of the Open Skies treaty, formal observation flights began in August 2002. During the first treaty year, state parties conducted 67 observation flights. In 2004, state parties conducted 74 missions. In 2007, Russia conducted overflights of Canada under the Treaty.

Since 2002 a total of 40 missions have taken place over the UK, and 24 quota missions were conducted by Russia, Ukraine and Sweden. There were 16 training flights by aircraft flown by Benelux, Estonia; Georgia, Sweden, US, Latvia, Lithuania, Romania, Slovenia, and Yugoslavia. The UK has undertaken a total of 51 Open-Skies missions.

The Treaty on Open Skies entered into force on January 1, 2002, and currently has 35 ratifying states, including the United States and Russia and their allies. It established a program of unarmed aerial-surveillance flights over the entire territory of its participants. The treaty is designed to enhance mutual understanding and confidence by giving all participants, regardless of size, a direct role in gathering information about military forces and activities of concern to them. Open Skies is one of the most wide-ranging international efforts promoting openness and transparency of military forces and activities.

The concept of "mutual aerial observation" had been initially proposed in 1955 by President Dwight D. Eisenhower; however, the Soviets promptly rejected the concept and it lay dormant for several years. The treaty was eventually accepted as an initiative of U.S. president (and former CIA Director) George H. W. Bush in 1989. The agreement was signed in Helsinki, Finland, in March 1992, having been negotiated by the members of NATO and the Warsaw Pact.

A Russian Defense Ministry spokesman stated in 2016 that Turkey had refused a Russian Open Skies mission to fly over areas adjacent to war-torn Syria, as well as over NATO airbases throughout western Europe. According to Russia, Turkey gave no explanation regarding the limitations, and claimed that their own overflights indicated illegal Turkish military activity in Syrian territory.

Both Russia and the United States have alleged that the other is violating provisions of the treaty. U.S. Secretary of State Pompeo cited for example Russia's access refusal in the Russian-controlled areas of Georgia. In 2019, the U.S. and Canada were denied access to a military exercise in central Russia.

In October 2019, according to documents from the U.S. House of Representatives, President Trump is considering a U.S. withdrawal from the multilateral Open Skies Treaty. Opposing the move are NATO allies and partners, in particular Ukraine, fearing it would give an excuse for Russia to reduce further Open-Skies overflights or ban them altogether, thus decreasing Western/NATO knowledge of Russian military movements.

In April 2020, it was reported that Secretary of State Pompeo and Secretary of Defense Esper agreed to proceed with U.S. withdrawal from the Open Skies Treaty. On May 21, 2020, President Trump announced that the United States would be pulling back from the treaty due to the alleged Russian violations. Of course he could make that happen; however, the treaty is a formal international agreement that benefits the United States just as well. In other words, the United States would then no longer be able to conduct or participate in the treaty-authorized relatively low-altitude flights over Russia and other nations of interests. Technical improvements in satellite earth surveillance no doubt make the Open Skies Treaty of less importance for verification purposes, but their absence would remove one more instrument from the proverbial tool box, making the unilateral U.S. move rather self-defeating (and spiteful).

Meanwhile, the United States has set aside $35 billion for the 2021 national budget to "modernize" the nuclear arsenal and pour billions of dollars into weapons while not providing adequate medical supplies to hospitals that are now overloaded by corona-virus victims. Each year, over the past five years, funding for the Department of Defense increased as it is poised to again next year. Just a single year of funding for nuclear weapons could buy 300,000 intensive care unit (ICU) beds, 35,000 ventilators, and pay the salaries of 75,000 doctors. Imagine how many face masks alone this year's nuclear-weapons budget of $35 billion could buy!

An Unexploded World-War II Bomb. Vividly I recall one incident in Trento, Italy, on a visit there. Driving from Milano, enroute to a professional meeting in northern Italy, my rental car was detoured in Trento because a UXO had just been discovered during scheduled pre-construction excavations in the school yard. Ironically, I was on my way to attend a conference that included the topic of detecting buried explosives.

The UXO unearthed was visibly a huge aerial bomb probably dropped by the Allies when the retreating German army had occupied the northern Trentino province just before being driven out of Italy. Trento was on a main Alpine route for German troops to defend or escape on their way out of Italy. Even bombs as old as that could (and occasionally did) explode with devastating consequences.

Years later, as I approached retirement at Argonne National Laboratory, the development of technology to detect UXOs became one of my major professional interests, and it included some field work and a presentation at one of the Oxford Gordon Research conferences.

A recent (2020) appeal by physicists including Frank von Hippel and Steve Fetter, has brought attention to developments that have raised the risk of nuclear catastrophe, pointing to increased world stockpiles of nuclear weapons, a collapse of negotiations for mutual arms control, the lack of reduction in nuclear-armed nations, and the risks of cyber insecurity.

Briefcases. Any male resembling a professional toted a leather briefcase, soft-sided or hard-cased, carrying not only documents and books, but also pens, pencils and in my case a slide rule. Eventually I favored for distant travel an over-the-shoulder case, into which was stuffed an emergency change of underwear, toothbrush, shaver, deodorant, mouthwash, pills, notebooks, maps....

Business-mode traveling often required graphic slides or viewgraphs, plus hard copies of presentations and technical papers. Quite often one had to bring home study or work material. (Laptops and thumbdrives weren't around then.)

For lunch at work in the late 50s, I recall starting out with the traditional thermos box — later simply a brown bag, supplemented at the cafeteria with a drink, like low-cal Fresca (still a favorite of mine).

CHAPTER X:
DOMESTIC POLITICS AND ACTIVITIES

As a matter of course during the Cold War, international situations largely drove domestic politics. However, there were some prominent exceptions, with the "*Progressive* Case" being one such notable example. Partly because of my first-hand involvement in the Case, it is recounted here. One reason for giving renewed attention is that its practical and constitutional lessons seem to have been largely forgotten, but those lessons should have been invoked in recently dealing with published books that have annoyed President Trump.

THE "PROGRESSIVE CASE"

This legal dispute was a matter that expanded into a *cause celebre* largely because of inordinate action initiated by well-meaning East-Coast "do-gooders."

Despite Wikipedia rendering a factually correct and comprehensive account as far as it goes (reported under the title *United States v. Progressive, Inc.*), I've had to assemble here my own insider first-hand version of the events and personalities.

What became known as the Progressive Case had become a unique nationally publicized litigious digression full of sound and fury. It was a federal legal dispute in which four of us at Argonne unintendedly got drawn into for about two years. It even made the national news and got us in hot water with our employer and our funding agency.

Sort of like an "own goal," the U.S. government, through the Department of Energy, brought widespread national public attention to certain findings of a free-lance journalist seeking to write something for a small-scale university news magazine. Instead — because of inordinate DOE actions, spurred on by some misinformed and overly alarmist Ivy League professors — the legal case became a national *cause celebré* (Figure 82) in which me and my colleagues got involved.

The Progressive was a left-wing American monthly magazine of politics, culture and opinion then with a circulation of around 40,000. In 1978, its managing editor, Sam Day, Jr., a former editor of *The Bulletin of the Atomic Scientists*, and its editor, Erwin Knoll, commissioned freelance journalist Howard Morland to write an article on the secrecy surrounding nuclear weapons production in America

Figure 80. A lapel pin that could be worn during the "Progressive Case" in support of those like us from Argonne who objected to government suppression of publication.

The Progressive Case was and remains unique in the annals of U.S. jurisprudence. Taking renewed note of this case is one reason why I hope this book you are reading will be of interest to a wider circle than those merely passing time constructively during the Covid-19 pandemic.

Although not mentioned in the Wikipedia account, I turned out to be a key participant at the center of the dispute: first, as one of the those frequently contacted by the aspiring free-lance *Progressive* magazine author-to-be, Howard Morland. He had called me and others, asking many probing questions, one after another, cross-checking with other sources, including some at other national laboratories, particularly including physicists Ray Kidder and Hugh DeWitt at the Livermore national nuclear laboratory.

Because I had an official Argonne leadership role and applicable technical experience, Morland telephoned me often, probing for additional information. (I had previously published some relevant nuclear-arms-control-related articles and opinion pieces in the open literature.) He also phoned my Argonne colleagues George Stanford, Ted Postol, and Gerry Marsh (which thus made us the Argonne group of four). And I vaguely recall that he came by to visit us at the Laboratory.

By then I had authorized access to actual classified information regarding nuclear and thermonuclear weapons as part of my official role in arms-control-treaty verification technology. Moreover, in prior years as part of my regular job assignment I had often made (slide-rule and computer) calculations of nuclear critical assemblies in various configurations, small and large.

Of course, in communication with Morland (or anyone without appropriate security clearance and need-to-know) we had to skirt any disclosure or comment on classified information. However, it was often difficult to appreciate the fine line that DOE had drawn between some of the classified and unclassified categories. DOE held (and forever has held) that Congress had deemed certain nuclear weapons information to be "classified" forever: i.e., "Born Secret." That's ultimately what became litigated in the federal courts in what became known as "The Progressive Case." Congress has never changed the Born Secret notion about nuclear-weapon design, even though events of the time and since then make ineffective such prohibition on fundamental nuclear-physics information.

The current **worldwide Cold-War nuclear weapons inventory**: nearly 70,000 altogether, counting spares. Even now, long after the Cold War ended, the number of deployable nuclear weapons stockpiled by the nuclear-weapon states totals ~15,000 warheads. Detonating even the smallest of these nukes could cause significant radioactive damage and public havoc.

You see, there's a huge difference between what is taught and learned in textbooks about nuclear fission and fusion, compared to what type of security-classified technical details are involved in making multi-stage nuclear-explosive devices. Moreover, about 140,000 nuclear weapons were produced during the Cold Wars.

Morland, being free-lance (that is, not under contract to a specific publisher, and thus rather freewheeling in spirt), also phoned or visited various professors around the country and anyone else whose ear he could gain. One of those professors on the East Coast became rather alarmed that Morland might learn about the real workings of the H-bomb (thermonuclear weapons). Actually (and as later confirmed), much of the generalized theory of multi-stage thermonuclear weapons had already pretty well made it into the public literature, and what wasn't out there ironically became public knowledge as a result of the ensuing federal court litigation that became known as the *Progressive Case.*

Long-story, sort: The Department of Energy unwisely and counterproductively brought suit in federal court, attempting prior restraint of publication, despite protections of the First Amendment to the U.S. Constitution (see below).

The First Amendment to the U.S. Constitution forbids the federal government from making laws which regulate establishment or free exercise of religion — or abridge freedom of speech, freedom of the press, the right to peaceably assemble, or the right to petition the government for redress of grievances. It was adopted in 1791 as one of the ten amendments that constitute the Bill of Rights.

Initially, the First Amendment applied only to laws enacted by Congress, and many of its provisions were interpreted more narrowly than they are today. Beginning 1925, the Supreme Court applied the First Amendment to States through the Due Process Clause of the Fourteenth Amendment.

In 1947 the U.S. Supreme Court drew on Thomas Jefferson's correspondence to call for "a wall of separation between church and State," though the precise boundary of this separation remains in dispute. Speech rights were expanded significantly in a series of 20th and 21st century court decisions which protected various forms of political speech, anonymous speech, campaign financing, pornography, and school speech; these rulings defined a series of exceptions to First Amendment protections. The Supreme Court also overturned English common law precedent in order to increase the burden of proof for defamation and libel suits, most notably in *New York Times Co. v. Sullivan* (1964). Commercial speech, however, is less protected by the First Amendment than political speech, and is therefore subject to greater regulation.

The free-press clause protects publication of information and opinions, and applies to a wide variety of media. In *Near v. Minnesota* (1931) and *New York Times v. United States* (1971), the Supreme Court ruled that the First Amendment protected against prior restraint — pre-publication censorship — in almost all cases.

It is a common misconception that the First Amendment prohibits *anyone* including private, non-governmental entities, from limiting free speech, but it actually only restrains federal-government-sanctioned officials.

Front covers of two books that emerged because of the ill-advised intervention by the U.S government, one by Morland and another coauthored by those of us ("the gang of four") at Argonne are depicted in Figures 81 on this page and 82 on the next page.

Another outcome is that societal involvement "of course" never did any favors for my professional career at Argonne. How could it? After all, higher management (from my Division Manager going all the way up through the Lab Director and into the University of Chicago) always cringed at every bit of attention I received either publically or officially. DOE bureaucracy at the Argonne National Laboratory site was never sympathetic or helpful, and DOE Headquarters in Washington was aghast, notably maintaining a *dossier* on me, keeping track of the number of transgressions.

While four of us here at Argonne were usually involved (and two more like-minded "troublemakers" at Los Alamos), I was the principal face of effrontery against the federal government and especially our funding agency, DOE. However, our two-year unexpected and awkward moment of fame dissipated quickly.

Figure 81. November 1979 cover of *The Progressive* magazine once the federal injunction was overturned.

Figure 82. Cover of our coauthored book, *Born Secret*, published June 1981.

Mind you, I'm not complaining — just setting the record straight, because it appears (from the Wikipedia) account about the *Progressive Case* to be in need of rectification.

LIVING UNDER THE NUCLEAR UMBRELLA

How did it feel being dependent on mutual destruction for the survival of you, your colleagues, your family, your neighbors, everything around you? In particular, were you any more secure when your federal government got adventuresome in the name of "national security"? From the very beginning of the Cold War, some scientists more knowledgeable than others about the common danger of nuclear weapons spoke out against nuclear armaments and proliferation and spoke in favor of some joint peaceful worldwide control.

By the time I became sufficiently aware of the dangerous consequences of nuclear war, limited or widescale, in defense or offense, there were so many nuclear weapons poised at each other and at their host populations that human survival was endangered. Certainly our comfort zone was imperiled. I was particularly and strongly influenced by technical colleagues who came from development of the atomic bomb intended to put a stop to World War II. After the wartime nuclear bombing of Japan, many having moved on to laboratories for peaceful nuclear development, saw the impending risk in worldwide proliferation of nuclear weapons.

At several point in time, just as part of my ordinary job assignment, I had occasion to visit some of our nuclear-weapons depots, where we had hundred of nuclear warheads stored. It was a life-changing experience, not just a moment of awe, that few have witnessed. We had as a nation funded and supported the development of nuclear weapons of all sizes, explosive yields, flavors, and devastation.

As the baton was passed on to my younger generation of nuclear scientists, we had to accept active responsibility for controlling the nuclear risk. That gave rise gradually to national and worldwide groups of non-military scientists and engineers who — partly because of their heightened knowledge of the risks — organized and spoke out in favor of nuclear-weapons limitations.

Here are tiles of the primary chapters in my book *Cold War Nuclear Challenges*: *Technical Controversies, Civil Disobedience, Government Infringements,*

Chapter 1: Cold War Convulsions
Chapter 2: Domestic Turmoil
Chapter 3: Public Anxiety
Chapter 4: Cold War Establishment
Chapter 5: Nuclear Controversy
Chapter 6: Government Control, Public Protest
Chapter 7: Government Oversight and Bureaucracies
Chapter 8: 21st Century Secrecy and Privacy
Chapter 9: Outlook for Democracy and Civilization

And here below are the contents of a preceding, more comprehensive Volume (first published 2017, revised and updated 2019-20):

Cold War Brinkmanship (Nuclear Arms, Civil Rights, Government Secrecy)
Preface

Chapter 1: Domestic Cold War Controversies
Chapter 2: International-Security Issues
Chapter 3: *Pro-Publico* (In the Public Interest)
Chapter 4: Ionizing Radiation
Chapter 5: Political and Nuclear Legacies
Chapter 6: Technical Challenges
Chapter 7: Autobiographical Supplement
Chapter 8: Documentation

JOHN BOLTON AND SECURITY-CLASSIFICATION INFORMATION

An ongoing brouhaha (this year, 2020) about Trump administration's Justice Department attempting to block a book being published by John Bolton brings me mixed considerations and emotions. I bring this up in conjunction with the "Progressive" Case, not to defend or impugn Bolton's long-standing right-wing views, but rather to highlight the irony of Bolton having to rely on the same constitutional protections reinforced when we went to Federal Court more than 40 years ago in that Case.

As described earlier, the full weight of the U.S. government was brought against *The Progressive* magazine in what turned out to be a failed attempt from 1978-79 at Executive Branch prior restraint of publication.

Who's John Bolton? He's a perennial hard-line right-winger Republican and Washington insider. For a year and a half he had been designated by President Trump as National Security Advisor, a position that does not require Senate confirmation.

Bolton has held government offices during the presidencies of Ronald Reagan and subsequent Bush administrations. Under President George W. Bush, Bolton was U.S. Ambassador to the United Nations from August 2005 to December 2006, but he resigned at the end of his recess appointment because he was unlikely to win congressional confirmation when the Democratic Party gained control.

Bolton is a former senior fellow at the American Enterprise Institute and has been a frequent Fox News Channel commentator since 2012. He was once a foreign-policy adviser to presidential candidate Mitt Romney. Bolton has been involved with numerous conservative groups, including being organization Chairman of the anti-Muslim Gatestone Institute and Director of the Project for the New American Century, which then favored going to war against Iraq.

Bolton is a foreign-policy hawk and has been an advocate for regime change in Iran, Syria, Libya, Venezuela, Cuba, Yemen, and North Korea. He has also repeatedly called for the termination of the Iran nuclear deal. Having been an advocate of the Iraq War, he supported the decision to invade. He has continuously supported military action and regime change in Syria, Libya, and Iran. A registered Republican, his political views have been described as conservative and American nationalist.

The **Iraq War** was a protracted armed conflict that began in 2003 with the invasion of Iraq by a U.S.-led coalition that overthrew the government of Saddam Hussein. The conflict continued for much of the next decade as an insurgency emerged to oppose the occupying forces and the post-invasion Iraqi government. An estimated 150,000 to 1,000,000 Iraqis were killed in the first three to four years of conflict. US troops were officially withdrawn in 2011. However, following the spread of the Syrian Civil War and the territorial gains of the Islamic State of Iraq and the Levant (ISIL), the Obama administration decided to redeploy US forces to Iraq in 2014. Many soldiers were employed by defense contractors and private military companies. The U.S. became re-involved in 2014 as the head of a new coalition.

The insurgency and some dimensions of the civil conflict continue. The Iraq invasion had occurred as part of the George W. Bush administration's War on Terror, following the September 11 attacks.

In 2002, Congress had authorized President Bush to use military force against Iraq should he choose The Iraq War began on 20 March 2003, when the U.S., joined by the U.K. and several coalition allies, launched a "shock and awe" bombing campaign. Iraqi forces were quickly overwhelmed as coalition forces swept through the country. The invasion led to the collapse of the Iraqi government; Saddam Hussein was captured in December of that same year and executed three years later. The power vacuum following Saddam's demise and the mismanagement of the Coalition Provisional Authority led to widespread civil war between Shias and Sunnis, as well as a lengthy insurgency against coalition forces. Many of the violent insurgent groups were supported by Iran and al-Qaeda in Iraq. The United States responded with a build-up of 170,000 troops in 2007. This build-up gave greater control to Iraq's government and military, and was judged a success by many. Under President Barack Obama, the winding down of U.S. involvement in Iraq accelerated and the U.S. formally withdrew all combat troops from Iraq by December 2011.

The Bush administration based its rationale for the Iraq War principally on the assertion that Iraq, which had been viewed by the U.S. as a "rogue state" since the 1990–1991 Gulf War, supposedly possessed an active weapons-of-mass-destruction (WMD) program, and that the Iraqi government posed a threat to the United States and its coalition allies. Some U.S. officials falsely accused Saddam of harboring and supporting al-Qaeda, while others cited the desire to end a repressive dictatorship and bring democracy to the people of Iraq. In 2004, the 9/11 Commission was unable to find evidence of an operational relationship between the Saddam Hussein regime and al-Qaeda. No stockpiles of WMDs or an active WMD program were ever identified in Iraq. Bush-administration officials made numerous assertions about a purported Saddam/al-Qaeda relationship and WMDs that were based on sketchy evidence, and that intelligence officials rejected. The rationale of U.S. pre-war intelligence faced heavy criticism both domestically and internationally.

A British inquiry into its decision to go to war, was published in 2016 and concluded military action may have been necessary but was not the last resort at the time and that the consequences of invasion were underestimated.

When interrogated by the FBI, Saddam Hussein admitted to having kept up the appearance of possessing weapons of mass destruction in order to appear strong in front of Iran. He also confirmed that Iraq did not have weapons of mass destruction prior to the U.S. invasion.

In the summer of 2014, ISIL launched a military offensive in northern Iraq and declared a worldwide Islamic caliphate, leading to Operation Inherent Resolve, another military response from the United States and its allies.

The Iraq War caused at least 100,000 civilian deaths, as well as tens of thousands of military deaths. The majority of deaths occurred as a result of the insurgency and civil conflicts between 2004 and 2007. Subsequently, the 2014–2017 War in Iraq, which is considered a domino effect of the invasion, caused at least 67,000 civilian deaths, in addition to the displacement of 5 million people within the country.

Bolton's memoirs, titled *The Room Where It Happened: A White House Memoir*, were published in June 2020. President Trump was upset and attempted to have the US Attorney General prevent publication. But federal-court-approved censorship would be unlikely, inasmuch as the *Progressive* Case rendered pre-publication restraint to be judicially doomed to frustration by the courts.

According to the *New York Times*, President Trump pushed out Bolton, his third national security adviser,

> amid fundamental disputes over how to handle major foreign policy challenges like Iran, North Korea and most recently Afghanistan.
>
> The departure ended a 17-month partnership that had grown so tense that the two men even disagreed over how they parted ways, as Mr. Trump announced on Twitter that he had fired the adviser only to be rebutted by Mr. Bolton, who insisted he had resigned of his own accord.
>
> A longtime Republican hawk known for a combative style, Mr. Bolton spent much of his tenure trying to restrain the

> president from making what he considered unwise agreements with America's enemies. Mr. Trump bristled at what he viewed as Mr. Bolton's militant approach, to the point that he made barbed jokes in meetings about his adviser's desire to get the United States into more wars.
>
> Their differences came to a climax in recent days as Mr. Bolton waged a last-minute campaign to stop the president from signing a peace agreement at Camp David with leaders of the radical Taliban group. He won the policy battle as Mr. Trump scrapped the deal but lost the larger war when the president grew angry about the way the matter played out.

Frankly, Bolton's historically chronic truculence was well known to Cold War activists such as me. Some of his many anachronistic allegiances and positions are recalled below. First, for background, the history of the Committee on the Present Danger should be recalled, although there is no indication that Bolton was a member.

Committee on the Present Danger. The Committee on the Present Danger (CPD) was a hawkish "advocacy organization" first founded in 1950 and re-formed in 1976 to push for larger U.S. defense budgets and arms buildups, in order to counter the Soviet Union. In 2004, The third incarnation of CPD was being planned, to address the War on terrorism. The CPD saw a parallel between the Soviet threat and the threat from terrorism.

Members of the 2004 CPD included Senator Joseph I. Lieberman, former CIA director R. James Woolsey, Jr., and Reagan administration official and Committee founder Max M. Kampelman. Other notable members listed on the CPD website included associates of the American Enterprise Institute, Heritage Foundation, American Israel Public Affairs Committee and the Boeing Company.

One day after the launch of the 2004 CPD, managing director Peter Hannaford resigned because it was reported that Hannaford, while working for his PR firm, had lobbied on behalf of Austria's Freedom Party, which is headed by right-wing nationalist Joerg Haider. Haider had been quoted as commending the "orderly employment policy" of the Nazi Third Reich government and paid a "solidarity visit" to Iraq dictator Saddam Hussein in 2002. Some CPD members defended Hannaford.

The CPD had been originally formed by top eastern-establishment luminaries. It was designed as a 'citizen's lobby' to alert the nation to the Soviet 'present danger,' and the resultant need to adopt the NSC-68 agenda in order to survive. NSC-68 was a top secret National Security Council document written by Paul Nitze promoting a huge military build-up for the purpose of rolling back communist influence and attaining and maintaining U.S. military supremacy in the world. In 1951 the CPD launched a three-month scare campaign over the NBC network. Sunday nights thereafter the group used the Mutual Broadcasting System to talk to the nation about the 'present danger' and the need to take action. Partly as a result of efforts such as these both in and out of government, the recommendations of NSC-68 were adopted. President Harry S. Truman promoted a policy of containment militarism, and the military budget escalated even more than the targeted factor of three times. Thus, the Cold War and an era of interventionist policies became a political reality in the United States.

The post-Vietnam era, however, saw the re-emergence in the American public of anti-interventionist sentiment. In Congress, new policies of detente and arms control reflected a more conciliatory attitude toward East-West relations. Such trends were anathema to the CPD's bipolar view of the world. Led once again by Eugene V. Rostow and Nitze, members of the CPD regrouped for action.

Revitalization in 1976 of the CPD grew out of an independent group called Team B authorized by President Gerald R. Ford and organized by then-CIA chief, George Herbert Walker Bush. The purpose of Team B was to develop an independent judgment of Soviet capabilities and intentions. Team B was headed by Richard Pipes and included Paul Nitze, Foy Kohler, William Van Cleave, Lt. Gen. Daniel O. Graham (ret.), Thomas Wolf of RAND Corporation and Gen. John Vogt, Jr. (ret.). Also a part of Team B were five officials then active in government: Maj. Gen. George Keegan, Brig. Gen. Jasper Welch, Paul Wolfowitz of the Arms Control and Disarmament Agency, and Seymour Weiss of the State Department.

The political base for CPD II was in the Coalition for a Democratic Majority (CDM), a group formed in 1972 by the hard-line, anti-Soviet wing of the Senate, led by the hawkish Sen. Henry M. Scoop Jackson. These "conservative" Democrats contended that communism was a great evil and that the U.S. had a moral obligation to eradicate it and foster democracy throughout the world. The 193 individual members of the revitalized CPD comprised a who's who of the Democratic Party establishment and a cross-section of Republican leadership. Eventually, 13 of the 18 members of the Foreign Policy Task Force of the CDM, lead by Eugene Rostow, joined the CPD. Notable among them were Jeane Kirkpatrick, Leon Keyserling, Max Kampelman, Richard Shifter, and John Roche.

The CPD and its cohorts became dominant with the election of Ronald Reagan. Thirty-three members of CPD received appointments in Reagan's first administration, more than twenty of them in national security posts. They included Kenneth Adelman, James Buckley, Max Kampelman, Kirkpatrick, Paul Nitze, Richard Pipes, Rostow, and George Shultz. In 1979, Reagan was initiated into the ranks of the CPD as a member of its executive committee. Dean Rusk, former Secretary of State was on the original board. Most of the super-hawks that populated Reagan's cabinet were culled from the CPD.

The Committee was organized by fanatically anti-communist neo-conservatives with little patience for the give-and-take of Richard M. Nixon/Jimmy Carter diplomacy.

Once viewed as extremists with minimal influence on policy debates, Reagan's victory brought the Committee to the center of power, the reigns of policy delivered into its lap. The arms-control process was hijacked, beheaded and left to rot besides the discarded corpse of détente.

Once in power, these right-wingers geared American policy toward forcing the Soviets to accept US strategic superiority. Outraged by Soviet nuclear parity enshrined in the ABM accord of 1972, the right-wingers sought to move beyond the stabilizing strictures of Mutual Assured Destruction into a world of first-strikes and laser defenses. In a series of extremely destabilizing public statements, they described nukes as effective offensive weapons, trying to make them sound ordinary and trying to make nuclear war appear not as inconsequential as conventional warfare. Such naivete brought out strong counter-reactions from those of us at Argonne who knew better.

Along with Harvard Professor Richard Pipes, who espoused a strong anti-communist point of view throughout his career at the university, Perle was the most vocal proponent of 'winnable nuclear war' in Reagan's first Administration.

Sovietology refers to the study of politics and policies of the USSR and former communist states generally, while **Kremlinology** was more like the Western-nation (NATO) study and analysis of the Soviet Union.

At Argonne, our employee-activist organization, the CAS, frequently took issue with these CPD hawks (which is one reason why many pages are devoted within this book in connection with hoopla over the political appointment and memoirs of John Bolton). As mentioned, I was a perennial chairperson of the CAS and a critic of hawkish views on nuclear-weapons policy.

John Bolton Returns from Obscurity

In a current-events internecine political struggle which could be best described as "they deserve each other," President Trump has been resorting to revilement against his former national-security advisor, John Bolton. That appears to be because Bolton wrote what was apparently a tell-all book *The Room Where It Happened: A White House Memoir* (2020) about his year and a half with the Trump Executive Office team. The falling out is somewhat amusing because of it's a clash between like-minded ideologues. And the public dispute inadvertently propelled sales into a best-seller.

Bolton, a right-winger's right-winger, has held opinions so controversial that they sometimes shocked his supporters. A hawkish regular on Fox News, he once advocated for war with North Korea, for U.S. invasion of Iraq, for aggressive postures toward Iran, and has been a perennial critic of multilateral institutions, international agreements, and free trade. Bolton had become one of the biggest anti-Iran hawks in the Trump administration. Here are some examples of his policy positions:

Bolton Has Called for an "End" to North Korea, Arguing for a Preventive First Strike

Like Trump, Bolton believes the nuclear deal that China, France, Germany, Russia, the United Kingdom, the United States, and the European Union signed with Iran is a sham that does little to curb Tehran's activities. But it his views about North Korea that have caused an internecine squabble.

Bolton had also been a political appointee in the Reagan and G. H.W. Bush administrations. He served at the U.S. Justice Department, the U.S. State Department, and the U.S. Agency for International Development in a variety of positions. His hawkish views on foreign policy won him many admirers (as well as critics), and he remained a polarizing figure during the presidency of George W. Bush.

As one knowledgeable critic noted: It is that sort of steadfastness in views — or, depending on your perspective, unapologetic hawkishness — that apparently impressed President Trump, a critic of the war in Iraq. Bolton has been a regular on Fox News, where he promoted aggressive postures toward North Korea and Iran. Bolton has even called for an "end" to North Korea and argued in *The Wall Street Journal* for a preventive first strike against the (well-entrenched and now well-defended) regime of Kim Jong Un.

Bolton, like Trump, is also a critic of multilateral institutions, international agreements, and free trade, and an advocate for a foreign policy based on what he sees as exclusively American interests. Regarding the war in Iraq, Bolton has maintained that deposing Saddam was worth the effort — even if the decisions made after the invasion weren't always right.

Bolton Tried to Upend the INF and New START Treaties

Bolton recently attempted to put a knife into Ronald Reagan's landmark INF Treaty which in 1987 broke the back of the nuclear arms race. Under the Treaty, it was the first time that the United States and the Soviet Union agreed to destroy, not just limit, nuclear weapons. Together, both sides eliminated nearly 2700 perfectly good nuclear weapons for which billions of dollars and many years had been spent. The INF Treaty consummated the process of massive Cold War nuclear arms reductions.

So now, could it have been Bolton who inspired President Trump to rail against extension of the INF Treaty? In October Trump suddenly announced he wanted to "terminate" the 1987 Treaty with the Soviet Union, even though the Treaty had long ago in effect ended after destruction of INF weapons. Such posturing raises concerns more about potential return of Cold War-style tensions over U.S. and Russian deployments of intermediate-range missiles in Europe and elsewhere and about the future of the 2010 New Strategic Arms Reduction Treaty (New START). While the INF weapons destruction cannot be undone, new weapons of long- and medium-range could always be fielded.

Bolton Trying to Let the New START Treaty Expire

On February 5, 2021, the New START treaty will expire on its own, unless the United States and Russia act to extend that last nuclear arms-control agreement for an additional five years.

No matter your political orientation, favoring a New START treaty extension should be a no-brainer — for a number of reasons. It keeps nuclear arsenals of both superpowers in check. If the treaty expires, there would be no constraints on US or Russian strategic arsenals for the first time since 1972. Its expiration would remove caps on how many strategic nuclear missiles and bombers the two sides can own and how many warheads that are carried on them. Russia could quickly upload about a thousand new warheads onto its deployed missile arsenal — without adding a single new missile; and the United States could upload even more because it still has more missiles and bombers than Russia.

At a time when NATO-Russian relations are at their lowest since the end of the Cold War, long-term strategic predictability is more important than in the past three decades. Allowing New START constraints to expire is obviously not in the US strategic interest or that of its allies. Very simply, New START is a good deal for both the United States and Russia; it cannot be allowed to expire without replacing it with something better.

The FAS has compiled several reasons for extending the strategic treaty. New START force level is the basis for current nuclear infrastructure plans. Both the United States and Russia have funded their nuclear weapons and industry modernization plans on the assumption that the New START force level will continue, or at least not increase. If New START falls away, those assumptions and modernization plans will have to be revised, resulting in significant additional costs that neither Russia nor the United States can afford.

New START offers transparency and predictability in an unstable world. Under the current treaty, the United States receives a notification every time a Russian missile is deployed, every time a missile or bomber moves between bases, and every time a new missile is produced. Without these notifications, the United States would have to spend more money and incur significant risks to get the exact same information through National Technical Means (i.e. satellites and other forms of site monitoring). Russia benefits in the same way.

New START has forced Russia and the United States to reduce deployed strategic nuclear forces. Why would we willingly give all that up, getting nothing in return (and actually paying a steep price for giving it up)?

In its collections of arguments in favor of New START, the Federation of American Scientists claims overwhelming bipartisan support — even among Trump voters. Not only is its extension a foreign policy priority for Democrats, but polling data has indicated that approximately 70% of Trump voters across the country are in favor of extending New START.

Trump's decision followed a years-long U.S.-Russian dispute about whether Moscow has developed and deployed a prohibited missile, and comes amid fears expressed by some government officials and defense policy experts that China, which is not a party to the INF Treaty, is gaining a military advantage in East Asia by deploying large numbers of treaty-noncompliant missiles. Hardly anyone with knowledge of this military history and strategy give the Trump viewpoint much credibility.

Because North Korea has demonstrated a potential capability to deliver nuclear-warheads against the continental United States, Bolton argued that "striking first" to eliminate the "imminent threat" from North Korea qualifies as "self-defense" and "is perfectly legitimate."

Bolton not-so-long-ago advocated pre-emptive strikes against North Korea and Iran. In March 2018, he suggested that South Korea invade North Korea and terminate the North Korean regime as the only "diplomatic option," and said that a pending war between the two countries is their problem and not a U.S. problem. Although Bolton was a supporter of the Vietnam War, he avoided combat through a student deferment followed by enlistment in the Maryland Air National Guard.

Bolton on First Invasions of Iraq

The British weekly on-line journal, *The Economist,* has called Bolton "the most controversial ambassador ever sent by America to the United Nations."

Bolton is regarded to have been an "architect" of the Iraq War. Following the first (1990) Gulf War, Bolton advocated for another U.S. invasion of Iraq calling on President Clinton to oust Saddam Hussein. Later, as under secretary of state for arms control, during President George W. Bush's first term in office (2001 to 2005), he told BBC that the U.S. was "confident that Saddam Hussein has hidden weapons of mass destruction and production facilities in Iraq."

The evidence used to go to war in 2003 has long been deemed mistaken or even contrived, and some of the war's most ardent supporters have expressed second thoughts since then, given the immense cost of human life and the resulting long-lasting degree of regional destabilization that occurred.

Other Bolton Political Positions

During his tenure under President G. W. Bush, Bolton was instrumental in derailing a 2001 biological weapons conference in Geneva convened to endorse a UN proposal to enforce the 1972 Biological Weapons Convention. He argued that the plan would have jeopardized U.S. national security by allowing spot inspections of suspected U.S. weapons sites.

From 2013 until March 2018, Bolton was chairman of the far-right anti-Muslim Gatestone Institute, which is prominent for disseminating false anti-immigrant and anti-Muslim information. From 1997 to 2001 Bolton was senior vice president of the American Enterprise Institute, a conservative think tank.

He also pushed for reduced funding for the Nunn–Lugar Cooperative Threat Reduction program to halt the proliferation of nuclear materials.

Bolton has often been accused of attempting to pressure the intelligence community to endorse his views. According to former coworkers, Bolton withheld information that ran counter to his goals from Secretary of State Colin Powell on multiple occasions, and from Powell's successor Condoleezza Rice on at least one occasion.

Bolton and President Trump

It is that sort of steadfastness in views — or, depending on your perspective, unapologetic hawkishness — that apparently impressed President Trump, a critic of the war in Iraq. Bolton was a regular on Fox News, where he called for aggressive postures toward North Korea and Iran. Bolton, like Trump, is also a critic of multilateral institutions, international agreements, and free trade, and an advocate for a foreign policy based on what he sees as exclusively American interests.

Like Trump, he believes the nuclear deal China, France, Germany, Russia, the United Kingdom, the United States, and the European Union signed with Iran is a sham that does little to curb Tehran's activities. His appointment increase the likelihood the president would withdraw from the agreement, as he did.

Trump had long wanted to name Bolton to a top Cabinet position, but in addition to the fact he would likely have faced strong opposition in the Senate, Susan Rice and other Republican *éminences grises* advised Trump against it. Yet, a little more than a year after he entered the White House, Trump went his own way, announcing that Bolton would replace H.R. McMaster to become the president's third national-security adviser. The position doesn't require Senate confirmation — a point that was also apparently relevant to Trump's appointment of his first national-security adviser, Michael Flynn, also controversial pick at the time and who has since pled guilty to lying to the FBI. Bolton, meanwhile, had the president's ear while on Fox News.

Having served in government as a political appointee in the Reagan and George H.W. Bush administrations, Bolton has also held a variety of positions at the U.S. Justice Department, the U.S. State Department, and the U.S. Agency for International Development. His hawkish views on foreign policy had won him many admirers (as well as critics). He remained a polarizing figure during the presidency of George W. Bush. Bolton was named, at Vice President Dick Cheney's insistence, as undersecretary of state for arms control in Colin Powell's State Department. There, he made the case for the U.S. withdrawal from the ABM treaty with Russia, but later helped negotiate a pact with Russia that saw both countries commit to large reductions in their nuclear-weapons stockpiles. During this time in office, he did not win many admirers among U.S. allies — UK officials, in particular, seeing him as an obstacle to negotiations involving difficult countries like Iran and Libya, and persuading Bush to keep Bolton off the negotiating teams.

Bolton — in his 2008 memoir, *Surrender Is Not an Option: Defending America at the United Nations* (Simon and Schuster, 512 pp) — made clear what he thought about the State Department:

> State careerists are schooled in accommodation and compromise with foreigners, rather than aggressive advocacy of U.S. interests, which might inconveniently disrupt the serenity of diplomatic exchanges, not to mention dinner parties and receptions.

He has creatively labeled the department's East Asian and Pacific Affairs Bureau (which works on issues including North Korea and China), the "EAPeasers." But such "State careerists" could be similarly skeptical of him.

Christopher Hill, a diplomat of long standing who conducted negotiations with the North Koreans during the Clinton administration, characterized President Trump's appointment of Bolton as a "major promotion." Hill noted that Bolton had "never had this level of responsibility before. [He was] always a kind of in-house free electron, amusing but not particularly consequential. All that changes now," said Hill.

That's an interesting and belittling analogy. An electron, in the science of physics, is a nuclear particle much less weighty than any others, such as neutrons or atoms.

During her time in office, Condoleezza Rice, who succeeded Powell as U.S. secretary of state, resisted the White House's efforts to make Bolton her deputy. Instead, Bolton was appointed as U.S. ambassador to the UN, a position for which he never achieved confirmation by the U.S. Senate..

Bolton — Longtime Critic of UN

Bolton has been a strong critic of the United Nations for much of his career. His opposition to the UN was rooted in a disdain for international organizations, who he believed infringed on the sovereignty of the United States. He also opposed the International Criminal Court.

In 1994, he famously said "The (UN) Secretariat building in New York has 38 stories. If it lost 10 stories, it wouldn't make a bit of difference." When U.S. senators asked Bolton what he meant by those remarks, he said he was making the case for a leaner bureaucracy in an organization notorious for its red tape. But comments like that, along with his other views, ensured that Bolton could never win over the Senate Foreign Relations Committee. President Bush named him to the UN post as a recess appointment, and he served in that position for about a year before stepping down.

Although Bolton's blunt assessments of U.S. allies and adversaries alike, as well as his brusque manner, has won him admirers, his conduct with colleagues has been criticized. Subordinates complained about abrasive behavior. During Bolton's nomination hearing for the UN job, Carl Ford, an intelligence official and assistant secretary of state, as well as a self-described conservative Republican, testified that Bolton bullied an intelligence analyst over evidence about Cuba's suspected weapons programs, prompting an intervention from Powell. At the time Ford said that Bolton is a "kiss-up, kick-down sort of guy" who "abuses his authority with little people.".

Former president George W. Bush later appeared to regret his choice of Bolton, reportedly saying he didn't "consider Bolton credible." Those remarks, made in the final days of Bush's administration, came after Bolton wrote a column in the Wall Street Journal, criticizing the Bush administration: "Nothing can erase the ineffable sadness of an American presidency, like this one, in total intellectual collapse."

The GOP's Trump-reelection-campaign effort to deflect criticism toward his Democrat opponent by labeling him as 'Beijing Biden' is undermined by Trump's former national security advisor, John Bolton. According to Bolton, "President Trump asked Chinese President Xi Jinping to help him win the 2020 U.S. election." That was the lead sentence of the *Washington Post*'s write-up of John Bolton's new tell-all book about his year-and-a-half as the Trump's national-security adviser. Now, Bolton alleges in his new book that President Trump indeed deliberately withheld Ukraine aid for political favors and straightforwardly asked the Chinese president to help him win 2020 presidential race. No wonder President Trump is fuming at Bolton! Moreover, Bolton has described Trump as "erratic" and "stunningly uninformed."

Bolton in Contemporary Times

Although it's philosophically difficult to feel sorry for John Bolton, my personal experience would have to consider him (not his political postures) sympathetically. But he's still a strident right-winger, hoping to move or keep American foreign policies further to the right, with little concern for domestic issues such as employment, health care, or civil rights.

And, having myself undergone and fought government efforts to suppress publication, I'd have to extend his him in his situation some sympathy, for what it's worth. His struggle to get his book published is likely to be time-consuming and costly.

Lest it seem that Bolton dominated my public-interest agenda at Argonne, read on. Following here are some of the many issues that I got involved in, all without looking for trouble (!). After all, activism did nothing for my professional work and potential promotion at Argonne. In fact, I was never elevated to the most Senior salaried employee status at the Laboratory. You'll see in the next subsection of this book why management often took a dim view of my self-appointed unofficial activities, mostly as head of the CAS.

As for Bolton's book, the recent attention by Trump has boosted sales, supposedly bringing in at least $2M.

ANOTHER DECADE OF MY ACTIVISM

Because of President Trump's short-lived appointment of John Bolton, we've detoured in recapping my professional career and activist involvement, and thus my qualifications to be a critic.

During the time frame between the 19879/80 Progressive Case and my ANL retirement in the year 2000, I continued to be engaged in civic activism for nearly another decade.

As a framework for explanation of my activism, consider the U.S. presidential sequence, time-ordered below during my involuntary vigil:

Kennedy — Johnson — Nixon — Ford — Carter — Reagan — GHW Bush — Clinton — GW Bush — Obama — Trump

John Fitzgerald Kennedy (JFK), a Democrat, served as the 35th president of the United States from January 1961 until his assassination in November 1963. His overwhelming challenge was the Cuban Crisis, in which he barely managed to keep the U.S. and USSR from escalating to nuclear blows, as discussed and critiqued in detail elsewhere in this book.

Lyndon Baines Johnson, often referred to by his initials LBJ, assumed the presidency following the assassination of President John F. Kennedy. Johnson served as the 36th president of the United States from 1963 to 1969, and previously as 37th vice president from 1961 to 1963..A Democrat from Texas, Johnson also served as a United States Representative and as the Majority Leader in the United States Senate. As Majority Leader, Johnson shepherded to passage the Civil Rights Acts of 1957 and 1960; the first civil rights bills passed by the U.S. Congress since the Reconstruction Era (1863–1877).

Johnson ran for the Democratic nomination in the 1960 presidential election. Although unsuccessful, he accepted the invitation of then-Senator John F. Kennedy of Massachusetts to be his running mate. They went on to win a close election over the Republican ticket of Richard Nixon and Henry Cabot Lodge Jr. On November 22, 1963, Kennedy was assassinated and Johnson succeeded him as president. The following year, Johnson won in a landslide, defeating Senator Barry Goldwater of Arizona.

In domestic policy, Johnson designed the "Great Society" legislation to expand civil rights, public broadcasting, Medicare, Medicaid, aid to education, the arts, urban and rural development, public services and his "War on Poverty.". Assisted in part by a growing economy, millions of Americans rise above the poverty line during his administration. Civil rights bills that he signed into law banned racial discrimination in public facilities, interstate commerce, the workplace and housing.

The Voting Rights Act prohibited certain requirements in southern states used to disenfranchise African Americans. With the passage of the Immigration and Nationality Act of 1965, the country's immigration system was reformed, encouraging greater immigration from regions other than Europe. Johnson's presidency marked the peak of modern liberalism after the New Deal era.

In foreign policy, however, Johnson escalated American involvement in the Vietnam War. In 1964, Congress passed the Gulf of Tonkin Resolution, which granted Johnson the power to use military force in Southeast Asia without having to ask for an official declaration of war. The number of American military personnel in Vietnam increased dramatically, from 16,000 advisors in non-combat roles in 1963 to 525,000 in 1967, many in combat roles. American casualties soared and the peace process stagnated. Growing unease with the war stimulated a large, angry anti-war movement based chiefly among draft-age students on university campuses.

Johnson faced further troubles when summer riots about the War in Vietnam began in major cities in 1965 and crime rates soared, as his opponents raised demands for "law and order" policies. While Johnson began his presidency with widespread approval, support for him declined as the public became frustrated with both the war and the growing violence at home. In 1968, the Democratic Party factionalized as anti-war elements denounced Johnson, and he ended his bid for renomination after a disappointing finish in the New Hampshire primary. Nixon was elected to succeed him, as the New Deal coalition that had dominated presidential politics for 36 years collapsed.

Johnson is ranked favorably by many historians because of his benevolent domestic policies and the passage of many major laws that affected civil rights, gun control, wilderness preservation, and Social Security, although he also drew substantial criticism for his escalation of the Vietnam War.

Johnson's successor, President Richard Nixon (1969-1974), a Republican, had to resign because he faced impeachment proceedings for his involvement in the Watergate scandal. In 1973, President Nixon appointed Gerald Ford to replace Spiro Agnew, who had resigned his position as vice president before pleading no contest to charges of bribery and tax evasion

The **Watergate scandal** was a political outrage involving the administration of U.S. President Richard Nixon from 1972 to 1974 that led to Nixon's resignation. The scandal stemmed from the administration's continuous attempts to cover up its involvement in their break-in of the Democratic National Committee headquarters at the Washington, D.C., Watergate Office Building.

After the five perpetrators were arrested, the newsmedia and the U.S. Justice Department connected the cash found on them at the time to the Nixon re-election campaign committee. Further investigations, along with revelations during subsequent trials of the burglars, led the U.S. House of Representatives to grant its judiciary committee additional investigation authority to probe into "certain matters within its jurisdiction," and the Senate to create a special investigative committee. The resultant Senate Watergate hearings were broadcast "gavel-to-gavel" nationwide, arousing public interest. Witnesses testified that the president had approved plans to cover up administration involvement in the break-in, and that there was a voice-activated taping system in the Oval Office. Throughout the investigation, the administration resisted the probes, which led to a constitutional crisis.

Several major revelations and egregious presidential action against the investigation in 1973 prompted the House to commence an impeachment process against Nixon. The U.S. Supreme Court ruled that Nixon must release the Oval Office tapes to government investigators. The tapes revealed that Nixon had conspired to cover up activities that took place after the break-in and had attempted to use federal officials to deflect the investigation. The House Judiciary Committee then approved articles of impeachment against Nixon for obstruction of justice, abuse of power, and contempt of Congress. With his complicity in the cover-up made public and his political support substantially eroded, Nixon resigned from office on August 9, 1974. It is believed that, had he not done so, he would have been impeached by the House and removed from office by a trial in the Senate. He is the only U.S. president to have resigned from office. Nixon's successor, Gerald Ford, subsequently pardoned him.

Altogether, 69 people were indicted and 48 — many of them top Nixon administration officials — were convicted. The term "Watergate" came to encompass an array of clandestine and often illegal activities undertaken by members of the Nixon administration, including bugging the offices of political opponents and people of whom Nixon or his officials were suspicious; ordering investigations of activist groups and political figures; and using the FBI, the CIA, and the IRS as political weapons. The use of the suffix "-gate" after an identifying term has since become synonymous with public scandal, especially political scandal.

In 1974. Gerald Ford, the former House minority leader became the 38th U.S. president,.the first person to reach the White House without being elected president or vice president. He held office from August 1974 to January 1977.

Jimmy Carter served as president, elected for one term, from 1977 to 1981, getting eclipsed out of a second term by the Ronald Reagan electoral steamroller. Carter had taken graduate work in reactor technology and nuclear physics and served as senior officer of the *SSN Seawolf* pre-commissioning crew.

As detailed elsewhere in this book, as well as in presidential history, Reagan served two controversial and partisan terms in office from 1981 to 1989.

The Intermediate-Range Nuclear Forces Treaty (**INF Treaty**) — formally the "Treaty Between the United States of America and the Union of Soviet Socialist Republics on the Elimination of Their Intermediate-Range and Shorter-Range Missiles" — was an exceptionally effective Cold War arms-control treaty between the United States and the Soviet Union (and its successor state, the Russian Federation). US President Ronald Reagan and Soviet General Secretary Mikhail Gorbachev signed it on 8 December 1987. The United States Senate approved the treaty on 27 May 1988, and Reagan and Gorbachev ratified it on 1 June 1988.

The INF Treaty banned all of the two nations' land-based ballistic missiles, cruise missiles, and missile launchers with ranges of 500–1,000 kilometers (310–620 mi) (short-, medium-range) and 1,000–5,500 km (620–3,420 mi) (intermediate-range). The treaty did not apply to air- or sea-launched missiles. By May 1991, the two nations had eliminated 2,692 missiles, validated by 10 years of on-site verification inspections. It has been turned out to be one of the most consequential and effective treaties between strategic adversaries.

However, on 20 October 2018, amidst continuing growth of China's missile forces, US President Donald Trump announced that he was withdrawing the US from the INF treaty due to supposed Russian non-compliance. Also, the US government officially asserted another reason for the withdrawal was to counter a Chinese arms buildup in the Pacific, including within the South China Sea. However, China was not a signatory to the INF treaty.

In what appears to be a purely symbolic measure, the Trump administration formally suspended the INF treaty on 1 February 2019, and in response Russia did so on the following day. The US formally withdrew from the INF Treaty on 2 August 2019. No meaningful change in the current strategic military balance is expected from these withdrawals.

After Reagan, George H. W. Bush, another Republican, followed as the 41st President (1989-1993). He was in office when the USSR dissolved 26 December 1991 — no thanks to Bush, but instead mostly due to increasing internal rot of the Soviet Communist system.

1990 was an extraordinary year of shocks and contrasts for the world economy. The Gulf conflict — apart from its immense human suffering — brought about regional destruction of infrastructure and a rise in environmental pollution; a sharp increase in energy prices; intensified economic difficulties for many countries; and a sudden erosion of consumer and business confidence in much of the world.

The dramatic early-90s developments in Eastern Europe and the Soviet Union ushered in an era of transition from the Communist-style command economy to the Western-style market system — a change that held great potential for the world economy but proved far more difficult than expected, and resulted in a sharp fall in the output of these economies. Some developed economies went into recession and others nearly did, ending their longest expansion in the post-Second World War period. Many emerging economies continued to stagnate under the burden of problems that persisted. These developments resulted in the slowest rate of growth of world output since 1982. *Per-capita* income declined in large parts of the world. The forecast for 1991 was zero-growth overall, with large-scale declines in the output of Eastern Europe and the Soviet Union and recession already visible in the developing market economies.

Yet a significant number of countries — both developed and developing — continued to grow strongly in 1990s, some even faster than in 1989. Most survived the Gulf crisis and the slowdown in world economy relatively unscathed. World trade retained much of its buoyancy, with exports of some countries growing vigorously.

Until leaving the Chicago area, moving West to California, I found myself unavoidably but passively active in nuclear arms-control issues, particularly with consummation of a couple of books providing a detailed nuclear history and analysis.

FAMILY TIME

This is a good point in this narrative to inject some brief biographic information about my own family and relatives and their evolution. My first wife, Helen, and I stayed together for some 20 years and brought up four children in Illinois, mostly in Lisle, a suburb southwest of Chicago. Son Paul still lives in the suburban Chicago area, but Marina set up home in Utah, Greg remains back in Lisle, and Dean in Baja Sur, Mexico.

A year or so after divorce from Helen, I met Judy, and we married and lived together for a couple of years before getting divorced. That was it for a while, until I met Mary Lou in California, and she moved to Illinois where we lived together until we separated and I moved to California for good.

While there is a large extended DeVolpi family on the Internet, about the only individual with whom I had substantive contact is Pete, whose father was from the Lockport (later, Michigan) branch of the family. This younger Pete worked in California for a while and now has his own family in the New York City metropolitan area.

THE G.W. BUSH WAR YEARS

The presidential administration of George W. Bush began on January 20, 2001, when he was inaugurated as 43rd leader of the United States, and ended after eight Mid-East war-torn years. The previous president had been Democrat Bill Clinton, from 1993 to 2001 (with his wife Hillary as Secretary of State).

Although some of my erstwhile colleagues and I had officially retired from Argonne National Laboratory by 2000, we continued to return to the lab at least one day a week, often carrying out some official work assignments and meeting together at the cafeteria during the lunch break. Meanwhile, the war in Iraq evolved, despite universal skepticism, particularly about alleged weapons of mass destruction that were never to be found, turning out to be an orchestrated Republican pretext for the invasion.

None of our private opposition to federal government war making could be accomplished without government scrutiny and retaliation, which led to our having to call for independent Inspector General oversight that officially cleared our actions.

An **Inspector General**, officially embedded in most U.S. government agencies, operates as independent auditor or investigator of expenditures and operations. Normally reporting directly to the agency head, IGs have significant visibility and importance. Their independence has been a bone of contention during the Trump administration, partly because President Trump didn't like the outcome of some of their reports.

George Walker Bush (born July 6, 1946) served as the 43rd president of the United States from 2001 to 2009. A member of the Republican Party, he was previously 46th governor of Texas from 1995 to 2000. G.W. became the fourth person to be elected president without a popular vote victory. His father, George H. W. Bush, served as the 41st president from 1989 to 1993.

In response to the September 11, 2001, terrorist attacks, G.W. created the U.S. Department of Homeland Security and mounted a "War on Terror" that began with U.S. military action in Afghanistan. He later in 2003 launched the Iraq War, with the administration arguing that the Saddam Hussein regime possessed an active weapons-of-mass-destruction (WMD) program, and that the Iraqi government posed a threat to the United States.

Some administration officials falsely claimed that Hussein had an operational relationship with Al-Qaeda, the perpetrators of the 9/11 attack. No stockpiles of WMDs or an active WMD program were ever found in Iraq.

In December 2007, the United States entered its longest post-World War II recession, often referred to as the Great Recession, prompting the G.W. Bush administration to obtain congressional approval for multiple economic programs intended to preserve the country's financial system.

G.W. was both among the most popular, as well as least popular, U.S. presidents: He received the highest recorded approval ratings in the wake of the 9/11 attacks, but one of the lowest such ratings during the 2008 financial crisis.

MY UNOFFICIAL INVOLVEMENTS AT ARGONNE

Demilitarization of plutonium was a chronic contentious issue that followed me past retirement from Argonne National Laboratory. My own detailed nuclear-criticality calculations, by worksheet and by computer at the laboratory, had emphatically confirmed that plutonium had to be of a minium fissile quality to be rendered into a nuclear weapon.

Nuclear arsenals were clearly not created with low-grade materials, particularly because military standards required that weapons had to detonate reliably and have predictable explosive yields. However, some academics, such as Princeton professor Frank von Hippel, who had little or no actual technical or engineering experience, reckoned otherwise.

Ironically, the misinformed professors were opposed to the only surefire means of rendering plutonium (and uranium) worthless for weapons. Now that the Cold War has ended, the public record on the specific number and recognition of nations that have produced nuclear weapons has been static. No additional nations have joined the nuclear-weapons "club." Plutonium is routinely produced in reactors, and all fissile materials are retained under strict national and international controls.

Even though the Cold War SDI program was resoundingly defeated, there have always been dismaying implications of a new space-weaponization race, inherent in recent programs to orbit weapons that might be capable of destroying satellites. Because of the nearly universal dependence of modern nations on orbiting satellites for communications and for monitoring of activities on Earth, any development of devices that might undermine the peaceful use of space endangers worldwide stability.

International nuclear arms control is also dependent on the growth of technical means for remotely monitoring nuclear-test explosions. This has been evident with the relevant degree of confidence that nations expressed after detecting North Korea's underground nuclear-explosive tests.

The **Comprehensive Nuclear-Test-Ban Treaty Organization** (CTBTO) is an international organization that will be established upon the entry into force of the Comprehensive Nuclear-Test-Ban Treaty, a Convention that outlaws nuclear test explosions. Its seat will be Vienna, Austria. The organization will be tasked with verifying the ban on nuclear tests and will operate therefore a worldwide monitoring system and may conduct on site inspections. The Preparatory Commission for the CTBTO, and its Provisional Technical Secretariat, were established in 1997 and are headquartered in Vienna, Austria.

The Comprehensive Nuclear-Test-Ban Treaty will enter into force 180 days after the Treaty has been ratified by 44 States that were designated to have a nuclear reactor or at least some advanced level of nuclear technology. As of March 2015, 41 of these states had signed the treaty and 36 had ratified. India, North Korea and Pakistan had not signed or ratified the treaty; China, Egypt, Iran, Israel and the United States had signed but had not ratified.

BOOKS PUBLISHED SINCE RETIREMENT

Much about"radical" involvements are recalled in my books published after formal retirement from Argonne, when no longer subject to scrutiny or administrative risk from bureaucrats at the Laboratory or DOE.

Nuclear Anxiety [2017/revised 2019]

Nuclear Anxiety: Challenges for American Governments, is an abbreviated and simplified analysis of national-security situations faced in modern-day American governance. It is derived largely from a pair of much more comprehensive volumes: *Cold War Brinkmanship: Nuclear Arms, Civil Rights, Government Secrecy* (Amazon, 2017; 684 pp, revised 2019) and *Cold War Nuclear Challenges: Technical Controversies, Civil Disobedience, Government Infringements* (Amazon, 2019; 684pp). Those two volumes include much more personal and technical narrative, as well as additional coverage of Cold War issues regarding civil rights and government secrecy.

Cold War Brinkmanship: Nuclear Arms, Civil Rights, Government Secrecy [2017/revised 2018] (Paperback)

Most of the public-interest issues in which I was involved in the decade before and after my retirement from Argonne are reported in my book, *Cold War Brinkmanship*: which carries the subtitle *Nuclear Arms, Civil Rights, Government Secrecy.* More about its content is contained it its sub-subtitle: *How we failed to stop the nuclear-arms race and human-rights violations.*

As a documented historical narrative, it covers specifically this boatload of topics:

Government Control, Public Protest, Privacy and Government Responsibility, Constitutional Rights, Public Information and Data, Government Information Control, Classified Nuclear Information, Cold War Protests, FOIA and Privacy Act, Being Investigated by the FBI; Government Oversight and Bureaucracies, Friction with Authorities, Big Brother/sister, Cold War Surveillance, Whistleblowing, Government Secrecy, Individual Privacy, Constitutional and Legal Issues; Government Accountability, Information and Privacy, Cold War Practices and Lessons, Surveillance and Secrecy, National Security and Counter-terrorism, Obama Administration and Congress, Outlook for Democracy and Civilization, Nuclear Arms Control and Human Rights, Privacy and Secrecy, Nuclear Heritage, Post-Cold-War Leadership, Contemporary Nuclear Issues; Today's Relevance.

Also available on Amazon is *Nuclear Brinkmanship: Challenges for the Trump Presidency*, a focused version of those two earlier Cold War volumes. Not just an insider, but also an active participant in Cold War events, experiencing and acquiring a detailed professional and technical understanding of nuclear weaponry and its strategic significance, I endeavored to simplify it all for the reader. This present volume focused on national-security demands — especially nuclear — facing the U.S. government.

Here's a list of the Chapters in *Nuclear Brinkmanship*:

Nuclear Brinkmanship: Challenges for the Trump Presidency (226pp, 2018)

CHAPTER 1   BECOMING INVOLVED
CHAPTER 2   INTERNATIONAL CONFLICTS
CHAPTER 3   DOMESTIC (NUCLEAR) CONTROVERSY
CHAPTER 4   SURROGATE WARS
CHAPTER 5   GOVERNMENT OVERREACH
CHAPTER 6   OUR NUCLEAR HERITAGE
CHAPTER 7   STRATEGIC ISSUES
CHAPTER 8   COLD WAR POLICY DEBRIS
CHAPTER 9   NUCLEAR CHALLENGES FOR TRUMP

And here's a subsequent and more comprehensive book that was well received:

Cold War Nuclear Challenges: Technical Controversies, Civil Disobedience, Government Infringements (Amazon, 2019)

CHAPTER 1: COLD WAR CONVULSIONS
CHAPTER 2: DOMESTIC TURMOIL
CHAPTER 3: PUBLIC ANXIETY
CHAPTER 4: COLD WAR ESTABLISHMENT
CHAPTER 5: NUCLEAR CONTROVERSY
CHAPTER 6: GOVERNMENT CONTROL, PUBLIC PROTEST
CHAPTER 7: GOVERNMENT OVERSIGHT AND BUREAUCRACIES
CHAPTER 8: 21ST CENTURY SECRECY AND PRIVACY
CHAPTER 9: OUTLOOK FOR DEMOCRACY AND CIVILIZATION

Paperback: 676 pages:
Customer Reviews: 5.0 out of 5 stars in 2 customer ratings
#2771 in Nuclear Weapons & Warfare History (Books)
#16925 in Military History (Books)

My books that have been reviewed have mostly been given 5* ratings.

Although never considering myself as a natural or charismatic leader, I found myself mostly by default being re-elected as perennial chairperson of the Concerned Argonne Scientists. No one else volunteered for the role (because of the visible workplace profile: you could never tell which manager above you was secretly antipathetic), and it became hopeless to find another CAS co-chair. There was no glory in that role, but sometimes professional grief. Administrators subjectively resented anyone who stirred the pot, even if it had nothing to do with them directly or professionally or administratively. Until civil-rights issues had settled, I had also continued participation in radicalized Chicago activities, particularly those under the umbrella of the Alliance to End Repression..

In this book, my account of that decade of activism (the 1980s) is shortened appreciably. Many details are available in my coauthored volumes of *Nuclear Shadowboxing: Contemporary Threats From Cold War Weaponry* (2004/2005) and my *Nuclear Insights* (2009) trilogy, both published after retirement (with the grateful financial assistance of W&L classmate Gerry Lenfest, a kindred spirit).

A reminder of reasons for my activism in the 1980s is reflected in the following classic illustration (Figure 83) reminding of an imperiled time in history when the United States and the Soviet Union held each other in a grip of mutual suicide during the Cold War. While only one of those illustrated multi-stage thermonuclear weapons could have been toted by a heavy bomber, and only about five of them were manufactured. Just think: each had enough explosive power to destroy an entire major metropolitan area, with considerable collateral damage coupled to radiation fallout over a wide geographic region.

The nuclear-bomb model shown in Figure 83 was in a museum in the Soviet Union just before the nation was to separate into present-day Russia. Let's leave the nukes in museums.

On one hand, this book recalls and celebrates humanity's escape from such horrendous abnormality, and, on the other hand, this book seeks to educate and strengthen awareness and barriers against such nuclear brinkmanship.

Figure 83. An iconic photo, standing next to a full-sized model of largest nuclear weapon ever built (150 Mt). My Argonne colleague Vladimir Minkov, is shaking hands with the Russian (former Soviet) chief nuclear-weapons designer. The bomb was only tested at about one-third of its capability.

POST-RETIREMENT QUASI-OFFICIAL ACTIVITIES

In early 1999 (8 January) I reached mandatory retirement age from Argonne (with standard benefits) after 40 years of employment at the laboratory. I don't recall if 40 years is a DOE or University of Chicago job-duration limitation. Comparable retirement ages were also being reached by my philosophical comrades at Los Alamos and Livermore labs. In any event, I had run out of officially useful and funded work assignments, while the Argonne lab and division roles shifted away from nuclear and more towards environmental R&D. After all, there was no longer much more need for further development or advancements in baseload nuclear power. Nor was the Cold War underway any longer.

As allowed at the other DOE labs, Argonne retirees were permitted return visits to the lab for either agreed part-time work or as guests. Like others, I continued to finish some incomplete officially authorized technical projects and to meet colleagues at lunchtime, once or twice a week at the Argonne cafeteria, and when someone else retired we joined socially in celebration.

CALIFORNIA, HERE I COME

After a decade or so staying in Illinois, I moved to southern California, San Diego area, with year-round weather much like that of the Como region in Italy. That was in 2010.

Since moving to California I've been able to fulfill several books, including the multi-volume Nuclear Insights. This book that you're now reading, *The Fox Millennium*, is my first to include substantial autobiographical and philosophical content. Although I retained membership in a couple of affinity (professional and ancestral) groups, this book is expected to provide my final published considerations.

Nuclear Shadowboxing

With respect to coauthoring books after retirement (but before leaving Illinois), first there was a collaborative two-volume pair — *Nuclear Shadowboxing*, written with my Argonne associates George S. Stanford and Vladimir E, Minkov, as well as our Russian (former Soviet) colleague Vadim A. Simonenko, Vadim was chief nuclear-weapons designer at the Chelyabinsk-70 nuclear laboratory.

Having initially met Vadim at one of the joint NGO-arranged meetings in Moscow, he thoughtfully helped me navigate the icey sidewalks when I was hobbling around on crutches, still recovering from hip-replacement surgery. In the course of time and after exchanging some East-West scientific ground-breaking visits, Vadim and I had built up sufficient rapport to collaborate in several books, foremost among them being *Nuclear Shadowboxing: Contemporary Threats from Cold War Weaponry* (2004).

Nuclear Shadowboxing: Contemporary Threats from Cold War Weaponry (Fidlar Doubleday) Alexander DeVolpi (Argonne National Laboratory, retired); Vladimir E. Minkov (FSU and Argonne, retired); George S. Stanford (Argonne, retired); Vadim A. Simonenko (Chelyabinsk-70, Russia).

Volume 1: *Cold War Redux* is a history of nuclear weapons and their development during the Cold War (Published December 2004).

Volume 2: *Legacies and Challenges* discusses the consequences after the Cold War of many nations having inherited nuclear weapons, fissile material, and radioactive substances (Published August 2005).

Figure 84. Cover of our E-W coauthored book, *Nuclear Shadowboxing*.

As we explained in our authors' response to a lukewarm critique of a collaborative 2-volume Cold War book *Nuclear Shadowboxing's* (cover design displayed in Figure 84):

The reviewer is perceptive in calling the two volumes "a labor of love." We could not find a publisher for this comprehensive and specialized tome, so we had to self-publish at our own expense; we have barely recouped our printing costs. Without remuneration, the four of us devoted more than twelve intense, part-time years to putting on paper the essentials of our unparalleled collective professional and personal experience during the Cold War.

Moreover, we do not "reiterate the existing consensus of academic physical scientists." Our experience goes well beyond the classroom. Between us we have first-hand knowledge of much of our subject matter, often acquired in the field — sometimes under dicey situations. While many historians and academics do a great job of canvassing, distilling, and interpreting historical events, we submit that Nuclear Shadowboxing adds a unique perspective.

We are now-retired nuclear physicists and engineers from both sides of the former Iron Curtain, with a unique combination of hands-on knowledge and skills in just about every aspect of nuclear weapons and arms control. We collaborated to provide, for the benefit of future evaluators of policy, a 1000-page (900,000-

*word) history and analysis of Cold War weaponry and lessons to be learned —
topics often viewed as complex, obtuse, controversial, and easily misunderstood.*

PERSONAL AND FAMILY MATTERS

Here are just a couple of pages about my families and friends, omitting most details, especially that covered in *Lover, Soldier, Reprobate*.

Readers who have tracked this book closely will have noted a mid-West perspective. Without saying that's good or bad, we often noted a difference of opinion compared to colleagues and friends at institutions on the East and West coasts.

Because of my four professional decades at Argonne, this book compensates for more prevalent intellectual treatments produced by East and West coast scholars and activists.

In particular, Chicago-area activism was vigorous and effective, even on matters dealing with national and international policy.

Deliberately I've endeavored to omit less interesting but always relevant episodes dealing with wives and children. Included is that which is largely centered about my peripatetic father.

Although not mentioned much in this book, I fancied myself a fisherman, using live and artificial lures. Often at dawn on weekends during salmon and trout upstream migration season, you could find me at the Berrien Springs dam spillway (Fig. 88), casting into the current for salmon

Probably because of the enjoyment I got from canoeing during summer camps in Virginia, I undertook a project to construct in my garage a fiber-glass canoe from a kit. I'm sure my kids rendered meaningful assistance.

With some friends and their kids, we regularly undertook camping trips, memorably to Maine and to Virginia, as well as more frequently in Michigan during summers. None of my wives were of the "outdoor" type. Too many bugs.

None of my progeny have expressed any interest or penchant in taking up public causes or writing books.

CHAPTER XI: A WEST-COAST PERSPECTIVE

This chapter, written largely for the curious and for the eternal record, fittingly invokes an ending that harks back to the beginning of the book, namely the pandemic scourges that wracked Italy 1000 years ago.

RELOCATION TO CALIFORNIA

The wintery and interpersonal Chicago-area climate (with Mary Lou) were major factors in my decision to pull up roots and relocate to southern California, specifically the San Diego area. Having visited the area often while on Argonne business, I had some friends who lived in southern California, particularly the San Diego area.

One accommodating couple were the Bartons (John and Claudia) who hosted me while I found new lodging in the area. They lived in Pacific Beach. The Bartons had both been on the professional staff at Argonne at one time, where I originally made their acquaintance, and we shared a commen technical interest in neutron radiography.

The accompanying Figure 85 is that of my wife Bobbi, who had two children, Greg and Paige, from before.

Three erstwhile colleagues whom a met while attending the local chapter meetings of the American Nuclear Society have been John Ross, Mehdi Sarram, and Vojin Joksimovich. John has been attorney of record for several patent filings tabulated below.

While at Argonne, I had three patents issued, and subsequently through John we've had five patents filed, four of which were granted, dealing variously with radiation production and monitoring of nuclear reactors.

Figure 85. Bobbi, my wife.

For a few years after moving to California, we incorporated as Nuclear Applications Corporation (NAC), engaging in a number of promotional nuclear activities that carried over from Argonne.

Besides periodically attending the local Italian affinity luncheon groups in the area, I was able to gradually fill in the gaps in my genealogical studies, eventually resulting in consummation of books such as *Lover, Soldier, Reprobate* and this one that you now reading.

It would be remiss of me not to mention my weekly participation in competitive tournament hold-em poker at Ocean's Eleven Casino conveniently located in Oceanside. Daily tournaments before the corona virus outbreak usually had five or six dozen players. I claim to have been holding my own in net tournament expenses and earnings.

FOIA APPLICATIONS

Eventually, residual curiosity — derived from glancing at the file cabinets I had shipped from Illinois — caused me to undertake a number of book-writing projects. It turned out that the U.S. government was a gold-mine of records about my involvement in civic and national affairs: All those background investigations to substantiate justification for my access to national-security information while at Argonne had led to a huge government-validated record. Since I hardly had any direct involvement in international affairs, the files were mostly about domestic political affairs.

Under FOIA, I was able to find out and document much more about the scope and intensity of government surveillance that extended from the federal all the way down to the local level. Simply joining an public-interest organization was enough to trigger a seemingly ominous information entry in federal government dossiers. For example, under a FOIA revelation, I found that my being a member of the FAS caused the FBI to add that tidbit of information to the (once-secret) file they kept on me.

While never keeping a diary as such, I had hung on to some private notebooks. Coupling that information to the FBI records obtain under FOIA, many of my past affiliations and public activities could be reconstructed: It was a goldmine of validated information. Lacking a diary or my Argonne laboratory workbooks, this was the next best thing. Thank you, Uncle Sam.

WRITING BOOKS

There were some unique experiences to recall, especially in time of continued tension about nations possessing nuclear weaponry. Substantiated by the FBI records, my initial books were the product of authorship partnerships with former professional colleagues. (I've had to produce this book on my own.)

Our two-volume collaborative pair of books, *Nuclear Shadowboxing; Contemporary Threats From Cold War Weaponry*, was described earlier. Both volumes came out before I left the Chicago area.

Perhaps my most readable book has been *Lover, Soldier, Reprobate* —mentioned a number of times and published in 2011.

As mentioned, the *Nuclear Insights* series was published with financial support from Gerry Lenfest, a Washington and Lee University classmate who had become a billionaire. Gerry was also supportive of some of my nuclear initiatives and inventions.

Titles: Nuclear Anxiety, Cold War Brinkmanship, and ***Cold War Nuclear Challenges.***

Nuclear Anxiety: Challenges for American Governments [2017/revised 2019], is an abbreviated and simplified analysis of national-security situations faced in modern-day American governance. It is derived largely from a pair of much more comprehensive volumes:

Cold War Brinkmanship: Nuclear Arms, Civil Rights, Government Secrecy (Amazon, 2017; 684 pp, revised 2019)

Cold War Nuclear Challenges: Technical Controversies, Civil Disobedience, Government Infringements (Amazon, 2019; 684pp).

The latter two volumes include much more personal and technical narrative, as well as additional coverage of Cold War issues regarding civil rights and government secrecy.

PUBLIC-ISSUE INVOLVEMENT

My continued membership in the American Physical Society, particularly its proactive Forum on Physics and Society, has provided contempary insight into some public issues. My other avenue for interaction had been the American Nuclear Society, particularly its San Diego chapter which usually met periodically in Oceanside (until the pandemic intervened).

Sometimes I met in North County with Mehdi and Vojin for lunch and occasionally gave an invited talk or attended a meeting that they had organized. However, during the corona-virus outbreak, much of my involvement lately has been more indirect, mostly through the books I have written.

Not having been much for on-line communication (e.g., Facebooking or otherwise, indirect through LinkedIn), I have gradually reduced my involvement in technical matters.

Partly because of the corona virus, I've withdrawn from periodic informal (quarterly) meetings in downtown San Diego with a World War I history group.

The pandemic has also reinforced my withdrawal from periodic and enjoyable luncheon gatherings of an Italian Genealogy group in North County. That group has had interests coinciding with the content of this book. Particularly for special-interest groups like that one, this book reinforces a lesson of vital interest to those involved in genealogical studies: that you must go to Italy (or wherever your family originated) in order to fully comprehend your family relationship (as exemplified by the nameplate of the Bari library, Figure 19).

Thus, my involvement in public issues is now indirect, through the books I've published.

CHEERING FROM THE SIDELINES

"The Back Page" column of the July/August 2020 *APS News* recently caught my attention with an article that included coauthors Steve Fetter and Frank von Hippel, writing about the present-day peril of nuclear weapons. Referring to the Spanish influenza in 1918 (17–100 million deaths) as an epidemic on the scale of the current corona virus, they see a parallel in the worldwide threat of unchecked nuclear weapons during our present-day pandemic. I agree mostly. Despite their chronic and misleading exaggeration of the threat from what they call "weapons-usable" fissile materials, we're nevertheless in accord on the need to maintain everlasting containment and possession of weapons-grade materials. There's no need to amplify the threat that's already recognized.

Some other public issues that have drawn my attention are described in the following pages.

Guns

Gun control continues to be a frequent and divisive issue. Nations have various ways of managing the ownership of weapons, such as firearms and I have gone through many changes in attitude and surrounding attitudes.

At Staunton Military Academy where I completed all of my grade-school and high-school-level education, we were issued and marched with rifles and sidearms (of course without firing pins). Unofficially I had possession of some rifles (and samurai swords) that my uncle sent from the Pacific theater of World War II and hid under my bunk mattress. (He worked in the Army Post Office, so he could get away with shipping them). One I recall was a British Enfield.

Without authorization I would hike to nearby quarries and fields for real fire practice, but, usually too scared to hit an animal or varmint. Ammunition was not difficult to come by. I think most hardware stores carried ammo.

We had a practice rifle range at SMA, and we often marched with rifles over our shoulders. In fact, we had to march with rifles on our shoulders to rid ourselves of demerits. I don't recall having a gun while in college, except of course when on weekly or annual naval-reserve training.

Aboard one LST assigned during my years in the Navy, I was the gunnery officer, in charge of bombarding helpless Vieques Island goats. There wasn't any resistance to report.

After active duty in the Navy, I don't recall being obliged to tote a sidearm during training sessions in the Virginia or Illinois research reserves, nor while on assignments at the Navy Research Laboratory in Washington, DC, or the Naval Radiological Defense Laboratory in San Francisco.

A good friend of mine in Illinois had been a Chicago cop, and he got me to join his fishing club. However, I had to quit after a year or two because the club, comprised of retired Chicago city policemen, was blatantly and vocally racist and sexist.

At our home in Lisle, Illinois, decades after being mustered out of military service, I still had a 22-caliber rifle stored in the garage, never firing it. By then I had transitioned to fishing and canoeing as my primary outdoor hobbies. One day I rediscovered the rifle and gave to local police because our family had young children who were becoming curious around the house.

Virginia-Tech Shootings. In 2007, a berserk student systematically shot and killed 32 people, mostly students and faculty, wounding 17 more, in one of the deadliest single-shooter incidents in U.S. history. America is home to 5% of the world's population, yet incurs something like 31% of mass shootings.

Partly because of my years as a student at the Virginia Tech campis long ago in Blacksburg, the 2007 slaughter impelled me to write to newspapers and various gun-control organizations. Here are extracts of one letter published in the *Chicago Tribune's* Voice of People ("Gun Ownership Public Safety," 19 April 2007), stressing the constitutional legitimacy of intensified taxing of most guns and ammunition, somewhat like we tax cars and gasoline:

> *Too often our society is paying the price for untempered possession of handguns, especially semiautomatics. This is not a 2nd-Amendment issue about rights to gun ownership. It is about the failure of Congress to provide the public's general welfare. Section 8 in Article I of the United States Constitution mandates:*

> *The Congress shall have power to lay and collect taxes,*
> *duties, imposts and excises, to pay the debts and provide*
> *for the common defense and general welfare of the United*
> *States; but all duties, imposts and excises shall be uniform*
> *throughout the United States....*
>
> *And To make all laws which shall be necessary and proper*
> *for carrying into execution the foregoing powers, and all*
> *other powers vested by this Constitution in the government*
> *of the United States, or in any department or officer*
> *thereof.*

With the public bearing societal costs for gun ownership, it would seem obligatory for appropriate levels of local, state and federal government to levy compensatory taxes and surcharges.

Money collected ought to reimburse costs of medical care, liability, incapacity, rehabilitation, victims, families, courts, property damage, physical and mental screening, law enforcement, prisons, restitution, business loss, emergency response other public burdens related to gun ownership in the United States. Just as it is with income taxes, those who don't file or pay are subject to being charged and judged, possibly resulting in lawful penalty if failing to comply.
The 2nd Amendment is just fine: the right to bear arms, but how many tragedies will it take before Congress exercises its constitutional powers to provide the general welfare of the people?

The *San Diego Union-Tribune* printed a shorter version of that Letter-to-the-Editor just after the Las Vegas shooting which killed 58 people, setting a record for gun-deadliness in the United States.

Gun-Violence Restitution — Public Costs. Aside victims of gun shootings, the public large bears heavy costs gun ownership: That's why I suggest taxes surcharges to levied local, state federal jurisdictions the privilege responsibility of gun possession. once Navy Gunnery Officer longtime gun owner, helps make one realize that society should compensate harm caused few. After all, we reimburse victims many types of accidents, their prevention consequences:

costs of law enforcement, medical treatment, public liability, individual incapacity, hospitalization rehab, victim compensation, family impact, court costs, property damage, physical mental screening, imprisonment, business loss, emergency response, many other personal public burdens.

The gun-ownership tax money collected within the various jurisdictions could help compensate such harmful consequences public expense related to gun violence. Some rural districts might choose not to levy taxes, while more populated areas (such as present-day Chicago) might assess taxes at levels sufficient to compensate some of the communal gun-related costs.

Sandy Hook, Riverside, Orlando, Baton Rouge. The statistical database regarding gun-enabled slaughter continues to grow. More than 30,000 people killed annually in the United States firearms. Nationally, the number of gun-related deaths in the United States per year is about the same as fatalities from vehicle accidents.

For few if any of these tragic situations, is it likely that better-armed citizenry would reduced the death toll? Instead, many gun-related tragedies before since Virginia Tech occurred, with Congress having abdicated its constitutional powers to provide the general welfare of the people.

PESTILENCE AND VIRUSES

The pandemic associated with the 2020 corona virus (Covid-19) is reminiscent of various scourges that ended up with considerable upheaval in the middle ages.

Viruses. A virus is an infectious agent that replicates only inside living cells of an organism. Viruses can infect all types of life forms, from large animals and plants to small microorganisms, even bacteria. Since just before the 19th century began, millions of viruses have been found in the environment in almost every ecosystem on Earth, and they are the most numerous type of biological entity.

When infected, a host cell is forced to rapidly produce thousands of identical copies of the original virus. When not inside an infected cell or when in the process of infecting a cell, viruses exist in the form of independent particles. Most virus species are too small to be seen with an optical microscope.

Origins of viruses in the evolutionary history of life are unclear. Viruses have been an important means of horizontal gene transfer, which increases genetic diversity in a way analogous to sexual reproduction.

Viruses spread in many ways. One pathway is through disease-bearing organisms known as vectors: for example, viruses are often transmitted from plant to plant by insects that feed on plant sap, such as aphids. Viruses in animals can be carried by blood-sucking insects. Influenza viruses are spread by coughing and sneezing. Norovirus and rotavirus, common causes of viral gastroenteritis, are transmitted by the fecal–oral route, passed by hand-to-mouth contact or in food or water.

Viral infections in animals provoke an immune response that usually eliminates the infecting virus. Immune responses can also be produced by vaccines, which confer an artificially acquired immunity to the specific viral infection.

Examples of common human diseases caused by viruses include the common cold, influenza, chickenpox, and cold sores. Many serious diseases such as rabies, Ebola virus disease, AIDS (HIV), avian influenza, and SARS are caused by viruses. The relative ability of viruses to cause disease is described in terms of virulence. Other diseases are under investigation to discover if they have a virus as the causative agent, such as the possible connection between human herpesvirus and neurological diseases such as multiple sclerosis and chronic fatigue syndrome.

Viruses have different mechanisms by which they produce disease in an organism, which depends largely on the viral species. Mechanisms at the cellular level primarily include the breaking open and subsequent death of the cell. In multicellular organisms, if enough cells die, the whole organism will start to suffer the effects. Although viruses cause disruption of healthy homeostasis, resulting in disease, they might exist relatively harmlessly within an organism. An example would include the ability of the herpes simplex virus, which causes cold sores, to remain in a dormant state within the human body. This is called latency and is a characteristic of the herpes viruses, including Epstein–Barr virus, which causes glandular fever, and varicella zoster virus, which causes chickenpox and shingles. Most people have been infected with at least one of these types of herpes virus. These latent viruses might sometimes be beneficial, as the presence of the virus can increase immunity against bacterial pathogens, such as *Yersinia pestis*.

Some viruses can cause lifelong or chronic infections, where the viruses continue to replicate in the body despite the host's defense mechanisms. This is common in *hepatitis B* virus and *hepatitis C* virus infections. People chronically infected are known as carriers, serving as reservoirs of infectious virus. In populations with a high proportion of carriers, the disease is said to be endemic.

SARS. Severe acute respiratory syndrome is a contagious and sometimes fatal respiratory illness caused by a coronavirus. SARS appeared in 2002 in China and spread worldwide within a few months, though it was then quickly contained. The SARS virus is transmitted through droplets that enter the air when someone with the disease coughs, sneezes or talks. No known transmission has occurred since 2004. Fever, dry cough, headache, muscle aches, and difficulty breathing are symptoms. No treatment exists except supportive care to mitigate symptoms and avoid retransmission.

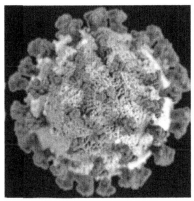

Figure 86. Image of the SARS-CoV-2, a member of the Corona virus family.

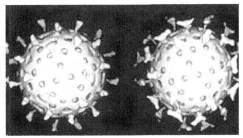

Figure 87. Two images of a rotavirus, which is similar but different from the Corona virus : the one on the right is coated with antibodies that prevent its attachment to cells and thus impede infection.

COVID-19 is is the name of an illness caused by a specific coronavirus labeled SARS-CoV-2. Older adults and people who have severe underlying medical conditions, like heart or lung disease or diabetes, seem to be at higher risk for developing the more serious complications from COVID-19.

It is thought to spread from person to person mainly through respiratory droplets produced when an infected person coughs or sneezes. These droplets can deposit in the mouths or noses of people who are nearby or possibly be inhaled into the lungs. Spread is more likely when people are in close contact with one another (within about 6 feet). It may be possible that a person to get COVID-19 by touching a surface or object that has the virus on it and then touching their own mouth, nose, or possibly their eyes. This is not thought to be the main way the virus spreads, but we are still learning more about it.

The virus that causes COVID-19 is spreading easily between people. Information from the ongoing COVID-19 pandemic suggests that this virus is spreading more sustainably than influenza, but not as efficiently as measles, which is highly contagious.

As of mid-2020, the COVID-19 virus was responsible for at least 170,000 people dying — mostly elderly — of about 5.5 million people thought to have been infected.

Simply citing written records of my Volpi family in Italy is enough to reinforce some tribulations of history. As described in Chapter 2, the family's move to Bari was carried out all the way from northern to southern Italy. That's almost 600 miles that now could be done on modern *autostrada* through many tunnels and bridges. How many of them, and over what period of time they migrated is not a matter of record found so far, but their respective coats-of-arms memorialize the relocation. Their move, back in the 1300s, was likely necessitated by incentives of survival in a time of deadly virus, of which there were several pandemics that decimated populations on the Italic peninsula.

Moving 600 miles with family and possessions in those days (by horse or donkey and cart) must have been quite a trek. A typical distance traveled in the United States by wagon trains across the West was 10 to 20 miles a day.

Scientists and medical researchers have differed over the exact definition of a pandemic (is it a pandemic, or an epidemic?), but one thing most everyone agrees is that the word describes a widespread occurrence of disease, in excess of what might normally be expected in a geographical region.

Cholera, bubonic plague, smallpox, and influenza are some of the most brutal killers in human history. Outbreaks of those diseases across international borders, are properly defined as pandemic. This especially applies to smallpox, which throughout history, has killed between 300-500 million people in its known 12,000 year existence.

Cholera is an infection of the small intestine that causes a large amount of watery diarrhea. The main symptoms are profuse diarrhea, vomiting, and abdominal pain. Transmission is primarily through contaminated drinking water or food. The severity of the diarrhea and vomiting can lead to rapid dehydration and electrolyte imbalance. Primary treatment now is with oral or intravenous rehydration solutions. Nowadays, antibiotics may in certain cases be used. Cholera is a major cause of death in the world. It was one of the earliest infections to be studied by epidemiological methods.

Cholera likely has its origins in and is endemic to the Indian subcontinent. The disease originally spread by trade routes (land and sea) to Russia, then to Western Europe, and from Europe to North America.

Due to filtering and chlorination of water supplies, cholera is now no longer considered a pressing health threat in Europe and North America, but it still heavily affects populations in developing countries. For example, in late 2010, long after a disastrous earthquake in Haiti, a cholera outbreak in the capital, Port-Au-Prince, had already killed over 200 people.

Because Cholera is waterborne, chlorine can be added to potable water to help contain the bacterial infection. Also important as preventative measures are washing hands with soap and disinfecting drinking water.

Smallpox. Thousands of years ago, variola virus (smallpox) emerged and began causing illness and deaths in human populations, with outbreaks occurring from time to time. Thanks to the success of vaccination, the last natural outbreak of smallpox in the United States occurred in 1949. The World Health Assembly in 1980 declared smallpox eradicated (eliminated), and no cases of naturally occurring smallpox have happened since.

Smallpox research in the United States continues and focuses on the development of vaccines, drugs and diagnostic tests to protect people in the event that smallpox would be used as an agent of bioterrorism.

The **Plague of Athens** was an flu-like epidemic that devastated the city-state of Athens in ancient Greece during the second year of the Peloponnesian War against Sparta (430 BC) when an Athenian victory seemed within reach. The plague killed an estimated 75,000 to 100,000 people and is believed to have entered Athens through Piraeus, the city's port and sole source of food and supplies. Much of the eastern-Mediterranean population also saw an outbreak of the disease, albeit with less impact. In addition, Pericles, the leader of Athens, died from the plague.

The plague had serious effects on Athens' society, resulting in a lack of adherence to laws and religious belief. In response, laws became stricter, resulting in the punishment of non-citizens claiming to be Athenian. The plague returned twice more, in 429 BC and in the winter of 427/426 BC. Some 30 pathogens have been suggested as having caused the plague.

Bubonic plague is one of three types of bacterium-caused plague. Flu-like symptoms can develop one to seven days after exposure to the bacteria,. These symptoms include fever, headaches and vomiting. Swollen and painful lymph nodes occur in the area closest to where the bacteria entered the skin. Occasionally, the swollen lymph nodes may break open.

Three types of plague (bubonic, septicemic and pneumonic) are the result of the route of infection. Bubonic plague is mainly spread by infected fleas from small animals. It may also result from exposure to body fluids from a dead plague-infected animal. In the bubonic form of plague, the bacteria enter through the skin through a flea bite and travel via the lymphatic vessels to a lymph node, causing it to swell. Diagnosis is made by finding the bacteria in the blood, sputum, or fluid from lymph nodes.

Prevention is through public-health measures such as not handling dead animals in areas where plague is common. Vaccines have not been found to be very useful for plague prevention; however, several antibiotics (including streptomycin) are effective for treatment. Plague without treatment has resulted in the death of 30% to 90% of those infected. Death, if it occurs, is typically within ten days. With treatment the risk of death is around 10%. In modern times globally between 2010 and 2015, there were over 3000 documented cases which resulted in 584 deaths. The countries with the greatest number of cases are the Democratic Republic of the Congo, Madagascar and Peru.

Plague was the cause of the Black Death that swept through Asia, Europe and Africa in the 14th century and killed an estimated 50 million people. This was about 25% to 60% of the European population. Because so many of the working population were killed, wages rose due to the demand for labor. Some historians see this as a turning point in European economic development.

The disease was also responsible for the Justinian plague originating in the Eastern Roman Empire in the 6th century, as well as the third epidemic affecting China, Mongolia and India originating in the Yunnan Province in 1855. The term bubonic is derived from the Greek word, meaning "groin." The word "buboes" also refers to swollen lymph nodes.

What about COVID-19 (The Coronavirus)?

Beginning in December 2019, in the region of Wuhan, China, a new ("novel") coronavirus began diagnostically appearing in human beings. It has been named Covid-19, a shortened form for "coronavirus disease of 2019." This new virus spreads incredibly quickly between people, due to its newness – no one had immunity because no one had it until 2019. While Covid-19 was initially seen to be an epidemic in China, the virus spread worldwide within months. The World Health Organization declared Covid-19 a pandemic in March 2019, and by the end of that month, the world saw more than a half-million people infected and nearly 30,000 deaths. The infection rate in the US and other nations began to spike in a year or so.

With the coronavirus pandemic, people all over the world have become more aware of best practices during a pandemic, from careful hand-washing to social distancing. Countries across the world declared mandatory stay-at-home measures, closing schools, businesses, and public places. Dozens of companies and many more independent researchers began working on tests, treatments and vaccines. The push for the humans to survive the pandemic became the primary concern. Research around the world ramped up.

The outcome of the Covid-19 pandemic is impossible to predict. But we can learn from history to determine our best courses. The bubonic plagues, cholera, small pox, Spanish flu and the AIDS pandemic have become our teachers — although of course there were no government or commercial medical insurance plans far back in time.

Malaria wasn't the only medical hazard that the soldiers faced. Because of poor sanitary conditions in their bivouacs – as you'll see, if you follow along with me – the troops also came down with typhus and typhoid fever, which I've been reminded are two completely different and ghastly illnesses.

Typhus is a bacterial disease spread by lice, mites, or fleas. It should not be confused with typhoid fever (see below), as the diseases are unrelated. The name comes from the Greek typhos, meaning smoky or hazy, describing the state of mind of those affected with typhus. The causative organism Rickettsia is a parasite and cannot survive for long outside living cells.

Epidemic typhus victimizes with chills, cough, delirium, high fever, joint pain, low blood pressure, rash, sensitivity to light, severe headache, severe muscle pain, and stupor.

The first reliable description of the disease appears during the 1489Spanish siege of Moorish Granada. These accounts include descriptions of fever and red spots over arms, back and chest, progressing to delirium, gangrenous sores, and the stink of rotting flesh. During the siege, the Spaniards lost 3,000 men to enemy action, but an additional 17,000 died of typhus.

Typhus was also common in prisons (and in crowded conditions where lice spread easily). It was known as jail fever, and often occurs when prisoners are frequently huddled together in dark, filthy rooms. Thus, "Imprisonment until the next term of court" was often equivalent to a death sentence. It was so infectious that prisoners brought before the court sometimes infected the court itself.

During World War I, typhus caused three million deaths in Russia and more in Poland and Romania. Symptoms of typhus may include: abdominal pain, backache, dull red rash that begins on the middle of the body and spreads, extremely high fever, hacking, dry cough, headache, joint pain, and vomiting. A few people can become carriers of typhus and continue to release the bacteria in their stools for years, spreading the disease. Prompt treatment with antibiotics now cures nearly every patient.

Typhoid Fever is a bacterial infection characterized by diarrhea, systemic disease, and a rash – most commonly caused by the bacteria *Salmonella typhi*.

Also known simply as typhoid, it is a common worldwide illness, transmitted by the ingestion of food or water contaminated with an infected person's feces containing the Salmonella bacterium.

The bacteria that causes typhoid fever spreads through contaminated food, drink, or water. If you eat or drink something that is contaminated, the bacteria enters your body, and goes into your intestines, and then into your bloodstream, where it can travel to your lymph nodes, gallbladder, liver, spleen, and other parts of the body.

Typhoid is characterized by a slowly progressive fever, profuse sweating, gastroenteritis, and non-bloody diarrhea. Less commonly, a rash of flat, rose-colored spots may appear.

Typhoid fever is common in poor or developing countries (such as Haiti, which has had a recent severe outbreak). Fewer than 400 cases are reported in the United States each year, most cases being brought in from overseas.

Early symptoms include fever, general ill-feeling, and abdominal pain. A high (over 103 degrees) temperature and severe diarrhea occur as the disease gets worse.

Flying insects feeding on feces may occasionally transfer the bacteria through poor hygiene habits and public sanitation conditions. Public education campaigns encouraging people to wash their hands after defecating and before handling food are an important component in controlling spread of the disease. Chlorination of drinking water has led to dramatic decreases in the transmission of typhoid fever.

Sanitation and hygiene are the critical measures that can be taken to prevent typhoid. Transmission is only from human to human. Careful food preparation and washing of hands are crucial to preventing typhoid.

Two vaccines are currently recommended by the World Health Organization for the prevention of typhoid.

Swine Flu. Swine influenza is an infection caused by several types of viruses endemic in pigs. It is common throughout pig populations worldwide. Transmission of the virus from pigs to humans is not common and does not always lead to human flu..

Symptoms in humans are similar to those of influenza, namely chills, fever, sore throat, muscle pains, severe headache, coughing, weakness, shortness of breath, and general discomfort.

In a 2009 swine flu pandemic, 11–21% of the global population (of about 6.8 billion people) contracted the illness. Fatalities were initially thought to be between 12,000 and 18,000, but a later study estimated more than 284,000 possible fatalities worldwide. In 2015, swine flu was reported in India, with over 1,800 deaths.

Hepatitis A is an infectious viral disease of the liver. Many cases have few or no symptoms, especially in the young. The time between infection and symptoms, in those who develop them, is between two and six weeks. When symptoms occur, they typically last eight weeks and may include nausea, vomiting, diarrhea, jaundice, fever, and abdominal pain. Around 10–15% of people experience a recurrence of symptoms during the six months after the initial infection.

It is usually spread by eating food or drinking water contaminated with infected feces. Shellfish which have not been sufficiently cooked are a relatively common source. It may also be spread through close contact with an infectious person. While children often do not have symptoms when infected, they are still able to infect others. After a single infection, a person is immune for the rest of his or her life. Diagnosis requires blood testing, as the symptoms are similar to those of a number of other diseases. There are five known hepatitis viruses: A, B, C, D, and E.

The hepatitis A vaccine is effective for prevention. Some countries recommend it routinely for children and those at higher risk who have not previously been vaccinated. It appears to be effective for life. Other preventive measures include hand washing and properly cooking food. No specific treatment is available, with rest and medications for nausea or diarrhea recommended on an as-needed basis. Infections usually resolve completely and without ongoing liver disease. Treatment of acute liver failure, if it occurs, is with liver transplantation.

Globally, around 1.4 million symptomatic cases occur each year and about 114 million infections (symptomatic and asymptomatic). It is more common in regions of the world with poor sanitation and not enough safe water. In the developing world, about 90% of children have been infected by age 10, thus are immune by adulthood. It often occurs in outbreaks in moderately developed countries where children are not exposed when young, and vaccination is not widespread. Acute hepatitis A resulted in 11,200 deaths in 2015.

Concluding Remarks

Although it is somewhat depressing to end a book with such negative realities as posed by the presently ubiquitous corona virus, there is a certain irony associated with comparing the beginning of this book with its ending at a time when the virus has surged throughout humanity. This challenges our ability to overcome the same kinds of problems that our families and humanity were facing at the beginning of this book, namely ruinous health epidemics 1000 years ago in northern and southern Italy.

LIST OF FIGURES

TABLE OF CONTENTS

INDEX

Made in the USA
Middletown, DE
18 September 2020